Shut Up and Train!

Also by the same author

I'm Not Stressed

Shut Up and Train!

A COMPLETE FITNESS GUIDE FOR
MEN AND WOMEN

DEANNE PANDAY

RANDOM HOUSE INDIA

Published by Random House India in 2013
1

Copyright © Deanne Panday 2013

Random House Publishers India Private Limited
Windsor IT Park, 7th Floor
Tower-B A-1, Sector-125
Noida-201301, (UP)

Random House Group Limited
20 Vauxhall Bridge Road
London SW1V 2SA
United Kingdom

978 81 8400 313 0

This book is sold subject to the condition that it shall not, by way of trade or otherwise, be lent, resold, hired out, or otherwise circulated without the publisher's prior consent in any form of binding or cover other than that in which it is published and without a similar condition including this condition being imposed on the subsequent purchaser.

Typeset in Sabon by Saanvi Graphics, Noida

Printed and bound in India by Replika Press Private Limited

To both my moms

*Queenie Woodham Rogers
and
Dr Snehlata Panday*

Contents

Foreword by Shahrukh Khan — ix
Acknowledgements — xiii
Meet Our Panel of Experts — xiv
Introduction — xv
Why this Book? — xxi
How to Use this Book — xxiv

Part One

1. The Way We Move — 3
2. The Way We Eat — 49

Part Two

1. History of Bodybuilding — 157
2. Before You Start Exercising — 185
3. Programming — 270

Conclusion	372
Afterword by Salman Khan	377
A Note on the Author	382

Foreword

Being fit is important in my line of work. My fitness thought is to be able to beat my son at the game that he plays till he is 21 and my daughter till she is 18. I am 47 now, and in another 7 years, I want to be in peak physical condition.

To be able to work for 12 hours a day—from 7 in the morning to 7 in the evening—you need to have a certain level of fitness. Plus I hate it if my shadow in the bathroom has a paunch. I detest feeling fat, looking fat, thinking fat. In my profession, everyone has bouts of stress. I believe you have to cut high stress with high energy. It's like diamond cutting diamond. You can't have low energy and try to cut stress.

But to develop physical strength, you first need to have mental strength. I always tell my children you don't need to have big biceps, but a big heart; your mind has to be tougher than your quads. The rest will follow. The physical attributes—the manifestation of a strong mind—will be seen in a strong body. It will never be the other way round. When I talk about strong body, I don't mean having a six-pack and being muscular. Take Gauri's father, for example. Even at 75, he is the fittest man I have ever come across. He is not aggressive at all. He is quiet, he does yoga, plays golf, does his exercise. And it's this internal strength which gives way to physical strength. So when my son asks me, 'You think Nana can beat you up?', I know he can!

During my younger days, I tore my knee while playing football and it keeps coming back. Then I once broke my toe during shooting. Once I was jumping on a mattress during a film sequence, but I slipped and landed on the floor, hurting my left shoulder. I think I have a congenital problem with my shoulder bone. It has grown beyond the size it should and it now cuts into my skin. Yes, so injuries are part and parcel of the game.

With so many injuries over the years, people always ask me, 'Are you normal?' I am normal not because I can do certain things, but because the body learns to adapt itself to different situations. It's the theory of evolution and it is visible in your body. I think the human body was designed to take pain, and God has given us is the ability to heal ourselves. Everyone can develop a threshold for pain if you think strong. But this does not mean you go ahead and bang your head against the wall to see how much pain you can take. Think strong, think positive, sit back, and let your body heal.

Also I think any injury is a sign that you need to rest. Because I have a high threshold for pain, I think I don't rest enough when I get a small injury. Deanne was the first person to teach me TRX. I am a big believer in weight training, but I don't believe in having a huge body than I can carry. The best way to look at your body and feel good is not under the top light of a gym. It's when you take a bath, look at yourself in the mirror, and say 'I am okay'.

People love to talk about the number of hours they spend at the gym. I think working out for an hour is adequate if you do it with full concentration. If you're faffing around, the same routine will take four hours. I think gymming out should be taken as having lunch at home or breathing or

Foreword

watching news or reading a book. Don't take it as a job, enjoy it. But get to it and look forward to finishing it. Now I spend 40 minutes—at its peak, 50 minutes—in the gym, not more.

My concept of gym and working out is completely different from other people. I am averse to music, air conditioning, chit-chatting, and resting. I go to the gym to enjoy the workout, I don't go in to enjoy the music. I can workout in a gym, in a tent, or on the floor, or in a 7-star hotel. As a matter of fact, I prefer the one in a tent because the most important part would be that I will have a great time exercising—not because I was chatting with friends or sipping juice at the bar.

I don't like being overweight at all. It's a phobia I have. I get very offended by it. I understand that people have their own body weight, their own physiology. But I know my physiology allows me to remain thin. I am 47 and my jeans size hasn't changed since I was 25. As a matter of fact, I used to wear a 31-inch jeans then and I wear a 29-inch jeans now. For me, that's just a shrinkage of the butt.

Two things have helped me develop strong glutes.—one that I am a Pathan, so I'm gifted genetically. Secondly, when I was young, I was a wicket keeper for the longest time. So the fact that you are always going down on your haunches in a 5-hour match makes a lot of difference. When I was very young, I got trained by few excellent coaches. They were not of international standards, but they made us work out a lot. What you do at a young age kind of retains longer than what you do at an age of 25.

I feel good when I put my hand on my stomach and feel a six-pack. I know a lot of friends who are very fit but don't have a six-pack. A six-pack is not overrated, especially if you are a father to a 15-year-old. It's like an acquired taste.

I have a natural diet, I don't eat roti and chawal. I love my grilled chicken. I enjoy my pizza too. My food is very basic. The only bad thing I have is black coffee with sugar. When

I work out, I eat four times, not six. I eat much less than the average person. I rarely eat rich food like dal chawal and biryani. When I am working out, I have grilled fish, chicken, or egg white. I have never drastically changed my diet. I find protein shakes and drinks make me feel very healthy.

I think you have to think fit, believe fit. Right now there are world-class training methods and trainers like Deanne. You know why there are so many people who come out with new workouts? It's because there is a different workout for everybody. Some of us like who are trained like Deanne can figure out a way which helps them. So make your own workout. **Your fitness regimen is as individual to you as your fingerprint.**

lots of love

SHAHRUKH KHAN
June 2013

Acknowledgements

A big thank you to Dabboo Ratnani, Haider, Subi Samuel, Soumyajit Nandy, Kavish Sinha, Sayan Sur Roy, Francois Matthys, BB Love Yourself, and Jitu Savlani for the star pictures, Tina Dehal for my book cover's photo shoot, and Meghna Butani for the hair and make-up. Thanks also to all the three experts—Dr Aijaz Ashai for giving his inputs on the injuries section in the book, Kinita Kadakia Patel for providing the break-up of calories, and Susana Garcia for the yummy recipes.

To Raksha, Milee, Gurveen and everybody at Random House India who helped give my book its final shape.

Lastly, to Mihir and all the stars who are part of the book—Arjun, Bipasha, Dino, Farhan, Lara, Priyanka, Salman, and Shahrukh. Thank you for making this book so special.

Meet Our Panel of Experts

Thank you so much Dr Aijaz Ashai for your expert advice on injury prevention and treatment, Kinita Kadakia Patel for the break-up of calories, and Susana Garcia for the scrumptious recipes in the book.

Dr Aijaz Ashai
Physiotherapist

Kinita Kadakia Patel
Sports nutrition consultant

Susana Garcia
Mediterranean fusion cook

Introduction

Being fit is a way of life for me, the foundation of what makes me strong and resilient. At 44, it is what I attribute my good health to and it is what continues to make me feel empowered—physically and mentally. Mentally because it allows me to push boundaries and face the barriers that come my way. Physically because it puts me in a high energy zone—I have more energy to do routine tasks more efficiently, I can avoid unwanted injuries as I age, I can let loose and dance till sun-down at a friend's party even after the rest of the gang has called it quits, and I can play with my son's friends who are half my age and yet last longer than them, even after most have given up!

Now when I look back, I truly believe I have my Granny lifestyle to thank for it. I don't mean it in the sense of being old but reliving the way my grandparents lived—with discipline, balance, and following a fixed routine.

A typical day for me is choc-a-bloc with activity. Two teenage kids, husband, in-laws, help, secretary, employees, clients, friends—there are a number of people that demand my attention. Not to forget my hyperactive pet cats, tortoise, and dogs. To deal with so much in a day, one needs to be fit, both physically and mentally. But I can manage all of it without a dip in my energy by being disciplined and following a balanced approach to life, just like our ancestors. It's a lifestyle that is available for you too if you go about it the right way.

In the years that I have managed to cultivate this disciplined lifestyle, my most treasured formula has been weight training. It goes by many names—strength training, resistance training, weightlifting. I have been lifting weights for two decades now. Not only has weight training made me stronger, it has helped me understand every muscle in my body. It keeps my immune system in top gear. I sleep better, and I have more energy during the day. It has enabled me to handle whatever is thrown my way.

India is a country where weightlifting is seen mostly as the domain of men or sportspeople. Go to your local gym and you'll see most women either doing light exercises or jogging on the treadmill. The weights lie in one corner of the room, collecting dust.

There have been times people have come up to me and said, 'I don't think you should be lifting weights. You will lose your femininity.' I simply laugh at their naivety. I know better than to take their misconceptions to heart. To break these obsolete myths about a fitness activity I have grown to love over the years is one of the main reasons why I wanted to write this book. First of all, you don't gain muscle overnight if you train with weights. Secondly, women have less testosterone, the muscle growth hormone, than their male counterparts. So there's no way women can develop those freakishly huge muscles. Tell me, will you become any less feminine if you have a lean waist and a tighter butt? If at all, weight training will make your body more toned and supple.

Weightlifting also allows me to have the foods of my choice without worrying about the calorie content. While most women will put themselves on unrealistic diets, I can afford to have my cheat meals every day and still lose weight due to an increased metabolism from weightlifting. And as I'm sure most of you know, the higher the metabolism, the easier it is to shed weight.

I grew up in a big family. We're six siblings, and looking back I'm sure we were quite a handful for our parents. Born to a half-Scottish–half-Nepalese father and a half East-Indian–half-Portugese mother, I have a large gene pool that I strongly believe works to my advantage.

I was always a sports-loving child, having taken inspiration from my father who was an athlete in his school days. So while my sisters were at home studying or playing video games, I was always outside engaging in physical activity. As a shy teenager, playing sports not just made me feel liberated, it also gave me a sense of accomplishment whenever I doubted myself. I believe that being an exceptional physically active individual all my life led me to my desire to pursue a career in the field of exercise and fitness.

In 1999, I began getting calls from magazines asking me to write about fitness because they said I looked really fit. I took up writing primarily because it allowed me to work from home without having to worry about my children. But I didn't want to dole out wrong information to the readers, so I decided to take up a two-week course in Australia to learn more on the topic of fitness. That's how my journey into health and fitness began.

In 2000, the *Times Group* came to me with the offer of training that year's Femina Miss India contestants. What surprised me the most was that in the history of the competition, the girls had never lifted weights before! I was, in fact, the first to introduce them to weight training.

As my children got older, I took on more clients and signed on stars like Bipasha Basu, Lara Dutta, Preity Zinta, and the likes. But working for so many hours at a stretch without a break was taking a toll on me. I stopped training personally when I set up my gym 'Play' in Mumbai—a one-of-a-kind gym in India which housed not just treadmills and weights but also balance accessories, agility equipment, and trampolines.

Then came my first book *I'm Not Stressed: secrets for a calm mind and healthy body*. I chose to write a book on stress first, even though I could have started off with a book on fitness since that is my forte, because I feel that once you know how to handle any situation with a balanced mind, any goal becomes easy to achieve. So I suggest whether your goal is to lose weight, get a toned body, or run a marathon, read *I'm Not Stressed* first and then pick up *Shut Up and Train*!

I strongly believe in the saying: 'What the mind can conceive and believe, the body can achieve'. Though *Shut Up and Train!* is about health and fitness, the basis of it is weight training. If you want your body to be fit and injury free, your muscles to be strong, your bones to be healthy, and your organs to be in good shape, you need to train with weights.

Ask yourself honestly—Have you lost weight but still feel flabby? Do you have a problem maintaining your stamina throughout the day? Do you constantly suffer from injuries? Are you suffering from lower back pain? Do you have premenstrual syndrome (PMS)?

If your answer is 'yes' to even one of these questions, you're only honest solution is weightlifting. I believe it is the most scientific way to modify your body without hurting yourself. It's very simple—when you weight train, you break down your muscle fibre. The body needs calories to repair these muscle fibres and to rebuild better quality muscles. That's the reason why you need to rest those muscles for 24 hours. You not only burn calories while resting, you also become strong. By boosting your metabolism, weight training helps you burn fat faster than other forms of exercise. So if you want to lose fat or change the way you look or become stronger, make weights your best friend. Weight training not just raises your metabolism, increases muscle in your body which helps you burn fat, strengthens bones, improves balance, and

Introduction

helps you avoid injuries, it also improves the functions of the nervous system, helps prevent diabetes, keeps cardiovascular diseases at bay, and helps avoid the loss of joint flexibility during old age.

Weight training is also seen to have profound effects on the musculoskeletal system, contributes to the maintenance of functional abilities, and prevents sarcopenia (loss of body mass) and lower back pain. Not just that, it also reduces the risk of diabetes, lowers high blood pressure, reduces the risk of breast cancer (by reducing high estrogen levels linked to the disease), minimizes the risk of osteoporosis, reduces symptoms of PMS, and even decreases colds! Lifting weights tones skeletal muscles which are responsible for supporting the skeleton and helping it move. The stronger these muscles are, the better physical condition your body is in.

Now if all those benefits of weight training don't motivate you enough to give it a try, nothing will! Through *Shut Up and Train!*, I plan to guide you through the right methods, the right kind of education of your body, and also the steps that you need to follow for this foolproof method to work. From the importance of doing functional moves likes squats, twists, and dead lifts to the real truth behind steroids and the method of going about training the right way, the book provides you with a blueprint to a fit and healthy body.

My fundamental goal is to educate people so that they don't fall for marketing gimmicks and unnatural methods of losing weight. Nowadays, everybody is a fitness expert or has some sort of a take on healthy food. While it's nice to see people educating themselves about fitness and health, it is shocking what is being peddled out there in the name of fitness.

When I visit gyms across the country, I see trainers mismanaging clients, not taking the time to teach clients the right form and technique, and worst of all, selling unnatural products which can cause harm to the body. It's almost like

Introduction

getting away with 'murder'—So many people end up with severe spinal problems, knee pain, and so on.

I believe in creating awareness in the purest way possible. I pride myself on being a 'lifestyle coach' because my objective is to make you reach a goal or bring about a positive change lifelong. I have decided I am not giving in to the giant supplement industry or the junk food generation who wouldn't want to back me because they are against good health. I don't promote marketing gimmicks, gadgets, diet pills, and supplements, even though it's the easiest way to make a quick buck.

Through *Shut Up and Train!*, I want to reach out to you and tell you that no matter what fitness training method you follow, you need to make weight training the base. Building strength is of foremost importance to get a toned body and strong muscles. The more you strength train, the more flexible you'll be. You will also have a lesser risk of muscle pull and knee or back pain because the body will build muscle around that area. As you strength train, you will see how you will be able to go about your daily activities like walking up the stairs, carrying a heavy box, or bending down to pick up a piece of paper with greater ease.

Remember that Elizabeth Arden ad featuring a beautiful woman where the ticker went, 'If you wish to look like this when you're 40, start when you're 20'? To keep yourself healthy lifelong, you need to start forming healthy habits now! Achieving this body will take time, but it will be worth it in the end. Go beyond the aesthetics, change your perspective, and think about how much you can benefit from a healthy body.

It's time to SHUT UP and get ready to TRAIN!

DEANNE PANDAY
Twitter: @deannepanday
Instagram: deannepanday
Email: deannepanday@gmail.com

Why this Book?

Can you easily bend down to tie your shoelaces without spraining your back?

Are you running on the treadmill all day long but still not losing an inch?

Are you bloating without having even touched a chocolate muffin in the recent past?

Do you realize you're training for aesthetics alone and not concentrating on the injuries you may get?

Do you feel like your personal trainer is pushing you over the edge without understanding the demands of your body?

It's time you start listening to your body and understanding how it works. You need to train to be fit and not get an injury. Understand the importance of organ cleansing, toxin removal, and their connection to weight loss. By concentrating on aesthetics alone, you are not only looking at your body superficially, you are also causing it internal damage.

I always have clients telling me they want to look like their favourite sportsperson or Bollywood star. What they don't understand is that no two bodies are the same—what works for them might not work for you and vice-versa. Plus, everyone approaches fitness with a different objective and you need to approach training keeping this in mind.

Why this Book?

And who says exercise can't be fun? One of my favourite workouts is AntiGravity Yoga which combines traditional yoga poses and principles with elements from aerial arts, dance, gymnastics, Pilates, and calisthenics. Since all the exercises are done on a hammock, one can obtain all the benefits of yoga without the impact or strain required to achieve the same movements and positions on the ground. But the biggest benefit of AntiGravity Yoga is that it decompresses the spine through its technique of zero-compression, or in other words, hanging upside down by a hammock.

Like AntiGravity Yoga, there are so many other fitness routines that you could try. See what works for you and your body. Make your exercise routine fun. Not only will your body become more flexible and agile, it will also have the strength to do routine tasks without feeling low on energy.

READY, GET SET, GO…

What if on the very first day of your life, you are offered a big, fat cheque to begin a Health Bank Account? And here's the sweetener—you can begin depositing small amounts into this Health Bank Account and the payback is a guaranteed hundred times more in less than six months. Of course, you will jump at this opportunity, right?

The big cheque that you have got in hand is your own body—with muscles, bones, heart, lungs and various organs, ligaments, cells, and your nervous system. Your body is the biggest wealth you have. And every single day that you wake up and follow a simple, healthy routine, you are depositing cash into your Health Bank Account.

The days that you starve yourself or decide to guzzle fat-burners or worse still, jump into crazy training routines that will cause injuries to the body, remember that you are not just skipping an opportunity to put in money into your account. You are, in fact, swiping your Health Credit Card

Why this Book?

and the debt will surely catch up with you. Through *Shut Up and Train!*, I will guide you to make huge deposits into your Health Bank Account. You need to keep that Credit Card safe in your wallet for special occasions! I'm not telling you not to enjoy that samosa or even that cold beer. But those moments need to be saved for special moments, and should not become part of your daily routine.

It's high time you stopped running up your Health Credit Card bill and fooling yourself.

How to Use this Book

Shut Up and Train! is divided into two parts. Part One educates you on how to lay the foundation for a holistic lifestyle.

In Chapter 1, 'The Way We Move', my attempt will be to create awareness about how your body moves so that you are less injury prone and have more improved performance. From explaining why some people are better at running in marathons than others to why high heels are bad for women—this chapter will tell you everything you need to know about your body—it's composition, movement and so on. I talk about the concept which forms the core of the training programme I believe in—functional fitness. I want to emphasize that it's not just your big muscles which work; it's also your stabilizing muscles that work in tandem for movement. When you work all your muscles in the way that your body meant for you to function, you know you are on the right path—and this means doing functional moves like squats, twists, deadlifts, pushing and pulling moves, walking, and running. In this chapter you will also learn how the body ages and how it is most important to train, bearing age in mind.

Chapter 2, 'Diet', will teach you how to get rid of toxicity in your body through five basic commandments. It will also

How to Use this Book

highlight how good gut health, liver, and endocrine glands are crucial to fulfilling your weight loss goals. Through this chapter, I will show you how to eat right by boosting your fibre intake and choosing the right carbs, proteins, and fats as well as methods to curb your sugar cravings. Have a blast whipping up the recipes that I have given in the second half of the chapter—it includes not just weight loss recipes but recipes which will help detoxify your system as well as help build muscle. There is also a section on cellulite that will explain what causes this unsightly fat to appear, why women are more prone to it, and what are the cures that can prevent its occurrence.

Part Two focuses on the method of weight training.

Chapter 1, 'History of Bodybuilding', shows you how bodybuilding went from a beautiful sport to a defamed one in a matter of years due to the use of unnatural supplements and steroids. I explain how the use of steroids have a harmful impact on the body—in both men and women. I also reveal the truth behind protein supplements, creatine, and glutamine. I make use of a case study of Mihir Jogh, a young 23-year-old boy who built his body the natural way to show you that one doesn't need to resort to such methods.

Chapter 2, 'Before You Start Exercising', explains the basic terms you need to get acquainted with before you start training. It explains in great detail the different ways in which you need to prepare before you begin your programme—from how many repetitions and sets to medical tests you need to take—it is a guideline to training the right way. It explains how factors like your fitness goal, age, and body type and shape are crucial to choosing a specific form of training. Make sure you go through the pointers on how to choose the right personal trainer too! The chapter will also show you why it is important to include variety into your routine and also briefly talk about the four pillars of fitness—strength, endurance, flexibility, and balance. There is a detailed section on injuries which is the main cause of concern for most fitness beginners and enthusiasts these days. From explaining specific injuries like shoulder, rotator cuff, elbow, wrist, spine, slipped disc, hip, knee, and ankle to solutions and treatment methods, everything has been given in detail. Use it as a guideline to educate yourself, not as a method of treatment.

Chapter 3, 'Programming', will teach you how to go about training the right way. Learn about the four pillars of fitness or 4PFs as I call it—strength, endurance, flexibility, and balance—and the different methods of training (with sample programmes) under each of these categories. Here I will bust some myths about toning and stretching and will also give some timeless moves like squats, lunges, deadlifts, push-ups, and pull-ups. As adults, we forget to incorporate fun and play into our routine. I have talked about something quite close to my heart—making fitness more than just an activity. So I have given you a list of accessories that you can work with. Your body will work wonders for you when you start having fun with your workouts.

Part One

1

The Way We Move

UNDERSTANDING THE BIOMECHANICS OF THE BODY

Try this: straighten your arm out in front of you and try to touch your wrist with your fingers. You can only touch your palm, right? If you push yourself any further, you will probably cry out in pain. Think of your arm action when you throw a ball. You can do a 360 degree rotation because your arm is connected to the shoulder joint which is a ball and socket joint. This allows movement in any direction. But if you do a similar action with your forearm, you will cause damage because your elbow joint does not allow you to go beyond a certain angle.

How we sit, stand, run, twist—all our actions should be in tandem with how nature intended us to move. Our bodies are a vast network of bones, muscles, tendons, ligaments, cartilages, nerves, and organs which work together in a precise manner to perform the action required.

Simply put, biomechanics is the science of movement of the skeletal, muscular, and nervous systems of the human body. All systems must work together and be properly aligned to produce movement efficiently. Proper biomechanics is needed to function normally in everyday life. Correct alignment of the body helps put minimum pressure on the muscles and joints. Athletes and sports coaches use the study of biomechanics to maximize performance. Improper biomechanics can result in a sudden injury or an injury over time.

The Slouch

Take your typical daily routine—we spend most of our time either sitting in front of the television, driving, or working at a desk job. I have seen that most people tend to slouch in front of the TV or computer screen, leading to a rounded shoulder posture. They stay in this position for long hours, without taking a break to move around.

While working on this book, I started neglecting my training sessions. To top it, my bad posture or stooping while writing led to a stressed-out spine. For almost two months, I gave up on yoga and strength training—something I had never done in my life before. Once I got back to my old training routine, one day while doing a body combat class, I felt a pull in my hamstring. I realized the injury was a result of having neglected my training sessions and in order to recover, I had to get back to my fitness routine the way it was before. Despite being a fitness expert, I had taken my body for granted. My experience should help you realize this can happen to anybody.

> I studied in the army school in Bangalore and they would make us walk like this (folds elbow and puts arm behind back and holds the crook of the other arm). I realize the importance now—you keep the shoulders back and you walk straight. And it was so good. You grow up that way—you walk straight, you stand tall. They caned you if you didn't do it. At that time, we would laugh and now I realize the importance of it. Body posture, form, and alignment are very important. It also adds to your outlook towards life. In very small ways, they do add to your confidence and your attitude.
>
> DINO MOREA, ACTOR

The spine is designed to bend forward and backward; it also rotates and bends to the side. Instead, what people do is that they compress their spine with bad posture. The lower back takes excessive and repetitive stress due to this, resulting in faulty body mechanics. Over time, it results in postural defects, frozen shoulder, tense neck and shoulder muscles, also leading to radiating pain in the lower back region and the leg, tight hip flexors, and various other problems. Breathing also becomes harder because your lungs are compressed when you round your back. You have to maintain the flexibility of the spine if you want to avoid problems. That's why I encourage taking breaks within 45 minutes to an hour when you are primarily have a desk job. You could just take a short walk or stretch.

If you're looking for another way to incorporate fitness into your routine desk job, you could try substituting your regular chair with a chair that has a Swiss ball built into it. It's all the rage in the West these days. While a normal chair compresses your spine, a Swiss chair supports your lower back and keeps your spine more flexible. It also helps to improve your posture in the long run and helps in getting immediate relief from muscle tension and stiffness. So incorporate an element of play in your mechanical 9 to 5 desk job and reap the benefits! But make sure you don't play around with it too much or you could end up hurting yourself.

It's a pity our lifestyles have become extremely sedentary. Our ancestors, if chased by a man-eating tiger in the woods, would be able to climb the nearest tree with ease. But the modern man can barely move from point A to point B. Faced with the same situation, the modern man would in fact be devoured by the tiger before he can even think of running! The point I'm trying to make here is that our ancestors were doing a lot more functional moves in their time—climbing, running, twisting, picking, bending, and so on.

Do you remember the last time you squatted in a traditional Indian toilet or did your own jhadu–pocha? In today's time, with domestic help and chauffeurs in every household to do our work for us, the importance of functional moves has long been forgotten.

Before you understand the role muscles and joints play in our body, you must know that the body is meant to move in a certain way. You need to know about the biomechanics of the body to maintain the highest level of efficiency with the lowest possibility of damage or injury. The more awareness you have about how your body functions, the lesser will be the risk of injury. Educating yourself about your bodily movements and the cause of those movements helps to achieve fitness goals in a quick and safe way and it will also decrease the risk of personal negligence against you if you're working with a personal trainer.

The word 'biomechanics' is derived from the Greek word 'bio' meaning 'living' and 'mechanic' meaning 'forces'. The primary purpose of biomechanics is to evaluate a body's motion as well as its applications of force. Biomechanics plays a role not just in prevention of an injury but in performance enhancement as well. Whether you are weekend runner or a national level sprinter, an understanding of biomechanics can help you develop more efficient movement patterns. Studying biomechanics will also help you understand how the body responds to different types of exercises, angles, and positions. For instance, if you're doing squats to strengthen the legs, biomechanics can help you know if you're going about it the right way. If you have poor form and technique, biomechanics can help you understand the pressure that will be exerted on surrounding joints and tissues.

I know this chapter may seem very boring to you, but it shouldn't discourage you from reading further. The first step to a great body is knowing what your body is made of.

AT THE JOINT OF IT ALL

All our movements occur at the joints. A joint exists wherever two bones meet. Each joint has a 'plane' of movement—the direction in which the bones are intended to move. When we brush our teeth every morning, we use our elbow and shoulder joints in the plane of movement which comes naturally to us. You don't twist your hand around your head to keep your teeth sparkling clean, do you? Think of the joints in your body as a machine which was developed to work in a certain way. Just like you can't manipulate a machine to do something else, the same way, our joints were made to move only in a specific way.

During strength training or any other activity, if you are not aware of the plane of the joint, you may push yourself. What happens then is that you might feel a slight ache or pain and you may neglect it. And if you continue to train in the wrong manner, very soon it will show up as an injury. Then it's bye-bye exercise and hello doctor. That's why it's important that you educate yourself about your own body and the joint movements, and the next time you feel pain, you will immediately know that you are doing something wrong.

Joints are divided according to structure:

1. Fibrous joints: Also called immovable joints because they do not move (Example: bones of the skull)
2. Cartilaginous joints: Are connected entirely by cartilage which is a flexible connective tissue. Allow more movement between bones than fibrous joints. (Example: disc between vertebrae)
3. Synovial joints: Joints that can be moved the most. The ends of this joint are enclosed in a capsule containing a thick, slippery liquid called synovial fluid. This lubricating liquid helps reduce friction between the bones. (Example: hip, elbow)

Synovial joints are the most important and can be divided into six major types:

- Ball and socket joint: Ball moves within a socket so as to allow rotary motion in every direction. (Example: shoulder, hip)
- Pivot joint: Allows only rotary movement. (Example: in the neck region, the first and second cervical vertebrae, called the atlas and the axis, allows rotation)
- Hinge joint: Movement is like the opening and closing of a hinged door. (Example: elbow, knee)
- Gliding joint: Found between surfaces of two flat bones that are held together by ligaments. (Example: bones in the wrists and ankles move by gliding against each other)
- Saddle joint: Resembling a saddle. Bones can go back and forth, and side to side. (Example: joints in the thumb)
- Condyloid joint: Lies between the convex surface of one bone and the concave surface of another. (Example: certain joints in the wrist)*

DO YOU KNOW YOUR RANGE OF MOTION (ROM)?

Each joint has its own 'range of motion', meaning the distance and direction a joint can move to its full potential. Stand upright, tuck in your lower tummy slightly, bend forward, and try to touch your toes. Be honest here; don't push yourself because you will only end up hurting yourself. Are you falling short of touching your toes? Can you reach your calves or just your knees? This simple stretch shows you the range of motion of your spine. Ideally, the way your spine is built to flex (bend forward), you should easily be able to touch your toes. But if your muscles are stiff or your spine is inflexible, you will have limited range of motion of the spine.

---

* To read more on joints, you can visit this weblink: http://www.innerbody.com/image/skel07.html

The Way We Move

Many people mistakenly think that it is stiff hamstrings that keep them from touching their toes. In reality, it's not just one muscle that's the culprit. Our entire body—including muscles, bones, and organs—is sheathed with a thin film of connective tissue called 'fascia'. So even if one muscle in the body is stiff, it can affect the movement of the joints. In the above case, if you couldn't touch your toes, the problem could be the muscles of your lower back or your calves or even the muscles at the bottom of your feet. That's why it is important to follow a good strengthening and stretching routine to ensure healthy joints and strong and supple muscles.*

Terms for Joint Movements

Flexion: Bending parts at a joint so that the angle between them decreases and the parts come closer together. Everyday example: when you bring a cup of tea to your mouth to sip, you flex your elbow joint, reducing the angle between the upper arm and forearm.

Extension: Straightening parts at a joint, so that the angle between them increases and the parts move farther apart. Everyday example: when you close a door, you straighten your elbow by pulling your forearm away from your upper arm.

Hyperextension: Excess extension of the parts at a joint, beyond the anatomical position. Everyday example: if you bend your head back beyond the upright position, you can cause an injury in the neck.

Dorsiflexion: Bending the foot at the ankle toward the leg. Everyday example: imagine lifting and flexing your foot while seated to see your toes.

---

* Read up more on fascial adhesions here: http://destroychronicpain.wordpress.com/fascial-adhesions-2/

Plantar flexion: Bending the foot at the ankle away from the leg. Everyday example: standing on tiptoes.

Abduction: Moving a part away from the mid-line of the body. Everyday example: raising your arms up to your sides laterally, away from the body. Imagine the wings of a plane.

Adduction: Moving a part towards the midline of the body (bringing it back towards the body). Everyday example: raising your thigh towards your chest, as if you are marching in a band.

Rotation: Moving a part around an axis. Medial rotation involves movement toward the mid-line of the body, whereas lateral rotation involves movement in the opposite direction. Everyday example: twisting the head from side to side to say 'No'.

Circumduction: Moving a part to follow a circular path, Everyday example: doing the butterfly stroke while swimming.

Pronation: To rotate the forearm so that the palm is downward. Everyday example: opening a door with a key.

Supination: To rotate the forearm so that the palm is upward. Everyday example: like when you stretch your arm to take money from somebody.

Elevation: Raising a part of the joint. Everyday example: shrugging the shoulders.

Depression: Lowering a part. Everyday example: dropping the shoulders.

Joint Actions

Spinal column: The vertebral column has the following normal ranges of movement: flexion, extension, lateral flexion, and rotation.

Shoulder girdle: The shoulder girdle has the following normal ranges of movement: elevation, depression, adduction, and abduction.

Shoulder joint: The shoulder joint has the following normal ranges of movement: flexion, extension, adduction, abduction, and medial rotation.

Elbow joint: The elbow joint has the following normal ranges of movement: flexion, extension, pronation, and supination.

Wrist joint: The wrist joint has the following normal ranges of movement: flexion, extension, adduction, abduction, and circumduction.

Hip joint: The hip joint has the following normal ranges of movement: flexion, extension, adduction, abduction, medial rotation, and lateral rotation.

Knee joint: The knee joint has the following normal ranges of movement: flexion and extension

Ankle joint: The ankle joint has the following normal ranges of movement: plantar flexion, dorsi flexion, inversion, and eversion.

This makes clear that our body is built to flex, extend, rotate, and twist in a certain manner. If you extend the joint beyond its natural range of motion, you will end up damaging your joints. That's the reason why in yoga so much emphasis is put on alignment and not pushing the body to the point where it hurts. Many people twist their necks and backs unnaturally because they are under the notion that the more they stretch, the better they will be at yoga.

Over the last decade, I have witnessed a significant increase in the number of sports injuries. One of the reasons for this is the fact that now most sportspeople like to play only the game of their interest or skill while earlier, one would play multiple sports. Concentrating on only one game leads to overtraining and muscle imbalance. Take a soccer player for example. Kicking the ball a certain way for a considerable period of time puts the joint used for the movement under a lot of stress. It's more problematic if the athlete does not understand his joint or plane of movement. If he kicks the ball the wrong way, it will definitely lead to an injury. Sports coaches are hired for this very reason—to evaluate the athlete's fitness levels and educate him on how to prevent himself from getting an injury.

The important thing to keep in mind is that you need to do movements biomechanically and, more importantly, at the plane of the joint. If you are bending your elbow, it should be bent up (flex) and down (extend) according to the plane of the elbow joint. If you bend it in any other direction, it will cause damage. And don't hyperextend it; that will cause pain. Similarly in the knee, if it flexes and straightens, you can't take it inwards and outwards. This is how knee damage is caused. If you hyperextend it, it causes injury to the joint.

Remember, when you do any exercise, you have to keep in mind the movement of the joint. Don't do any action which is unnatural or away from the range of motion of the joint.

KNOW YOUR ANATOMY

Tendon: A flexible but inelastic cord of strong fibrous collagen tissue attaching a muscle to a bone. Example: achilles tendon

Ligament: A short band of tough, flexible, fibrous connective tissue that connects two bones or cartilages or holds together a joint. Example: anterior cruciate ligament

Cartilage: A tough, elastic, fibrous connective tissue found in various parts of the body, such as the joints, outer ear, and larynx. Example: hyaline cartilage

Nerve: Any of the cordlike bundles of fibers made up of neurons through which sensory stimuli and motor impulses pass between the brain or other parts of the central nervous

The Way We Move

system and the eyes, glands, muscles, and other parts of the body. Example: optic nerve

Bones: Any of the pieces of hard, whitish tissue making up the skeleton in humans and other vertebrates. Example: carpals and tarsals

> ### Tendons vs Ligaments: What's the Difference?
>
> Along with biomechanics, it's also important to know a bit about the connective tissues that help hold your body together. People often refer to tendons and ligaments as if they are the same thing because both are made up of two types of fibres—collagen which provides strength and stiffness and elastin which allows the joint to extend. But while both are made up of the same fibrous tissues, they perform different functions in the body. While a tendon connects muscle to bone, a ligament connects bone to bone. Most of you may be familiar with the Achilles tendon which connects the muscles of your calf to your heel.
>
> Athletes and dancers stretch their ligaments to make their joints supple, and to prevent injury. Both tendons and ligaments have a high risk factor of getting ruptured or torn. These injuries are most common in athletes, especially in sports such as football, rugby, hockey, and basketball because of the high level of strain put on the knee through pivoting and lateral or twisting movements in the legs. Half-squats and half-lunges help to strengthen these tissues and prevent an injury.
>
> Another reason why weight training is important is that stronger muscles help to improve your tendon and ligament strength. High-resistance training forces you to work your tendons and ligaments more than you usually would due to the amount of the weight.

MUSCLE YOUR WAY IN

Mention the word 'muscles' and the first thought that comes to mind is bulging biceps, isn't it? Most people think of muscles that they can see. But there's a whole lot more than meets the eye. The human body has over 640 muscles. When you read, you use your eye muscles. When you sing, you use the muscles of the larynx, mouth, and tongue. In fact, the tongue alone has 8 muscles! For any action, there are several muscles being used, without you even knowing it. Aren't you surprised because till now you only knew about the most commonly known muscles like biceps, triceps, and quads?

Muscles help your body turn fuel into motion. They are not meant to be developed only for aesthetics—they help you express yourself, be it singing, dancing, skipping, jumping, writing, or even just blabbering! Muscles grow stronger when you use them efficiently and they repair themselves when you rest. The benefits of strengthening muscles are many. Stronger muscles not only improve body composition (more muscle mass, less body fat), they also lead to an increase in the metabolic rate, thus helping you burn kilos faster. With stronger muscles, your body will be less susceptible to injuries. Not just that, your bone density will increase, thus reducing the risk of osteoporosis. Strong muscles are also said to improve glucose metabolism, which can reduce the risk of diabetes. With so many added advantages, only a fool would ignore his muscles.

There are three types of muscles:

Skeletal muscles: Are attached to the skeleton. We control these muscles by our own will to perform any action. That's why they are also called voluntary muscles. For example, if you want to kick a ball, you voluntarily use your leg muscles.

Cardiac muscles: Are muscles of the heart that work together to pump blood throughout the body, and back and forth from the heart.

Smooth muscles: Are muscles which are not controlled by will, but by your brain. They are also called involuntary muscles. They are the muscles found in the digestive system, blood vessels, airways, bladder, and the uterus. So when you breathe, the muscles in your airways work like clockwork, you don't have to will them to function.

KNOW YOUR MUSCLES

The reason why I lay emphasis on the importance of knowing about the muscles that make up your body is so that you can work on them efficiently to achieve your fitness goals. Your muscles are attached to bones, so building good quality muscles allows efficient joint action, takes impact of any kind of stress, and helps prevent an injury. Also, knowing about each muscle and its corresponding location and action will not just help you figure out how best to stretch or develop the muscle, it will also prevent you from getting an injury. With the right information, you will know if you're working on a muscle too little or too much.

Each muscle has an origin known as proximal attachment. It ends at a distal attachment called insertion and contracts to produce a specific action. Knowing the anatomy of the muscles helps you visualize when you workout.

Upper Body

Arms

#BICEPS

Location: Muscle at the front of your upper arm.

The biceps have a 'short head' and a 'long head' that work as a single muscle. The tendon that connects the biceps muscle to the shoulder joint in two places is called the proximal biceps tendon. The tendon that attaches the biceps muscle to the forearm bones (radius and ulna) is called the distal biceps tendon. Everyday example: striking a match.

#BRACHIALIS

Location: Lies between the upper-arm bone and biceps.

Brachialis is not known by most, but it's a muscle that shares elbow-bending duties with the biceps. Unlike the biceps, the brachialis does not insert on the radius, and therefore cannot participate in pronation and supination of the forearm. It only flexes the elbow joint. Because of its broad origin and it having only one action, it can be considered the strongest flexor of the elbow. Everyday example: turning a corkscrew.

#TRICEPS

Location: Rear-side of the upper arm.

Triceps means 'three headed'—it has a long head, lateral head, and a medial head. Triceps is actually twice the size of biceps and accounts for two-thirds of the upper arm's muscle. Many men focus on their biceps and neglect their triceps because they suffer from the 'bulging bicep' syndrome. On the other hand, I have noticed many women overdoing triceps exercises to get rid of their 'wobbly arms'. That's not how strength training works; you have to strengthen all the muscles to build strong arms, protect the joints, and perform stronger, powerful actions. Everyday example: turning the steering wheel.

#FOREARM

Location: Distal region of the hand, between the elbow and the wrist.

There are several muscle groups in the forearm. The most important ones are the flexor pollicis longus and the flexor digitorum superficialis. Again, many people skip strengthening their forearms, wrists, and hands and this causes muscle imbalance in the body. Everyday example: turning your palm down to pour liquid out of a container.

You know there was this old Latai they used to do to build forearm strength. Everything is about your forearm strength and grip—if you don't have that, you are not strong. You don't say you are going to bench-press 350 pounds and not build forearm strength. Your strength is in your forearms and your legs.

—SALMAN KHAN, ACTOR

Salman is bang on! Your grip will never be strong if you keep neglecting forearm muscles. Something as simple as squeezing a stress ball or a hand gripper can help strengthen your forearm and grip.

Shoulders

#Deltoids

Location: Triangular-shaped muscles on the shoulder.

They are the main muscles of the shoulder. The deltoids have three heads—the front, the middle, and the rear—named as per their location on the shoulder joint. Everyday example: swinging your arm while walking.

#Rotator Cuff

Location: Group of four muscles which surround the shoulder joint. Each muscle originates on the shoulder blade or scapula and inserts on the arm bone or humerus.

The rotator cuff muscles include the infraspinatus, subscapularis, suprascapularis, and the teres minor. These muscles have the important job of stabilizing the shoulder as well as elevating and rotating the arm. Many weightlifters and sportspeople tend to ignore these muscles and suffer from rotator cuff tears or shoulder injuries. The external rotators are the most commonly injured. Everyday example: lifting a container.

#Teres Major

Location: Lower 1/3 of the lateral border of the scapula (shoulder blade).

The ball-and-socket joint of your shoulder moves in multiple directions. The teres major muscle powers several of these movements. It's not part of the rotator cuff muscles. When you reach for something on a high shelf, several muscles spring into action to raise your arm. Your teres major muscle helps you lower it again. Everyday example: rowing.

#Rhomboids

Location: Rhombus-shaped muscles associated with the scapula (shoulder blade).

There are two rhomboid muscles—rhomboid major and rhomboid minor. Rhomboid major is larger and positioned below rhomboid minor. Chins and dips are excellent activities for developing these muscles. Everyday example: pulling a drawer open.

Chest

#Pectorals

Location: Situated in the chest.

Men use these muscles to flex their chest! In females, the muscles lie underneath the breasts. The pectoralis major is the largest, superficial muscle. Lying beneath it is the pectoralis minor. Everyday example: bringing the arm across the chest.

#Serratus Anterior

Location: Upper nine ribs at the side of the chest.

The serratus anterior muscle is used in activities which draw the scapula forward. It is used strongly in push-ups and bench presses. Everyday example: reaching out to open the window.

Back

#Latissimus Dorsi

Location: Starts from under your armpit and covers sides of middle and upper back.

Commonly known as 'lats', these are the broadest muscles of the back and one of the largest in the body. Once large enough, they help give men the coveted 'V-shape'. Latissimus dorsi muscles are also called 'wings' because of their flared,

The Way We Move

wing-like look when they are well-developed. They are powerful extensor muscles of the arm and are used extensively in chinning and climbing. Everyday example: pushing the arms of a chair while standing.

#Trapezius

Location: Diamond-shaped muscle that covers your upper back, shoulders, and neck.

The trapezius is divided into three sections as per location—upper, middle, and lower trapezius. Its main function is to move the shoulder blade, assist in neck movements, and support the arm. Its degree of tightness or looseness affects the neck's flexibility. For people who work at desks and computers, or who spend many hours driving, the upper trapezius often becomes very sore and painful. Everyday example: shrugging the shoulders.

#Spinal Erectors

Location: They line the spinal column from the lower to the upper back.

The spinal erectors are not just one muscle, but a bundle of muscles and tendons. They are paired and run more or less vertically. They help you straighten and bend your back. The spinal erectors are made up of three major muscles—iliocostalis, longissimus, and spinalis.

As most of us know, the back is the most neglected area in the human body. Since the erector spinae muscles help hold up the spine, they are the most important muscles to train. These muscles go all the way up to your spine, supporting and protecting it. Thus it is important to strengthen these muscles if you don't want to suffer from back pain. Everyday example: Picking up a newspaper

Lower Body

Hips

#GLUTEAL MUSCLES

Location: Buttocks.

There are three gluteal muscles viz. the gluteus maximus, the gluteus medius on the outer surface of the hip, and lastly, the baby one—the gluteus minimus—which lies beneath the medius. If you want a nice and round-shaped butt, these are the muscles you need to target. Everyday example: getting out of a car.

> **DON'T MAKE IT THE BUTT OF JOKES!**
>
> Generally, people assume that the main weight-bearing muscle of the body is either the calf muscle or the back. Here's the truth—it's the gluteus medius muscle that makes up the outer surface of the hip. That is the muscle which takes your body load when you walk or run and balances your CG— the centre of gravity of your body.
>
> If the gluteus medius muscle is weak, you are going to limp when you walk. If this muscle is strong, it will hold your legs and upper body in position, making your walk smooth. When you see a sprinter running, it's basically their gluteus medius which takes the proper weight of the body, making the sprinter run faster.
>
> Lateral resistance band walk is the best exercise to strengthen the gluteas medius muscle. You tie a resistance band around your ankles and walk laterally. Whenever you exercise in the gym, you need to start strengthening the gluteus medius muscle while doing a standing exercise so that the load is taken on both sides equally. By building muscle, all your movements—walking, running, sprinting—will become perfect.

#HIP FLEXORS

Location: Front of your upper thigh and just below your hips.

Hip flexors are a group of muscles which include the psoas major, psoas minor, and the iliacus. Most people don't pay much attention to their hip flexors. But know this—when you experience back pain, knee pain, and hip stiffness, it's often due to tight hip flexors. This is largely due to our modern lifestyle, which is characterized by too much sitting and a lack of stretching. It helps to get up and walk around every 1 hour if you have a desk job. Stretching this muscle is needed on a daily basis. Everyday example: sit-ups.

Legs

#GROIN/HIP ADDUCTOR MUSCLES

Location: Inner portion of the thigh.

Comprising of the adductor brevis, adductor longus, adductor magnus, gracilis, and pectineus, this is the group of muscles most girls at the gym want to tone up to pass the hot swimsuit test! I have seen women sit for hours on the hip abductor–adductor machine which target the outer hip and inner thigh. Please know that there is rarely a need to train these muscles separately. If you do a quality weight training programme with squats and lunges, they get trained automatically.

The reason people use this machine is because they think that if they work on the inside and outside of the thighs, they'll be able to melt the fat off those areas. It's such a false belief! If you want slimmer thighs, using this machine every time you workout will do nothing to help you towards that goal. What will work for you is a combination of cardio, overall strength training, and good nutritional habits that will help you tone and lose fat everywhere, including your thighs. Everyday example: cycling.

#TENSOR FASCIA LATAE & ILIOTIBIAL BAND (IT BAND)

Location: Outer portion of the thigh.

The tensor fasciae latae is a small muscle which attaches inferiorly to the long thick strip of fascia, known as the iliotibial (IT) band. Fascia is a layer of fibrous tissue. The IT band assists in moving the hip forward and outward. Rotating the hips inward is another action the muscle does. Since it's used for so many movements and is in a shortened position when seated, the IT band becomes tight easily. You need to strengthen and stretch this important muscle. If there is pain near the hip and knee and difficulty maintaining balance while the opposite leg is raised, it usually indicates an IT band strain. Everyday example: keeping one foot in front of the other when walking.

#Quadriceps

Location: Front of the thigh.

Quadriceps has four heads of muscles which meet just above the knee cap. Their main function is to straighten the knee joint from a bent position. The four muscles that make up the quadriceps are rectus femoris, a hip flexor which lies on the middle of the thigh and covers the other 3 muscles; vastus lateralis: which lies on the lateral (outer) side of the thigh; vastus medialis: which lies on the medial (inner) side of the thigh; and vastus intermedius: which lies in between the vastus lateralis and medialis, deep below the rectus femoris. Everyday example: picking up a box from the ground.

#Hamstrings

Location: At the back of your upper leg.

Tight hamstrings muscles are a common problem. If you can't touch your toes, one of the reasons could be inflexible hamstrings. The hamstring muscles comprise biceps femoris, semitendinosus, and semimembranosus. They help to flex or straighten the knee. Everyday example: jumping.

#Gastrocnemius

Location: Rear part of the lower leg.

Gastrocnemius is the largest and most superficial of the calf muscles. It runs from its two heads—lateral and medial—just above the knee to the heel, and is involved in standing, walking, running, and jumping. Everyday example: standing on tip toes.

#SOLEUS

Location: Rear part of the lower leg.

The soleus is a powerful muscle which runs from just below the knee to the heel, and is involved in standing and walking. Together gastrocnemius, soleus, and plantaris are known as triceps surae. These are the major muscles in the calf. Usually when people say that somebody has good legs, they mean shapely calves. The major factor in play here is genetics, but don't despair if you have spindly or thick trunks for calves. You can aspire for a better shape if you train right! Everyday example: standing upright.

> ### THE SECOND HEART IN OUR BODY
>
> The calf muscle is sometimes referred to as the 'second heart' because when standing, the soleus is constantly contracting to help pump blood upwards in order to aid the heart in circulation. It is the muscle which circulates blood to both legs. It is the muscle which helps you stand for long durations and run faster. If your calf muscle is weak, pressure will be felt on the joints. Numbness and stiffness is caused by weak calves. That's why it is important to do calf raises and strengthen the muscles. Don't start with weight bearing machines. You can use the leg press machine. Without bending the knee, push it with the calf. If someone has a shin problem, you can slightly turn your toes inside and push it so that it works on the lateral side of the calf.

#TIBIALIS ANTERIOR/SHIN MUSCLE

Location: Outside of the shin bone (tibia).

The shin muscle controls balance as well as foot and toe mobility. The muscle is used in everyday activities such as walking, running, and standing. This is the most active muscle when running and therefore, also the most frequently injured. The shin muscle is what makes up the fleshy part of the outside of the shin bone. It can usually be seen when flexed from the front of the lower leg. The shin muscle helps to stabilize the legs when standing or preparing to kick a ball. It is used to dorsiflex the foot and ankle, when the toes point upward towards the body. Everyday example: Walking by lifting the foot up and clearing the ground.

Abdomen

#EXTERNAL OBLIQUES

Location: Lowest 8 ribs.

The external obliques wrap around the trunk on each side to form our waist. They join to the linea alba, a band of connective tissues running down the front of the abdomen. Everyday example: raking leaves.

#INTERNAL OBLIQUES

Location: Lower 3-4 ribs; lie beneath the external obliques.

The internal obliques wrap around the waist and insert into the linea alba, a cord like strip of connective tissue running down the centre of the abdomen. Everyday example: Bhunjangasana (upward facing dog) pose in yoga.

#TRANSVERSE ABDOMINUS

Location: Deepest muscle; lies beneath the internal obliques.

The transverse abdominus holds all your internal organs in place. When you suck your lower abdomen in, you work this thin strip of muscle. Everyday example: stomach hollowing (sucking the stomach inwards) exercises

#Rectus Abdominis

Location: Paired muscle running vertically on each side of the anterior wall of the abdomen.

The rectus is crossed by 3 (rarely 4) fibrous bands called the tendinous intersections. This causes the formation of 6 muscle bellies, giving rise to the overhyped 6-pack muscle. The muscles don't really help out in having a good posture like the other muscles and you can maintain it only for a while. It's the most superficial of all muscles. It's only for aesthetics and does not really protect your spine. Everyday example: moving from lying to sitting position.

The below diagram highlights the major muscle groups that have been talked about so far. Knowing the exact location of each muscle is crucial in understanding how these muscles work.

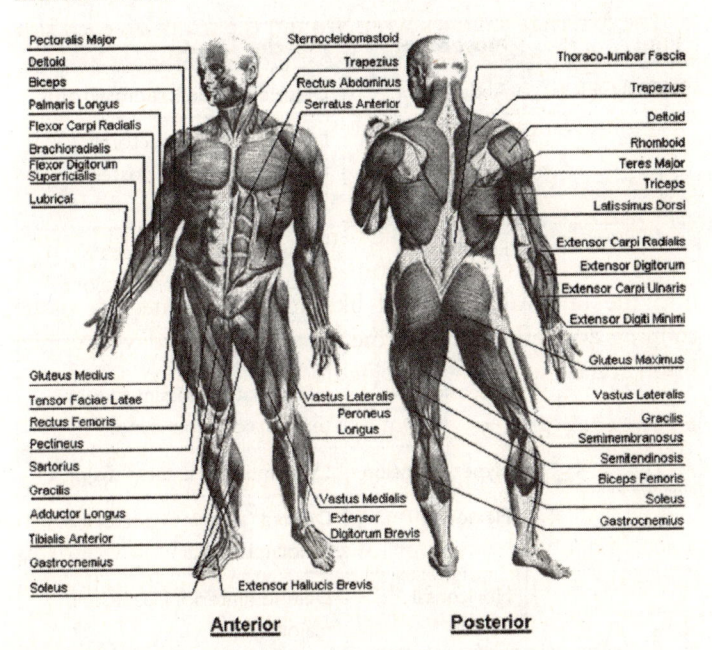

Photo credit: www.health-advisors.org

Now you understand how a particular muscle helps you in a particular action and that it's not just one muscle but a lot of muscles that work with a particular movement. You need to train all muscles equally. Avoid focusing on one area of your body and never ignore training any of the major muscle groups.

Take the shoulder joint for example. For a medial rotation movement at the shoulder joint, the major muscles used are latissimus dorsi, pectoralis major, teres major, and the subscapularis. Medial rotation is a rotation that occurs towards the midline of the body from the anatomical position. When swimming butterfly, for example, medial rotation at the shoulder takes place when the arms enter the water.

Given below is a list of muscles that are the prime movers for a given joint action.

Joint	Movement	Muscles Used
SHOULDER	Abduction	Deltoid (middle), supraspinatus
	Adduction	Latissimus dorsi, pectoralis major, teres major, posterior deltoid
	Extension	Latissimus dorsi, pectoralis major (sternal), teres major, posterior deltoid
	Horizontal extension	Deltoid (posterior), infraspinatus, latissimus dorsi, teres major, teres minor
	Hyperextension	Latissimus dorsi, teres major
	Flexion	Deltoid (anterior), pectoralis major (clavicular)
	Horizontal flexion	Deltoid (anterior), pectoralis major

The Way We Move

Joint	Movement	Muscles Used
	Lateral rotation	Infraspinatus, teres minor
	Medial rotation	Latissimus dorsi, pectoralis major, teres major, subscapularis
SHOULDER GIRDLE	Abduction (protraction)	Pectoralis minor, serratus anterior
	Adduction (retraction)	Rhomboids, trapezius (middle fibres)
	Depression	Pectoralis minor, subclavius, trapezius (lower fibres)
	Elevation	Levator scapulae, rhomboids, trapezius (upper fibres)
SCAPULA	Upward rotation	Serratus anterior, trapezius (upper and lower fibres)
	Downward rotation	Pectoralis minor, rhomboids
ELBOW	Flexion	Biceps brachii, brachialis, brachioradialis
	Extension	Triceps brachii
RADIOULNAR JOINT	Supination	Supinator, biceps brachii
	Pronation	Pronator quadratus, pronator teres
WRIST	Abduction (radial flexion)	Flexor carpi radialis, extensor carpi radialis longus, extensor carpi radialis brevis
	Adduction (ulnar flexion)	Flexor carpi ulnaris, extensor carpi ulnaris

Joint	Movement	Muscles Used
	Extension/ Hyperextension	Extension carpi radialis longus, extensor carpi radialis brevis, extensor carpi ulnaris
	Flexion	Flexor carpi radialis, flexor carpi ulnaris, palmaris longus
TRUNK	Flexion	Rectus abdominus, internal oblique, external oblique
	Extension/ Hyperextension	Erector spinae group, semispinalis
	Lateral flexion	Internal oblique, external oblique, erector spinae group, multifidus, quadratus lumborum, rotatores
	Rotation	Internal oblique, external oblique, erector spinae group, multifidus, rotators, semispinalis
HIP	Abductors	Gluteus medius, piriformis
	Adductors	Adductor brevis, adductor longus, adductor magnus, gracilis, pectineus
	Extensors	Biceps femoris, gluteus maximus, semimembranosus, semitendinosus
	Flexors	Iliacus, pectineus, psoas major, rectus femoris
	Lateral rotation	Gemelli, gluteus maximus, obturator externus, obturator internus
	Medial rotation	Gluteus medius, gluteus minimus

Joint	Movement	Muscles Used
KNEE	Extension	Rectus femoris, vastus intermedius, vastus lateralis, vastus medialis
	Flexion	Biceps femoris, semimembranosus, semitendinosus
ANKLE	Extension (plantar flexion)	Gastrocnemius, soleus
	Flexion (dorsiflexion)	Extensor digitorum longus, peroneus tertius, tibialis anterior
FOOT (Intertarsal)	Eversion	Peroneus brevis, peroneus longus, peroneus tertius
	Inversion	Flexor digitorum longus, tibialis anterior, tibialis posterior

Source: *ACSM's Health & Fitness Certification Review*

THE PRIME MOVERS

Now that we've understood the different type of muscles used in a particular joint movement, it is also important to understand that for any type of movement—walking, squatting, running—a muscle fulfils three types of roles.

Prime Mover/Agonist: Is responsible for producing a certain movement.

Antagonist: Is a prime mover muscle that opposes the agonist.

Synergist: Helps the prime mover muscle perform the action.

The difference between agonist and antagonist muscles is that they work in the opposite directions to complete an action.

For example, when you want to kick a ball, you need to straighten your knee joint. Here, the quadriceps helps you straighten the leg—so they become the prime movers. The hamstrings works in the opposite direction, becoming the antagonist muscle in this action.

The agonist and antagonist are usually found on opposite sides of a joint. Depending on the action that is performed, each muscle serves as the agonist at some times and as the antagonist at other times. In order to initiate movement, the agonist always contracts while the antagonist stretches and lengthens to allow the movement. The reverse will happen to return the body part to a normal position. Then the agonist muscle that initiated the original movement will become the antagonist to allow the original antagonist muscle to contract and return to the normal position.

Take a look at the picture below:

The biceps muscle is located on the front of the arm, while the triceps muscle is on the back of the arm. If a person is exercising while using a triceps pushdown machine, the

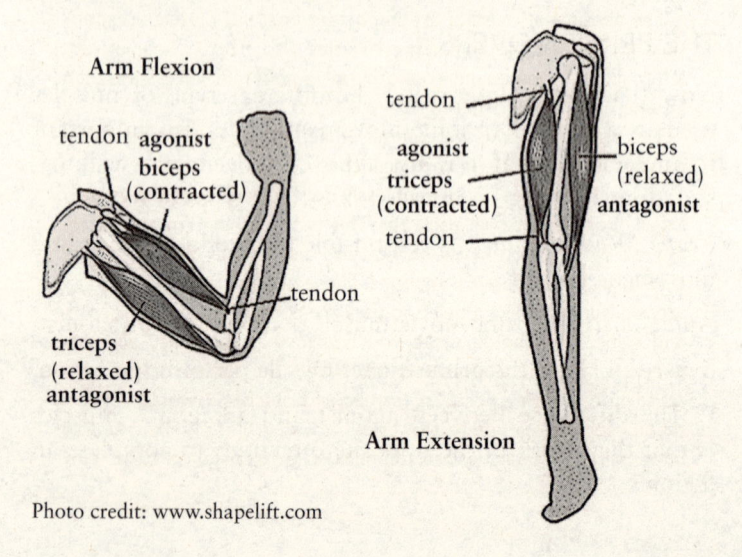

Arm Flexion

tendon — agonist biceps (contracted)

tendon

triceps (relaxed) antagonist

tendon

agonist triceps (contracted)

tendon

biceps (relaxed) antagonist

Arm Extension

Photo credit: www.shapelift.com

triceps are the agonist muscles. Meanwhile, the biceps muscles act as the antagonists. However, if the person then decides to perform biceps curls, the roles are reversed. The biceps change into agonists and triceps, the antagonists that react to the motions of the biceps.

Now that you know that the muscles are attached to bones and that so many muscle are required to perform a particular action. Don't lust after bulging biceps because you know that you will need to train the triceps equally. All muscles are interconnected and dependent on each other to perform a particular movement. Even the smallest muscle has a particular function and you need to devote equal amount of time to train all muscles and allow your body to move the way it is meant to.

STRENGHTENING YOUR AB MUSCLES THE RIGHT WAY

Ab muscles are most fitness buffs' favourite muscles to work out at the gym! Unfortunately 90 percent of them do not have strong abs because they don't train the muscles properly.

The abdominal muscles are important postural muscles responsible for flexing the spine. The muscles also help in keeping the internal organs intact and in creating intra-abdominal pressure, such as when exercising or lifting heavy weights.

The biggest mistake we commit while exercising our abdominal muscles is that we begin with 'crunches'.

You will often see people endlessly doing crunches at the gym to attain those elusive six-pack abs. This is something I'm absolutely against. By now you know it's not just one muscle but four layers that form the abdominal muscles. These abdominal muscles wrap around our waist like a belt and they are connected to the hip, ribs, and spine. This should make you realize that the most effective exercises for the abdominals are when the body rotates in a standing or lunging position. Instead of crunches, I would recommend movements where the body moves diagonally like the axe chop with a medicine ball, dumbbells, or resistance band. Any

> movement where your torso is twisted will help you strengthen your abdominal muscles.
>
> Another important factor to keep in mind is always begin by strengthening your back muscles first, and then move on to working on your abdominal muscles. Remember when you do any kind of ab exercise, you are essentially putting pressure on your back and hip since they are all connected. You can easily end up damaging your spine. First condition your body for a week or two by strengthening your back muscles, then work on isolation moves like plank and plank variations, and then begin working on your abs.
>
> The nine months of carrying a baby leads to muscle imbalance and overuse. New mothers should focus on slowly getting back to their workout programme by strengthening overused muscles of the core. Upper back and posterior shoulder exercises, squats, and deadlifts will help support the new roles of carrying, feeding, and lifting your newborn. You can also do gentle stepmill sessions.

FAST-TWITCH, SLOW-TWITCH

Have you noticed how some people are better at short sprints while others are better at marathons? It's because the composition of their muscles are different. Our skeletal (voluntary) muscles are made up of two main fibres—slow-twitch and fast-twitch. They are named such because of the speed at which they contract when stimulated. Slow-twitch fibres contract for long periods of time but with little force. They are responsible for endurance and help you run long, never-ending marathons or to go long on a treadmill or cycle. With more slow-twitch fibres, you can perform long cardio sessions and multiple repetitions of a lighter weight. On the other hand, fast-twitch fibres contract quickly and powerfully but fatigue very rapidly. They give your body explosive power and strength, helping you to jump and sprint. Similarly in weight training, it you want to lift heavy weights, you need more fast-twitch fibres which help you to lift heavy weights for a few repetitions or for short, very high intensity anaerobic exercises. The way to building more fast-twitch fibres is by including a mix of short periods of activity which involves power and strength—like a sprint or lifting heavy weights. This of course depends on your fitness level.

Sprinters target the fast-twitch fibres because their aim is to focus more on a regime of high intensity interval training to increase their anaerobic threshold and build muscle mass for power. Swimmers are more concerned with endurance, so they focus more on endurance workouts. You need to train your muscles according to your fitness goals.

To avoid creating 'bulk', women generally go for light weights with multiple reps. While this does enhance the ability of the muscle to lift weights, it does not build muscle. And without muscle, they can never get the toned, sculpted look they desire. Women should keep in mind that they have less muscle fibres as compared to men because of the high level of estrogen in their body, which is why they can never develop 'unfeminine' muscles. So don't dread weights for the fear of building unsightly muscles!

THE SHE-HULK SYNDROME

A lot of women come up to me and say, 'We don't want to attempt weight training since we don't want to end up looking like a man!' This is one of the biggest myths. Women have fewer fast-twitch and slow-twitch fibres, so they will not bulk up like men. Not just that, they have less testosterone levels as compared to men. So rest assured, unless you are lifting extremely heavy weights and taking testosterone injections, you will not become a She-Hulk!

> Most women are very scared of weight training. They are scared of building muscle. They think that by building muscles, they will become like men. It's a very weird concept. I will tell you when I was not working out, I used to dream of wearing white racer-back

> *ganjis* and jeans. I used to see all these Baywatch women on TV and I used to love their toned arms. I did not ever think that I would be able to achieve it. Now I believe that you can achieve what you want. But you have to get over the fact that you are going to build that much muscle like a man. Weight training is very important. It is something that is most essential. Most women are scared of weight training and they only keep doing cardio. It's not a smart thing to do.
>
> BIPASHA BASU, ACTOR

LISTEN TO YOUR BODY, IT'S SMARTER THAN YOU

So now you know how many muscles work to perform a particular action. It's not just about training the biceps or just the triceps. There's a whole lot more that needs to be taken account of when you are strengthening your body.

Any particular action involves three kinds of muscles—primary, secondary, and auxillary.

Primary muscles: These are the largest muscles capable of producing the most work (thigh, chest, and back muscles) and contributing to the overall strength development.

Secondary muscles: These are smaller muscles (sometimes called synergists) that contribute to the work produced by the primary muscles directly or help with balance or control.

Stabilizer muscles: These muscles stabilize an adjacent segment. Their main function is to hold a joint in place so that the exercise may be performed. Strong stabilizers help to prevent injuries and just give you an all-round better lift.

For example, in a shoulder press (when a lady lifts a coconut basket, the action of 'lifting' is overhead shoulder press) while using dumbbells, the primary muscle used is the anterior deltoid. The secondary muscles that assist the anterior deltoid are lateral deltoid, supraspinatus, triceps brachii (the triceps is actually only a two-headed muscle), middle trapeziusand pectoralis major, while the long head of the triceps, short head of biceps brachii (funnily enough, the biceps is a three-headed muscle), and upper trapezius act as stabilizers, holding the joint in place.

Anatomy in Motion

Perhaps the easiest sport to articulate the importance of

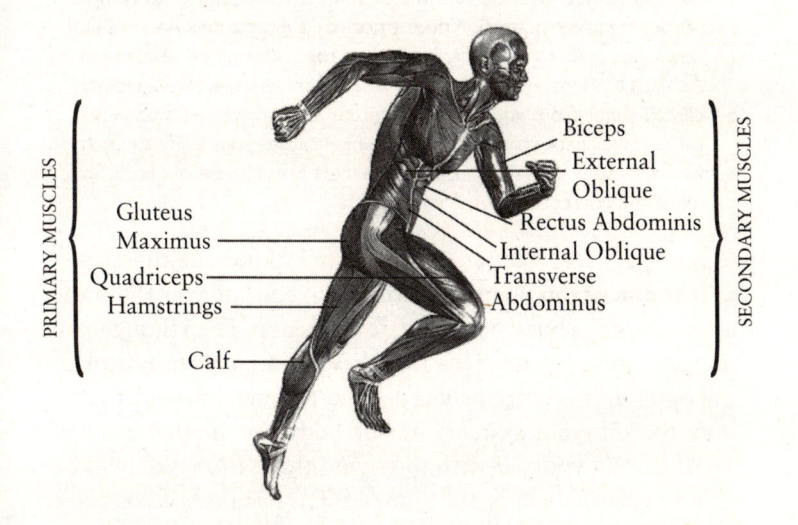

PRIMARY MUSCLES
- Gluteus Maximus
- Quadriceps
- Hamstrings
- Calf

SECONDARY MUSCLES
- Biceps
- External Oblique
- Rectus Abdominis
- Internal Oblique
- Transverse Abdominus

understanding biomechanics is running, since about three times the athlete's body weight is transmitted to their feet each time their foot strikes the ground. The force of the impact has a visible distortion on a lean runner's body.

The primary muscles involved in running are hamstrings, quadriceps, gluteus maximus, and the calf. The secondary or support muscles used are the biceps and the upper and lower abdominals. There are no auxiliary muscles used in running.

> ### Are Your Feet Killing You?
>
> Are you one of those women who can't just do without your high heels even though you know it's bad for your back and feet? Women may love wearing high-heeled shoes, but they cause so much harm to your feet. Any heel above 2 inches is considered 'high heel'. Such a shoe creates three to six times more stress on the front of the foot than a regular shoe. If you wear flats, the entire foot will absorb this impact. Humans are meant to walk heel-to-toe, with the leg at about a 90-degree angle to the foot and the ankle joint employing a 60-degree range of motion during normal daily activities. As a result, heels can lead to bunions, heel pain, toe deformities, shortened Achilles tendons, and trapped nerves. The ankle, knee, and hip joints can all suffer from your footwear preferences. High heels can also cause lower back strain because the heel causes your body to pitch forward more than normal, putting excess pressure on the back. So make the correct footwear choices.

The aim of this chapter is not just to educate you about the anatomy of the body but to create awareness. Even though you may feel what you have read so far was extremely technical, in my opinion it is extremely crucial in helping you understand how the different systems in our body our interconnected. By educating yourself with the right information, you will be able to visualize yourself inside out. For instance, if you have a knee problem, you know it could have originated in the spine. So many joints work together in order to make every move efficient. For your body to function at its optimal best, you need to work on each and every muscle. They all have to be strengthened equally to avoid imbalance of any sort.

I can't stress on the importance of functional training enough since it allows individuals to perform the activities of daily life more easily and without injuries.

Envisage a day when you are trying to run after a bus that has already left. You'll be able to catch the bus only if

The Way We Move

certain key muscles used in the movement are developed. As you move your leg forward, you use mainly the quadricep muscles at the front of your thigh. They bend your hip and straighten your knee. The quads also stabilize the knee and help absorb the shock of impact as you land.

As your body moves forward, the action switches to your hamstrings, the muscles at the back of your thigh, which straighten your hip and begin to bend your knee. The hamstrings also work to help you lift your knee behind you.

At the same time, the muscles of your lower leg, the soleus (inner calf) and gastrocnemius (outer calf) extend and flex each foot as you land and push off. These muscles also help absorb impact and give your stride spring.

To be able to catch that bus even after it has left, you need to train all of the aforementioned muscles equally to facilitate efficient movement.

Sometimes when you are excessively tired and feeling guilty of not having worked out, you push yourself. The truth is that you will only end up with an injury. So take time to pay attention to how your body works. The human body is meant to work like a well-oiled machine. The only time it doesn't is when you have done something wrong and caused an imbalance. Listen to your body as it gives you signs. It tells you when you are doing something wrong. Now that you have educated yourself as to how vast the network of muscles, joint actions, ligaments, tendons are in your body, you have no choice but to be intelligent and smart about your exercise and training methods.

AGEING

Option A. Healthy

Option B. Not Healthy

What would you choose?

The answer is pretty easy, right? Then why do most people find it so difficult to apply it to their lives? Here's what I want you to know—no matter what your age or condition, the first option will always be the right one: Healthy.

I am 44-years-old. I can arm wrestle with my kids. I can dance with my friends for hours and enjoy every moment without worrying about muscle cramps. I can choose to have my prawn curry rice in Goa or share a bowl of instant noodles with my teenage daughter and not feel guilty about it. I can twist my body into difficult yogasanas and yet manage to keep my mind steady. And do you know why I can do all of this? It's because I have made a conscious decision to eat and live healthy. It's not a punishment for me, it's not something I am forced to do; it's a way of life—like breathing or brushing my teeth. Over the years, my mind has become very strong. So even with a physical challenge like 50 push-ups, I can pull through the barrier of pain after the 40th push-up and reach my goal. As I age, I am amazed at how much my body and mind allows me to do because I have treated it so well over the years.

Ageing is a natural process—everybody goes through it. Our body suffers wear and tear over the years, and it affects us in many ways—our reflexes get slower, our joints get stiffer, and our food requirements change. But you have no excuse to not stay fit, no matter what your condition is. Seek help, ask for advice, go to a doctor, hire a personal trainer, go for a walk—take inspired action to just get off the couch. Even if you have never attempted exercising or eating healthy, you shouldn't spend the rest of your life that way. I keep going back to this—there's just one option: Healthy.

Research has proved that exercising helps increase bone density, regularizes blood pressure, and increases muscle mass, strength, and endurance. A study at McMaster University found that the ageing process occurs because of defects at the very cellular level—our mitochondria—which are the 'powerhouses' where energy production takes place. The study found that with regular endurance exercise, we can prevent premature ageing in nearly every organ of the body. Now that should be a good enough reason to exercise, shouldn't it?

So what's your excuse?

I often hear people using aches and pains that are a natural outcome of ageing as an excuse to not workout. Or they say 'I am too old to do that.' Someone rightly said: you are only as old as you think you are. Then, there are people who suffer from 'no time, lots of responsibilities' syndrome. The reasons vary—'I have to travel a lot for work', 'I have two kids and my life's crazy between making meals and taking care of their school stuff', 'I have to work long hours to provide for my family'…the excuses are endless. I want to say to you that you have it backwards. You first need to take care of yourself before you can take care of anybody else. Any form of exercise reduces stress, boosts energy levels, keeps lifestyle diseases like high blood pressure, heart attack, stroke, obesity and diabetes at bay, and slows down the ageing process. Fitness not only helps you stay active, it also helps you avoid injuries in old age because it strengthens the neuromuscular system.

> Fitness for me is a necessity, just like eating food or drinking water or breathing. It is just a part of all of us, so how can it be boring? I enjoy each and every workout I do or prepare. I have known Deanne for many years and have seen her get obsessed with the science of our bodies. Yes people get fanatical but then you stop having fun. Why do anything in life that isn't going to be something you are not going to enjoy?
>
> ARJUN RAMPAL, ACTOR

I truly believe that it is never too late to start getting fit, even if you are a couch potato. Why do you see people who have suffered and overcome problems like heart attack or diabetes getting active and healthier after the health scare has passed them? It's out of fright. They also become more aware of their body. Fitness helps you prevent these problems in the first place. The best part of your life is being able to control it and mastering how it ages. No matter what your age, or your ability to do things, you are designed to move. The more sedentary you become using age as an excuse, the more problems you are going to face.

Have you noticed how doctors tell new moms to start walking within a few days of giving birth to their baby? The reason is that the new moms have to be up and about so that they can take care of the newborn. Similarly, you should see fitness as a responsibility to take care of your body. Don't use age as an excuse. You can begin small—just 20 minutes of daily exercise that elevates your heart rate. If you have time to watch your favourite sitcom or go to a party or a satsang, then you DO have time to workout.

You need to break your love affair with your couch. Walk to the market to buy vegetables, walk to the temple, walk up the railway subway, or just walk up the stairs. Jog, swim, play cricket, dance, do what you love. Enjoy your life to your last breath and you can make it possible. It's all in the mind; it's all about having the will—just keep moving. My grandfather lived till 100 and he died of old age. When was the last time you heard of people living their life without aches and pains? Besides blindness caused due to old age, he had no other health conditions. That's how I'd like to live my life. We had a grand funeral to celebrate his life. I don't remember crying when he died. We have forgotten what it is to die of old age. Cancer, heart attacks, stress, and various other diseases are the cause of death now.

Get moving. Your older self will thank you.

Even though a lot of people over the age of 40 or 50 know that exercise is the key to healthy ageing, only a small percent follow it. The two most common problems of ageing are injuries and arthritis. Injuries occur as our reflexes become slower due to slower neuromuscular coordination. On the other hand, arthritis is the regular wear and tear of bones as we age.

I was at the gym one day and learnt that a good friend of mine, Neha, had joined a CrossFit class. Not only was Neha well past 50, she also had a history of osteoporosis which her trainer knew nothing about. Now CrossFit is a high intensity workout and is usually recommended to people below 30 years of age or if you are above average fit (if you have no medical history of joint issues, if you have well-conditioned muscles that can take the stress of this workout, or of you have an athletic background). I instantly knew that if Neha did CrossFit the wrong way, she would surely injure her spine and joints. Your muscle quality deteriorates over time and cannot take the impact of such a demanding training session. Understand that your organs are ageing internally and may not be functioning as smoothly in your 50s as they did in your 30s. But I'm not stopping you from doing something altogether either. In Neha's case, an ideal workout for her would be a bit of CrossFit mixed with TRX or yogasanas.

I will advise her against plyometric box jumps or kettlebell moves. One wrong kettlebell move could damage her spine because she already has a high history of osteoporosis which has already led to a considerable amount of bone loss. Her brittle bones make her extremely vulnerable to an injury.

Follow a more slow, steady, and balanced approach to fitness bearing the age factor and fitness levels in mind. And *don't* ever forget to discuss your medical history to your trainer.

In the last two months, I have been experiencing a slight stiffness in my ring and little finger. The doctor says it is osteopenia, which is a pre-cursor to osteoarthritis, a condition which runs in my family. I have been advised to increase my Vitamin D3 levels by taking in enough of morning sunlight in order to increase my bone mineral density levels.

Just this year I noticed a gray hair strand for the first time as I looked at myself in the mirror. And guess what? I was really excited to see it. This is what I call the 'joy of ageing'. Everybody ages but you don't have to make it a painful process. It's going to happen irrelevant of your fitness levels. You can't stress about it. You have to be able to move past your aches and pains to make the rest of your life as joyful and peaceful as you can.

To read more on anti-ageing and foods that help, go to page 83.

How your body ages

Oxygen is very important to every cell in the body. Without it, your cells cannot produce energy. As you get older, getting oxygen to the cells takes more energy. You build up lactic acid in your muscles which makes you sore. Suddenly you find that your highly efficient body has now been replaced by a less efficient one. The more we exercise, the more oxygen you get into your cells.

Let's take a look at the changes inside our body.

THE HEART

This is the most essential organ that manages our blood flow, blood pressure, and provides our body with oxygenated blood. Over 50 years, if we take an average of 50 beats per minute, our heart produces 2.1 billion heartbeats. No wonder is the heart is the first organ that starts deteriorating. Wrongful habits like smoking and eating unhealthy food puts more pressure on the heart and as you go grow older, your heart becomes more susceptible to diseases and other problems. Your maximum heart rate, the ability of the cardiac muscle to contract, and the stroke volume—all start declining with age.

While this is natural, you can slow many of these heart problems by exercise, proper diet, and management of blood pressure and stress. When blood pressure rises, the heart adjusts by pumping blood harder. Also, the arteries—blood vessels which carry oxygenated blood from the heart to the organs—become stiffer and less flexible with age. This is what causes your blood pressure to increase. Thus, the wall of your left ventricle becomes thicker with age. This thickening causes the heart to pump more to the stiff arteries.

Also, as the heart ages, it becomes less responsive to chemical messages from the brain. In old age, our body cannot exercise as intensely as when we were younger. That's why older people often experience shortness of breath.

ARTERIES

It is important to understand what happens to your arteries during ageing and how we all know that cardiovascular diseases are one of the biggest risk factors. Arteries are the tubes of the heart that carry blood away from heart to your lungs and to the rest of your body. Arteries are made of muscles and like other muscles in our body they tend to stiffen with age. Hardening of the arteries is caused by smoking and eating fatty foods. In addition, as our muscles age, the blood vessels become narrow, making the heart work harder to push blood through narrower arteries. The heart naturally compensates by becoming bigger. Usually softer, supple arteries don't show up on X-rays but the hardened ones do. Hardening of the arteries is not inevitable; exercise keeps the arteries supple and also allows for more blood to flow to the brain.

LUNGS

Everybody gets out of breath when they run fast, even an athlete. How soon you start getting out of breath depends of how much your body is conditioned to exercise. For instance, you will notice that an obese person will experience shortness of breath even when doing a simple stretching exercise. When you breathe, oxygen attaches itself to the red blood cells to be carried to the muscle or tissue that needs it.

But factors such as age as well as smoking prevent oxygen from entering the lungs. The amount of air the lungs can hold decreases by about 250 ml per decade. With age, the lung capillaries start declining and the exchange of oxygen and carbon dioxide becomes less efficient. Exercises, yoga, breathing, and meditation—all of them enhance lung capacity.

MUSCLES

As we age, muscle fibres decrease, leading to an increase in muscle stiffness. We also lose lean muscle mass. That's why most doctors recommend weight training for seniors because it helps build good quality muscle. With age, we go into muscle loss called sarcopenia. It's the degenerative loss of skeletal muscle mass (0.5–1 percent loss per year after the age of 25), quality, and strength associated with ageing. Lack of exercise is currently thought to be a significant risk factor to sarcopenia along with smoking, eating unhealthy foods, and a sedentary lifestyle.

The Way We Move

The reason why our muscles start shrinking is because our fast-twitch muscle fibres, which are responsible for muscle power, shrink by 30 percent as we age. That's why our strides get shorter and our muscles get stiffer.

But it's not all bad news. Exercise can actually help build good quality muscle. Research shows that weight training results 5 percent increase in strength per day.

BONES

It is the only dynamic organ that is constantly changing and remodeling over a lifespan. Bones experience a lot of stress and load, making them stronger. They get weak when they don't experience stress. This loss of bone density can lead to bones getting frail and a greater possibility of fractures.

Bone mass keeps growing till the age of 30 after which it reaches maximum strength and density known as peak bone mass. Women tend to experience minimal change in total bone mass between the age of 30 and menopause. But in the first few years after menopause, most women go through rapid bone loss which can lead to osteoporosis. It's a well-stated fact now that weight training helps slow down the degenerative process—in fact, many can even increase their bone density levels. I tell them to do weight-bearing exercises because that helps in increasing bone density levels by restoring bone loss.

CARTILAGE AND AGEING

Many people complain of knee pain as they age. This is because the cartilage in the knee joints start thinning and wearing out. The pain occurs because there is no cartilage to protect the joint. Inactivity decreases the health of the cartilage and causes it to soften.

If you are an athlete, a runner, or above 40, you must take this factor into consideration. Take symptoms like a slight knee pain seriously and get it checked by a doctor. If you continue to ignore the pain, it will become worse. Slow down high impact activity and strengthen the muscles which are surrounding that joint. This is why I recommend swimming because it's physiotherapy in water. It helps with arthritis and is suitable for all ages.

BODY FAT COMPOSITION

That got your attention, didn't it? Fitness is unfortunately still limited to how we look. But now you know there is so much more to it than that, and fitness goes down to the cellular level. With age, the body fat composition in men and women rises. The good thing is that even a few weeks of regular exercise can make a change in body fat percentage levels.

It also makes a big difference as to where you carry the body fat. It's a bigger problem if you carry fat mainly around your belly than on your hips and thighs. Fat around the belly is called visceral fat and is more dangerous than peripheral fat which lies mainly under the skin. Fat stores excess energy and works as a hormone-making organ that can cause high blood sugar, high blood pressure, and inflammation of the arteries. Exercise helps decrease visceral fat and can change the way your body looks.

NEUROMUSCULAR SYSTEM

I strongly believe in the mind–body connection. As we age, we suffer from a loss of coordination, balance, flexibility, and an increase in proprioception (sense of how your own limbs are oriented in space). Regular exercise and balanced training helps slow down the rate of decline in many of these. Yoga and meditation too help in strengthening the neuromuscular system and also our sense of balance.

> I had started doing yoga many years ago. For me, the time that I spend on the yoga mat is almost more meditative. I have done all kinds of yoga—as Deanne knows—Ashtanga, power yoga, name it, we have done it all. So it's not really meditative yoga but it's more about getting the focus back to your breath. That itself becomes meditation for the hour–hour and a half—that you spend on your mat. Yoga has helped me align my mind with my body.
>
> LARA DUTTA, ACTOR

AGE: JUST A NUMBER?

Some people will read this chapter and recognize these changes are happening to their body. The more sedentary your lifestyle, the faster would be the ageing process. Therefore challenge your body with exercise at any age and see the benefits.

And start now, especially if you want to be a rockstar like my children's dadi (my mom-in-law)! She wakes up at 4 in the morning and comes home at 8 in the evening. A nutritionist by profession, she runs a staff of 50 people without breaking a sweat! In fact, she is the one who introduced me to concepts like drinking milk mixed with haldi or cooking with no oil. Even at 70+, she looks and behaves young.

She can touch her toes, kick like a professional martial artist, or beat you in a wrestling match! She's never missed her 4 am yoga class, not even for a single day. She truly emits energy and she has been a constant source of inspiration in my life.

The other person who inspires me immensely is Swami Yogi Krishnan, whom I met at an international yoga festival in Rishikesh. A vegetarian, he does the most advanced postures, even at 75! It may sound clichéd, but age is just a number. Manage your life well and enjoy it till the end!

To conclude, all this starts happening in the body internally. There are days when you may feel stressed. People are so caught up in their lives that they take their body for granted. You're not meant to be like that. The brain can take it but not your body. You need to train the body so well that it is capable to keep up with the mind.

However good you may look on the outside, what is more important is how fit the body is on the inside. Like food, the body also has a shelf life and our body organs slow down with time. But you can reverse the ageing process by many years by keeping yourself fit, eating a healthy diet, and flushing out the toxins from your body.

Even though your body is continuously ageing, your mind can be fresh. Take the Dalai Lama for example. At his age, he still greets you like a little child.

In my class too, people are amazed to see me pick up heavier weights than them even though I'm elder to most of them. My strength and fitness levels have been acquired after years of practice, discipline, and self-motivation. Remember, age is just a number.

2
The Way We Eat

CLEAN EATING AND LIVING—THERE'S NO OTHER WAY TO BE

In December 2012, I had gone to Goa—the town of beaches, sands, and surf—for a month-long course in Ashtanga Yoga. It was an eco-friendly resort in the middle of a jungle serving fabulous vegetarian dishes and raw salads made from organic fresh produce. The vegetables and fruits were grown in the plantations and there was special emphasis on water conservation. No toilet rolls were allowed because it was considered wastage of paper. The air was fragrant; everything from the flowers to the greenery was pleasing to the eye. For me, there is nothing more fulfilling than having clean air and clean food. I didn't need to meditate, I was already in heaven.

The food was served buffet-style, in open air terraces. Everything, from the organic, chemical-free food to the yoga, the cotton clothes that we were wearing at the resort, and the air that we were breathing was 'clean'.

Within two-three days of being in the resort, I felt an instant energy change. I was able to do hours of asanas with ease, work on my book, and go for walks on the beach. I would wake up every morning feeling positive about myself.

I had my cheat meals too. I believe in balance and moderation, so two evenings in the two weeks that I was in Goa, I stepped out of the resort to enjoy my prawn curry rice. There was no way that I was going to be in Goa and not have my favourite dish! But that did not affect my weight or energy levels at all. In fact, I had lost weight without realizing it and my body felt stronger and fitter than before. It was like the kilos had melted away and so had the stress. I got back to Mumbai and shot for the book cover. Tina Dehal, the photographer, told me that my skin was glowing and I looked years younger. I'm not boasting, but the image you see on the cover hardly required any photoshopping!

All I want to tell you is that this is how life should be—organic, fuss-free, energy-boosting, and fresh. I want to go a step further and say it's not just about healthy, nutritional food but it's about clean eating and living. I am convinced that if we want our bodies to perform optimally and maintain a constant energy level, we need to get our diet right. If weight loss or muscle building is your goal, then adopt the Clean Eating and Living Programme. You will not realize how the kilos literally fall off or how you start building good quality muscle. The benefits of such an approach will be that you will not feel fatigued and will look forward to your workouts and meals. I would say that almost 80 percent of a healthy living plan is about the clean food you eat.

PROJECT CLEAN EATING AND LIVING

I have been practising the concept of 'Clean Eating and Living' for over 15 years now and have come pretty close to perfecting it. How did I do it, you ask? The answer is to make a plan and take baby steps towards it.

I make sure all my meals are simple—from dal-chawal, chicken stews, and salads to simple curries and multigrain rotis. If I make burgers at home, I use multigrain bread. Everything from fresh fruits and vegetables to the oil used

The Way We Eat

is pure and organic. I don't use teflon-coated non-stick pans because they can release toxic gases when heated at a high temperature. The water bottles I use are made of glass, not plastic, because I like to reduce the use of plastic for environmental concerns. I believe this has gone a long way in maintaining optimal health for so many years. My kids are also on the leaner and fitter side—they eat French fries when they want but by and large, they love simple food.

I once read a poster somewhere—'Your food isn't making you fat; your life is making you eat. Put your life on a diet.' Nothing could be closer to the truth. I feel clean eating and living has helped me stay lean, fit, and youthful. The big secret is that it's not just about training programmes, lifting weights, or cardiovascular exercise. It's about the small changes that you need to make in your life to boost your body to get that 'perfect ten' physique.

> I eat like a boy sometimes. Everybody's body is different. You have to learn to know what your weaknesses are. Everybody knows the basics of clean eating—stay away from junk food, fried foods, or processed foods. These are the basics that we all know but don't follow. So if you want to get healthy, you should start following the basics.
>
> BIPASHA BASU, ACTOR

Eating disorders are the order of the day—teenagers and young moms are starving themselves to death. Younger people are suffering from arthritis and heart diseases. Not just that, many people are depressed because they just can't lose the last few kilos or they seem to yo-yo from fat to thin.

The fact is that we are surrounded by toxins and chemically-saturated food and it is destroying the natural rhythm of our body. This is the reason why people are struggling to lose weight and are not able to look fit and healthy.

Clean eating and living can help you lose the kilos and get a beautiful, toned body. It emphasises:

- ✓ Removal of toxins from every layer of our body
- ✓ Eating nutritious, organic, simple foods

Is There Toxicity in Your Body?

There was a time in my life when I was struggling with weight loss (yes, me!). On most days, I would feel extremely bloated and shedding the kilos seemed like a Herculean task even though I was eating healthy and working out. So what was causing the bloating, the gas, and the mild acidity? Why was I having difficulty losing the last three inches? My sister suggested I give this particular ayurvedic spa in Kerala named Somatheeram a try. Now my knowledge of Ayurveda was very basic, so I accepted her advice rather reluctantly. And boy was I pleasantly surprised.

According to Ayurveda, the body functions normally only when its doshas, dhatus, malas, and agni are in a state of equilibrium. When either of these factors are not functioning optimally, one falls sick. Their diagnosis revealed that I was a Pitha–Vatha and my doshas were not balanced. To get my doshas back on track, I was put on a specific diet for a week to help cleanse my stomach lining. By just the second day of the diet, I noticed that I had started sweating a lot. This was a sure sign that all the unwanted toxins in my body were being flushed out. I came back home to be greeted by compliments from my near and dear ones. They all wanted to know how I had managed to lose so many inches in just a week!

My experience shows that if I can knock off the inches in just one week by cleansing my internal organs, so can each one of you. Won't you agree that with age, our digestive system too is ageing and needs an occasional cleansing? It's not just about muscles and weight loss anymore. It's about making changes at the cellular level because only when we

The Way We Eat

break the toxic link do big changes occur in our bodies. It's about removing toxins bit by bit from your environment and diet to adopt a truly healthy lifestyle.

Toxins are poisonous substances produced by living organisms that can cause health problems and even death. Many of these toxins are dumped into water supplies and the food chain, which then impacts us.

If you want to lose weight or bulk up, you have to reduce the toxic levels in your body. The reality is many of you have high levels of toxicity and may not even know it.

Answer the questions below with a Yes or a No.

- Do you have trouble losing weight?
- Are you stuck at losing the last few kilos?
- Do you have food cravings most of the time?
- Do you feel fatigued or listless without any particular reason?
- Do you suffer from muscle aches and pains frequently (once a week)?
- Do you suffer from joint pains?
- Do you suffer from bloating, gas, or irritable bowel syndrome?
- Do you suffer from water retention?
- Do you suffer from problems in bowel movement, constipation, or diarrhoea?
- Do you have foul-smelling stools?
- Do you suffer from frequent acidity attacks or heartburn?
- Do you have foul body odour or bad breath problem?
- Do you have a coating on your tongue when you get up in the morning?
- Do you have difficulty sleeping or insomnia?
- Do you lack focus or have trouble concentrating on work?
- Do you have nasal congestion or sinus problems?

- Do you frequently experience headaches?
- Do you suffer from skin rashes, skin problems, acne, or eczema?
- Do you have watery eyes or nose most of the time?
- Do you have dark circles or puffy eyes?
- Do you suffer from skin and food allergies?
- Do you suffer from painful PMS or other menstrual problems?
- Are you moody, irritable, and angry most of the time?
- Are you a smoker?
- Do you have alcohol often?

If it's a yes to more than three questions, you have a high level of toxicity in your body.

Now, answer the questions about the environment you live in with a Yes or a No.

- Do you stay close to an industrial plant or chemical factory?
- Do you stay in a city where pollution levels are high?
- Do you stay close to a road where there is a lot of traffic?
- Do you drink or eat out of plastic containers, plates, and cutlery?
- Do you heat your food in plastic containers?
- Do you buy fruits and vegetables from stores which are exposed to car exhaust fumes?
- Do you eat fish brought from coastal areas where mercury levels are high?
- Do you eat a lot of processed and junk food?
- Do you eat a lot of street food or fried foods?
- Do you have constant cravings for salty or sweet food?
- Are you on a lot of medication?
- Do you have antibiotics at the drop of a hat?
- Do you take sleeping pills every day?

Even if you have answered yes to one of these questions, bingo! You have toxicity in your body and you need to keep a watch on it.

OK, I'M READY TO SIGN UP! BUT HOW DO I BEGIN?

Now that you are convinced, you do not need to sell off your city apartment and buy a house in the village or turn vegetarian or give up fast food in a day. When you start the 'Clean Eating and Living' programme, you need to go slow and steady. If you are a meat-eater, replace one meal a day with vegetarian dishes and salads. If you drink a lot of coffee, substitute one cup with a juice or decaf. If you are addicted to junk food, try eating only fresh produce for one entire week in a month. Once you build confidence and start seeing the changes in your body, you will be able to make many more changes to your lifestyle.

Drastic measures don't really work. You have to basically prepare your body to remove the toxins. For instance, the first time I went vegetarian for two weeks, I noticed that my hair started falling. My doctor told me it was because of a deficiency in vital minerals and vitamins because my body wasn't used to it. I adopted the slow and steady 'Clean Eating and Living' programme more than a decade ago, before I even realized what I was doing. Eight years back, I gave up eating red meat and then four years back, I also gave up protein shakes. I didn't enjoy the feeling of eating meat or consuming excess protein. Now I am literally off chicken and I mainly eat fish and vegetarian food. I also have a lot of natural products—from hemp protein to flaxseeds to almond milk. I also make sure all my cosmetics and fragrances are organic and toxin-free. I use simple soaps which are made of natural products. Most importantly, I love to relax, have fun, and be calm even in stressful situations. I believe that the biggest toxin in our body is negative emotions or stress. Stress is a 21st century disease and the medicine is free and known to all—be happy. So take time out to lighten up, laugh, and play.

FIVE COMMANDMENTS TO GET RID OF TOXINS FROM YOUR BODY

1st Commandment: Clean Your Pantry and Home

That grilled fish that you are enjoying with sautéed vegetables may just be a forkful of mercury you are putting into your mouth. That plastic bottle from which you are drinking your litre-a-day may actually be making you fat! And if you have been popping antibiotics, you probably suffer from water retention. I am not trying to scare you. The fact is that if you really want to lose that weight and be in the prime of your health, you need to look at everything that you use, eat, and drink a little more closely.

The First Step: Eat Clean

1. FRUITS AND VEGETABLES: GO GREEN, GO ORGANIC

#Shopping Smart: Buy organic fruits and vegetables to remove the toxins, unwanted hormones, and antibiotics from your body. Organic produce does not have any chemicals or pesticides. No pesticides also means healthier soil and water which means it's good for the environment. So why not do your bit and go green? I've seen many people taking to growing their own fruits and vegetables on their terrace and there's no reason why you can't do it too. Start simple with spinach and tomatoes.

#Produce by Perfection: Buy seasonal fruits and vegetables as much as possible. Buy mangoes in the peak of summer. Don't be greedy and buy the early varieties because they are ripened unnaturally. Have mooli, spinach, and methi in the winter months.

#*No Fumes on my Produce!:* Don't buy produce which has been lying forever near a busy road and has layers of car fumes and pollutants on it. Try and buy from vendors who sit away from traffic. Every small step makes a difference.

2. Make Sure that the Animal Products You have are Hormone-free

#*Something Smells Fishy!:* The Centre for Science and Environment has found that mercury contamination in India is reaching alarming levels due to industrial pollution. Mercury is poisonous is all forms—it can trigger depression, suicidal tendencies, paralysis, kidney failure, Alzheimer's disease, impotence, and allergies. Even small amounts of mercury exposure can adversely affect the cardiovascular system. It's difficult to know which fish varieties have mercury content in India. So eat everything in moderation. You need to burn what you consume. Make sure you limit the amount of fish you have in a week to twice or thrice. Be careful when you eat sushi or raw fish since they tend to be high in mercury content.

#*Buy Chicken and Meat which are Hormone-free:* There are certain hormones injected in chicken and young animals so that they can gain weight quickly. This in turn helps the meat and dairy industries make more profit because of the reduced waiting time for an animal to be slaughtered and sold in the market. Become friendly with your local butcher—ask him where the chickens are bred. Choose the farm-bred variety and look for the skinny chickens since the probability of a fat chicken being hormone-injected is far more.

#*To Drink Milk or not to:* Ages ago, we would get milk straight from the local cows in the farms. Now, that has become a luxury even in India. Adulterated milk is the biggest problem here. Time and again, in raids conducted across the country, authorities have found thousands of litres of synthetic milk and adulterated milk products like paneer, yogurt, and ghee are being used and sold. Cows are being injected with the hormone oxytocin to increase production. This has been linked to cancer and other such diseases. Try and find a place where you can get fresh milk. Make paneer, dahi, and ghee at home. I make it a point to drink hormone, chemical free, fresh farmer's milk that comes in glass bottles.

#Honey, I Shrunk the Kids: Vegan diets consider honey an animal product because the bees change the plant product, nectar, into honey. Recently, there was a furore when lab results found that well-known honey brands in India had high levels of antibiotics in it. That is appalling since so many of us have honey because we think it is good for health and considered a cure for many ailments according to ayurveda. Stick to organic options instead of the ones you can get in the market which are anyway loaded with sugar. If you have a chance to buy local honey when you travel to smaller towns and villages, go ahead and stock them. They will probably be the most nutritious and fragrant honeys you will come across.

3. STOP THE WHITE MENACE:

#Junk the Junk Food: Drop all kinds of fast food, processed food, fried food, 'white' food like white flour and white bread—you are just drawing up a death sentence for yourself. You know the risks—hypertension, diabetes, heart problems, and obesity. Even though you know that there are zero nutrients and vitamins in these kinds of food, why would you repeat consuming them day in and day out? The aloo parantha that is homemade with multigrain flour and local potatoes is healthier than the aloo tikki burger that you wolf down at a fast food restaurant. Yes, both have high calories but at least the parantha is full of vitamins and minerals and is not processed. Over time, instead of frying the parantha with loads of ghee, use healthy oils or reduce the ghee content. It's like taking the first step towards clean eating and living and then making incremental changes.

#Brown Bread or Caramel Colour?: Wondering why you have still not lost weight even after sticking to brown bread sandwiches? If your packet of brown bread has a list of things you can't pronounce, don't buy it. It should be just bread made from unrefined, whole wheat flour. In our stores, it is usually regular maida mixed with a little caramel colour. Sometimes, almost as if the companies felt a little guilty, a little aata may be added. Unless you are buying from a high-end bakery, you are better off sticking to whole wheat rotis and chapatis you make at home. An egg-white omelette wrapped in a chappati has more nutrition and fibre than the same slapped between two slices of fake brown bread. If you feel a little more adventurous, bake your own multigrain bread.

4. Is your Water Filtered Enough?:

There is a sea of pollutants in the water we drink, shower, or even gargle with. As more rivers are getting polluted, the municipalities are finding it difficult to treat river water to safe levels and supply it to the citizens. And if you think you are safe with bottled water, think again! The Centre for Science and Environment laboratory report analysed bottled water samples from Mumbai and Delhi. The samples contained a deadly cocktail of pesticide residues, some with even five different pesticide residues, in levels far exceeding the standards specified as safe for drinking water. Always boil your drinking water, even if it is filtered. My mother would strain the boiled water in a mulmul or muslin cloth to make sure we had clean drinking water.

The Second Step: Dump Plastic

Your Plastic Bottles Could be Making You Fat!

Plastic bottles contain Bisphenol A (BPA), a synthetic chemical agent that is used in plastic food and beverage containers such as baby bottles. It is also a component of the lining of canned metal food cans. BPA can leach out from the container and contaminate the food inside, particularly when exposed to high temperatures. Recently, BPA has been implicated in many adverse health conditions, including an increased risk of obesity. Research shows that BPA mimics the role of hormones in our body, making it a potential endocrine disruptor. This simply means it throws our hormonal system out of whack. Switch to stainless steel or glass bottles.

Say No to Plastic Bags

Something like a simple plastic bag can be a bagful of toxins. Use biodegradable bags instead. Carry your own cotton or jute bags to the market. Get rid of plastic toys for your children and instead buy wooden toys. Also make sure the toys or crayons you buy are non-toxic. Polyvinyl chloride (PVC), another form of plastic, is present in cling wrap and cooking oil bottles. So if you wrap a healthy sandwich in cling wrap, it gives out chemicals. Store your food in glass containers instead of plastic containers. Limit the use of plastic cutlery, unless it's BPA free; use kulhads, clay pots, good old stainless steel, or ceramic cups.

The Third Step: Do You Really Need that Medication?

Be Wary of Antibiotics; You Could Put on Weight

Don't pop antibiotics at the drop of a hat. They disrupt the natural healing process of our bodies. Only in India are antibiotics given so easily over the counter—be it a throat itch or a sneezing fit. Yes, they are good for you if you're really unwell, since they destroy the 'bad' bacteria in your system. But they also destroy the 'good' bacteria, the friendly ones which boost immunity. Research shows that good bacteria also plays an important role in regulating the hormone ghrelin which is responsible for controlling fat development and hunger. This could lead to obesity, type-2 diabetes, and inflammation of the digestive tract. Remember, anything anti means it works against the body's natural rhythm. Have antibiotics only when really required and under a doctor's supervision.

#Medications and the Dreaded Belly Fat

Most women suffer from yeast infections when they have antibiotics because the medication kills off bacteria that prevent the overgrowth of yeast, a fungus that lives in our intestines and produces chemical toxins which can make us dizzy and exhausted. Yeast causes water retention because the body is attempting to flush out the toxins. It also diminishes the thyroid function and increases sugar cravings, leading to weight gain and unwanted belly fat.

The Fourth Step: Get Rid of Non-stick Cookware

Think Your Non-stick is a Blessing? Think Again!

When non-stick pans were first introduced, everybody thought they were a godsend—you could cook with just a teaspoon of oil just like the doctor or dietician prescribed. But now we know better. The coating on your non-stick Teflon pans is Polytetrafluoroethylene (PTFE), a fluorocarbon based polymer known for its high resistance to solvents, acids, and bases. But what you don't know is that when PTFE heats up, it releases toxic gases that have been linked to cancer, organ failure, reproductive damage, and other harmful health problem. So what's the solution? Keep using your non-stick pans but don't heat it to a high temperature. Use old-fashioned utensils like cast iron pans or stainless steel. Opt for baking or steaming your food instead of cooking in a non-stick pan.

The Fifth Step: Your Household Cleaning Products May be Toxic

You are Cleaning Your House with Chemical Hazards

The cleaners you use are the worst offenders. If you suffer from respiratory problems or find it difficult to keep up your lung power, maybe the sprays you use are to blame. All-purpose cleaners often contain ammonia, linked to liver and kidney damage. Bleach is a powerful oxidizer which can burn eyes and skin. Many strong toilet cleaners give out noxious fumes. Switch to natural products like baking soda to unclog drains, and remove stubborn stains and stale smells from the kitchen and fridge—it is cheap, non-toxic, and has multiple uses.

What's that Smell?

Air fresheners may smell fragrant but they can choke you and cause all sorts of respiratory problems. Most of them have phthalates—chemicals that can cause hormonal abnormalities, reproductive problems, and birth defects. Instead, a non-toxic cleaning product which can work as a substitute is good old vinegar—it works well both as a disinfectant and deodorant. A bowl of vinegar kept in the microwave will absorb the smells of food. You can even simmer cinnamon and cloves in water and have a natural aroma of baking in the house. Or you can make your own fragrances by using a few drops of your favourite essential oil in tiny aromatherapy diffusers.

The Sixth Step: Eco-friendly Cosmetics and Soaps

Toxins in Your Make-up

Your skin is your largest organ. From shampoos and soaps to body scrubs, moisturisers, and perfumes, from your eyeliner to your nail polish, all of them contain several toxins which can penetrate the skin and even affect vital organs over time. Always check the ingredient list. If it has urea, it can cause skin irritations, allergies, and even joint pain. Parabens can mimic the hormone estrogen in the body and act as an endocrine disruptor. When the body's hormone system is not working optimally, visible symptoms will be exhaustion, food cravings, and weight gain. Turn to ayurvedic and organic products instead. There are so many options available out there, not just in the market but in our very homes as well. Remember the homemade products that were all the rage before—besan and milk for the skin, cream or malai to moisturize, or even pure almond oil. We should turn back to these options rather than load our skin with chemicals. Organic soaps are available even in several stores around the country.

These are simple ways to keep toxins from taking over your body and your life. Once you start following these tips, you will notice the changes in your body. The weight yo-yoing will stop and the food cravings will go away by itself.

The Route to Removing Toxins the Right Way

This is how you go about removing toxins from your body bit by bit:

Pre-Detox

Since your brain and body is used to a certain lifestyle, begin slowly—make one change in a month. A detox journal can be used to make notes of the changes that you have made. It could range from the foods you eat to the products you apply on your skin. If you prefer your laptop to a diary, create an excel sheet or you can make notes on your mobile phone, whatever is easiest for you. If you have more serious issues like obesity, do it slowly and under the supervision of a doctor. You can start with eliminating sugar or white bread. This is called pre-detox. Then you can try adding a lot of vegetarian, vegan, or organic food to your diet for better health.

Clean eating and living involves taking time to know what your food is made of and choosing to eat it in its most natural state. It's not about eating boring food, it's not about just sipping on detox juices—it's about feeling like every bite of food that you put in your mouth is good, healthy, and nutritious for your body. The closer the foods are to the soil, the purer and healthier they are.

Note the changes

Once you are well underway with the pre-detox process and have got down to eating healthy meals, start noting down changes that you feel in your energy levels and physical appearance in your detox journal. Are your inflammations disappearing? Do you still experience coughs, colds, migraines, or headaches? These signs are important to look out for since they tell you that you are well on track. Soon you will notice that your digestive system will start working like clockwork; your stressed liver will be functioning normally again. The anti-ageing process will be set in motion and people will start complimenting you. You will feel lighter, cleaner, and more beautiful. And though you will start losing kilos easily, that will cease to be your only objective. You will start seeing that negative emotions will go away and your perspective on life will change.

Adopting the Clean Eating and Living Lifestyle

Once you're in a pre-detox mode, you will find yourself automatically reaching for a healthy lifestyle. You will make sure that your sleeping patterns are right. Instead of going for a 3-day detox plan, try and do it for life. Nobody's telling you not to have cheat meals; it's all about striking a balance.

> I think it is very important to detoxify yourself and your body on a regular basis because we don't realize even when we eat healthy. We don't realize the build-up that happens in the lining of our stomach. I really advise this for people who have been stuck in a rut, or who are unable to lose weight—do a detox—it will help you eliminate a lot of toxins from your system. It will make your digestive system work again and it will give you that jump-start to weight loss.
>
> LARA DUTTA, ACTOR

DO IT FOR YOURSELF

Last but not the least, don't let others bully you into doing something that is not right for you. I recently went for a christening ceremony and they had a lavish spread with all kinds of meat and pastas and curries. But I chose to pile my plate with salads and took two pieces of chicken. I could hear people whispering, 'Oh, there she is, dieting again' or 'Come on, Deanne. Eat just this once'. But I didn't care. Once you get into the fit lifestyle, this becomes second nature to you. Remember to be light-hearted and laugh, but don't change yourself.

2nd Commandment: Fix Your Gut, Get Your Liver and Endocrine Glands to Work

If you're having trouble losing weight, good chances are that it's because of poor gut health. Your gut not only controls how efficiently you lose weight, it also controls your metabolism.

Have you ever used the phrase: 'I don't think I have the guts to do that'? What does the word 'gut' really mean?

The gut is the gastrointestinal tract in our body, a tube which runs from the mouth to the anus. It's about 15 feet long, consisting of the food pipe, stomach, intestines, and anus. The gut processes food, and though most people don't think about gut health in terms of weight loss, it is responsible for effective digestion, metabolism, fat breakdown, toxin removal, flushing out excess water, and thyroid and hormone regulation. A healthy gut is crucial to fulfilling your weight loss goals because the gut controls your metabolism and how efficiently you'll lose weight.

A healthy gut helps you to have constant energy levels and keeps inflammation at bay. Optimizing your gut health can help you lose weight and meet your athletic goals.

Did you know that 99 percent of all diseases begin in the gut? This list of diseases due to a malfunctioning gut is long and includes Irritable Bowel Syndrome (IBS), obesity, bloating, water retention, acidity, constipation, diarrhoea, chronic fatigue, allergies, depression, and many more. You may be struggling to lose your belly fat and may not realize that it's your inner tube which is the root cause of the problem.

That's why it's absolutely essential that you fix your gut if you want to be fit, toned, and strong, and lose weight.

Is Your Gut Killing You?

Each part of your gut has a different function—digestion, absorption of essential nutrients and minerals, and elimination of waste matter. There's also a whole lot more—whatever affects the health of your gut affects your hormonal function, nervous system function, and the immune system function. Your gut has a quite a few tasks to manage. These includes:

Taking care of Gut Flora: The gut is home to trillions of bacteria which form an interdependent ecosystem called the gut flora which helps digest food, remove toxins, and produce healing compounds which help keep the body healthy. A healthy adult has about two kilos of such bacteria in his gut. This ecosystem must be kept in balance. Harmful ones like yeast can seriously damage your health. By taking care of these bacteria, we can prevent and even reverse heart disease, autoimmune disease, obesity, allergies, or even cancer.

Keeping the Gut–Immune System Intact: If you want to remove toxins from your body, you gut must be absolutely healthy. Eighty percent of our immune system cells line the digestive tract and protect it. These cells prevent damage by unhealthy bacteria, caffeine, excess sugar, alcohol, processed foods, and antibiotics. If you consistently put these products into your body, one day the cells give up, thus activating the immune response mechanism in the body. This could lead to all sort of diseases including unexplained infertility, arthritis, skin diseases, allergies, etc. It could also lead to the 'leaky gut syndrome'—the food and toxins are not broken down for absorption and elimination and so they 'leak' through the damaged wall of the gastrointestinal tract directly into the blood stream. This is what causes inflammation, stress hormones in the body, and throws the detoxification abilities out of gear.

Gut Feelings Boosted by the Nervous System: The gastrointestinal tract is loaded with neuron cells that release the same neurotransmitters found in the brain: serotonin, dopamine, and so on. More than 70 percent of the body's serotonin is made in the brain. This is important because serotonin helps in the regulation of learning, sleep, and checking mood swings. It is also nature's very own appetite suppressant—it makes you feel satiated even when your stomach is not full. The result is weight loss! Anything which irritates or is harmful to the gut will send a message through the body's nervous system and will contribute to you feeling angry, irritated, anxious, or depressed. On the other hand, food that is nourishing and healing to the gut will keep you calm and relaxed.

> ### THE PROMISE OF PROBIOTICS: BOOSTING GOOD GUT BACTERIA
>
> The meaning of the word 'probiotic' is 'good for life'. Natural probiotics are foods that contain live good bacteria that contribute to the health and balance of the gut. Probiotics promote fast recovery after illnesses. They work great for certain types of yeast infections. Along with significantly lowering the risk of allergic reactions, they also lower the chances of developing respiratory tract infections and help fight urinary tract infections.
>
> If you want to boost good gut bacteria, have these natural probiotics:
>
> - Yogurt (which contain the bacteria lactobacillus paracasei and lactobacillus rhamnosus)
> - Buttermilk
> - Cottage cheese (paneer)
> - Any kind of aged cheese
> - Indian snacks made from fermented batter including idlis, dosas, dhoklas, khandvi, etc
> - Kefir (sour, fermented milk popular in Russia and parts of Europe)
> - Kimchi (spicy, fermented cabbage, a traditional Korean dish)
> - Miso (fermented soybean paste used in soups, popular in Japan)
> - Sauerkraut (finely shredded cabbage, fermented in brine)
> - Tempeh (fermented soybean product from Indonesia)
>
> Note: You can suffer from bloating or gas if you have too much of probiotics. Try to stick to natural products as much as possible and always take supplements under the supervision of a doctor.

Why You Need to Love Your Liver

Now you know the importance of keeping the gut in healthy condition if you want to lose weight quickly.

So how does the liver come into play?

Very few people know that the biggest secret to losing fat is keeping your liver (yes, you heard that right!) in top working condition. The liver is considered the biggest fat burning organ in the body. Not just that, it is also the prime detoxification organ. When the liver is unable handle the excess fat and sugar, the fat and sugar piles up in all the wrong places of your body. The liver is the heart of the toxin removal system and is responsible for performing many functions that are critical to your well-being. Your liver is the only organ in your body that has the ability to regenerate itself by creating new tissue. That means it can still function, even if a significant part of the organ is diseased or removed.

A quick look at all the important functions that the liver takes care of:

- ✓ Helps digest food by releasing bile
- ✓ Makes, stores, and releases sugars and fats
- ✓ Clears the blood of waste products and toxins
- ✓ Breaks down hormones and old blood cells
- ✓ Produces essential proteins, including blood clotting and enzymes
- ✓ Supplies vitamins, minerals, and iron to the parts of body where needed

Liver and the Weight Problem

Your Very Own Fat Processing Plant: The liver breaks down fat and compounds, and to boost the absorption of fat and fat-soluble vitamins, it produces bile. It stores the bile in your gall bladder where it can be disposed off to the intestine when needed. If there is excess fat in your body, the liver combines fatty acids and glycerol to form a storage molecule and sends it to your body's natural storage depots, like tissue just under the skin. When your energy levels are low, this stored fat is converted back into glycerol and the remaining fatty acids are used for energy. So if you want to process your fat better, be good to your liver!

An Energy Switch: It's a known fact that carbohydrates provide instant energy. But it's actually your liver which manages the release of this vital energy. Once the carbohydrates are broken down into glucose in the gut, the glucose enters the blood stream and it is taken to the liver. The liver cells either release the energy to you when it's needed or store it for later use when you need an energy boost.

A Protein Regulator: Proteins help you build muscle and the liver is in charge of processing proteins. Once proteins are broken down into amino acids in your intestines, they enter the blood stream and flow directly into the liver. The liver cells work on removing nitrogen from the proteins which would otherwise change into a highly toxic substance—ammonia. Your liver then converts this into urea to be eliminated through urine from your body. If the liver produces too much uric acid, the patient will have too much of the acid in the blood. This condition is called hyperuricemia. Supersaturated uric acid in the urine can crystallize to form kidney stones.

A Detox Machine: When harmful toxins enter your blood stream, the liver acts to destroy them. The toxins could be anything from a by-product of metabolism to alcohol to inhaled substances such as drugs. The liver filters your blood, removes dead cells, bad bacteria, processes nitrogen and cholesterol, and neutralizes harmful hormones. All toxins are then transported to the intestine or kidney for removal. When you eat clean, your liver automatically gets detoxed.

A Vitamin Health Store: Many vitamins and minerals are stored in the liver for use when the body needs them the most. It stores vitamins A, B12, D, E, and K as well as minerals like iron and copper.

Just like you would take care of your gut, you have to learn how to take care of your liver through healthy eating and exercise.

Your Body's Secret Weight Loss Weapons

By now you know that just eating right and exercising is not enough. In fact, if you understand how your body works, you

The Way We Eat

will experience such astonishing results that you would be kicking yourself as to why you didn't educate yourself earlier.

Hormones are like Your Body's Secret Weight Loss Weapons!

A majority of people with weight issues don't realize that they have an exhausted endocrine gland to blame. The endocrine system is made up of glands that secrete chemicals called 'hormones' into the bloodstream or surrounding tissues. An overstressed gland leads to hormonal imbalance, thus causing weight gain. This is why it's important that you understand the endocrine system since there is a vital link between weight loss, muscle gain, appetite, and your hormones, which are secreted by the endocrine glands. This is not a biology class; it's about understanding that the function of these glands to assist you in achieving your athletic goals. High level athletes and holistic fitness enthusiasts understand this and they work with their bodies to push it to its optimal level.

The major endocrine glands are the pituitary, pineal, thymus, thyroid, adrenal glands, and pancreas. Men produce hormones in their testes and women produce them in their ovaries.

Think of your hormone as a chemical messenger—the brain sends a signal, the hormones get secreted, and then they head towards the target cell to bring about a particular change in that cell. For instance, insulin acts as a chemical messenger and signals to the liver, muscles, and fat tissues to absorb glucose from the blood and store it as glycogen. As the glucose level in the blood drops to normal levels, the insulin release slows down or stops.

It takes only a tiny amount of hormonal imbalance to cause big changes in your body. That is why too much or too little of a certain hormone can be serious. It's like your body is running without any chemical messengers to guide it.

And this can result in several life-threatening diseases. Take the adrenals for example. They are tiny, grape-shaped glands, which are located at the top of the kidneys and produce hormones that regulate blood pressure and kidney function and protect the body against stress. When the adrenal glands do not work properly, it leads to adrenal imbalance. Acquiring a regular sleep-wake cycle, lifestyle changes, and avoiding stress can help repair the imbalance. Visit an endocrinologist to get your hormone levels checked annually. Below are the most important hormones which directly affect body weight, energy levels, and appetite.

Insulin (The Sugar Hormone):

Here's what mainly happens when the body's insulin signalling goes haywire.

Diabetes

- Can you imagine your body's cells attacking you? This is what happens in **Type 1 diabetes.** The body's own immune system destroys the insulin producing cells of the pancreas, causing a shortage of insulin. Studies today show that there is a rise in auto-immune diseases due to the high level of toxicity in our environment. It can also be caused by genetic factors.
- **Type 2 diabetes** is caused by chronically high levels of insulin in the body. When you eat a lot of sugary foods of sugary foods, the pancreas work overtime to release excess insulin in the body to drop the glucose levels to normal. But after a while, the body gets desensitized to the insulin's messages and stops listening altogether.

Metabolic Syndrome

Often called pre-diabetes, this syndrome is not understood very well.

The main cause for it is the decreased response to insulin in certain tissues like muscle and fat. Symptoms include high blood pressure, high cholesterol, and a very high waist circumference. You may have noticed people who have unusually large bellies as compared to their limbs. People suffering from metabolic syndrome are often overweight and are at a higher risk of cardiovascular diseases.

Insulin levels are regulated when you avoid sugary snacks and instead include whole grains, lean meats, and vegetables in your diet. If you are vegetarian, make sure you include healthy, plant-based proteins in your meals. Eat at regular times and don't go hungry for long periods of time.

Leptin (The Fullness Hormone)

Do you have uncontrollable food cravings? Do you go on crash diets only to drop off it and then gain more weight than you had in the first place? It's your high leptin levels to blame.

Leptin is a hormone that is tied closely to appetite, metabolism, and hunger. It is the single most important hormone that sends signals to our brain that we're full and can stop eating. When leptin levels are low, we feel hungry and crave food. People with leptin disorders eat uncontrollably.

Now here's the weird part. Leptin is produced by a particular fat in our body called the adipose tissue. The fatter you are, the more leptin your body produces. Obese people have high concentrations of leptin in their body. So when obese people eat a lot of food, they don't feel satiated because their leptin levels are low.

When you crash diet and suddenly lose a lot of weight, the body needs time to adjust to the big changes in the fat levels and leptin production. When leptin levels plummet, your brain stops getting clear signals about how full you feel. This is why you end up eating large amounts and just can't stop yourself. Unfortunately, you are chemically wired to do so. So put an end to crash dieting; it won't work in the long run.

Sleep and processed sugar are two other factors that play an important role in the fullness hormone production.

To keep leptin levels constant, you need to sleep properly. On the other hand, processed sugar makes your brain less sensitive to leptin, which in turn causes you to eat more and pack on the unwanted kilos. Recent research shows that eating a fish rich diet or one which includes healthy Omega-3 fats like fish oil capsules, walnuts, and flaxseeds increases the body's sensitivity to leptin.

Controlling leptin levels is pretty simple. Avoid crash diets or yo-yo diets. Sleep at regular times. Avoid any kind of processed sugar. Include fish in your diet or any other source of Omega-3.

Ghrelin (The Hunger Hormone)

If leptin signals to your brain that you are full, then ghrelin is the hormone that sends the signal to your brain that you are hungry. These are the two appetite hormones that you must learn to keep in balance if you want to get rid of your food cravings.

Your gut produces ghrelin when it's empty. Ghrelin levels are high before you eat and low after you eat. It's a simple funda—if you want your brain to stop signalling that you're hungry, don't keep your stomach empty for long periods of time. Have a meal or a snack every three–four hours, so that your body does not secrete high levels of ghrelin.

Research shows that intense exercise decreases ghrelin levels. Now you know why interval training or power walking is recommended. If you play any kind of sport like badminton, football, or tennis, try and include it once a week. It will help regulate ghrelin levels and will work as a wonderful stress buster too! High intensity exercises and regular meals help keep ghrelin levels in check.

Cortisol (The Stress Hormone)

During stressful situations, for example when you are in the middle of a heated argument with someone, your adrenal gland releases the stress hormone called cortisol. If you are under stress most of the time or if you are an extremely short-tempered person, you will probably have high levels of cortisol in your bloodstream. This can lead to several negative health conditions, one of them being weight gain. Cortisol is also the main culprit behind the dreaded belly fat.

Under normal circumstances, your body releases extra cortisol in response to stress and your levels drop to normal once the stress has passed. It's only when you are under constant stress that problems like low immunity levels, a dip in energy level, and all kinds of allergies develop due to the high levels of cortisol in your body.

Since cortisol is responsible for energy regulation in the body, it starts stimulating the metabolism of carbohydrates and fats. It also helps your body release insulin. All this leads to hunger pangs and food cravings. Add to that, the high levels of blood sugar cause the excess glucose to be stored as fat in the stomach and hip area.

You can regulate your cortisol levels by de-stressing with breathing techniques, meditation, yoga, leisure walks, and regularizing your sleep cycle.

Hgh (The Growth Hormone)

Often referred to as HGH, the growth hormone is secreted by the pituitary gland, a pea-sized structure at the base of the brain. It helps bone, muscle, and the organs to grow. So if you are looking to build good quality muscle, this is one of the main hormones required to do so.

Considered as the fountain of youth, HGH interacts with fat cells, assisting them to break down, and burns stored fat for energy.

Growth hormone can be increased through intense exercise like intervals or circuit training, weightlifting, and sleep. To maximize the fat-burning effect of growth hormone, train hard and sleep well.

> ### Attention Women: The Hormones That Make Your Hips and Thighs Fat!
>
> Estrogen and progesterone are hormones produced by women's ovaries and are vital to their health. These two hormones exist in a delicate balance, and when that delicate balance is thrown off, various health complications can ensue. They play an important role in keeping the waist of a woman tiny and melting away fat in major problem areas like hips and thighs. The important factor to remember here is that estrogen works against the action of insulin and progesterone works against the action of cortisol. Now you know that both insulin and cortisol—if produced in excess by the body—causes belly fat.
>
> Estrogen is the main hormone which increases fat storage in the hips and thighs. But progesterone works with estrogen to stop this. When a woman is stressed, this natural process does not occur. High stress level means higher secretion of cortisol, which in turn depresses the levels of progesterone. So if you are a woman and you see fat accumulating around your waist, you need to de-stress and raise the progesterone levels in your body. Do something that you like, be it yoga class (not power yoga), massages, walks, leisure swims—all these help keep your hormones in check.
>
> Estrogen balance is maintained when you increase the protein content in your diet and combine it with healthy carbohydrates like whole grains. As a woman ages, stress or environmental estrogen-mimicking chemicals, cause the ovaries to reduce the production of estrogen and progesterone. So it's a combination of eating right, de-stressing as well as living clean that puts your hormones back in balance. Isn't it nice to know that you don't have to bust your bottom on the treadmill to lose the fat on your hips and thighs? Instead just eat right, lift weights to increase HGH, and spend a day shopping, or at the spa. Do yoga, take up Tai Chi, de-stress—your hips and thighs will thank you for it!

Serotonin (The Mood Neurotransmitter)

Serotonin is a neurotransmitter that sends messages to the brain about mood, learning, sex drive, sleep, eating patterns, pain threshold, and social behaviour. While both neurotransmitters and hormones are chemicals secreted within the body, neurotransmitters are produced at our nerve terminals whereas hormones are secreted by our endocrine glands.

With normal serotonin levels in our body, we feel happy and relaxed. When the body becomes overly stressed, it begins to use higher levels of serotonin. If the stress level remains high, the body is not able to produce more serotonin to replace the reserves. This is when we slip into depression. The lower the level of serotonin, the deeper the depression.

People with low levels of serotonin also suffer from:

- Low self-esteem
- Social withdrawal
- Lack of focus
- Chronic fatigue
- Food cravings
- Sleep disturbance
- Low libido

Serotonin is vital to the functioning of the gut muscles. It causes the contraction of our intestines and acts on gut nerves which signal nausea and pain. If you eat something that upsets the stomach cells, the gut releases vast amounts of serotonin. Depending on how bad the irritation is to your stomach, you may vomit or suffer an attack of diarrhoea!

You should include serotonin-rich foods in your diet such as walnuts, tomatoes, plums, kiwis, bananas, and pineapple. Light exercises, walks, yoga, and meditation also boost serotonin levels.

Why We Reach for Carb-Rich Foods When We Are Depressed

Do you know why sad and depressed people reach out for junk food? When your serotonin levels drop and you start feeling depressed or stressed, your body makes you crave foods rich in 'tryptophan', an amino acid which is key to the production of serotonin. Which foods are high in tryptophan? Duh! Carbohydrates. No wonder you reach for instant noodles, pizza, or a burger. It's a vicious cycle—the serotonin levels will rise but so will your insulin levels. And that will just set you off on more weight gain.

So what's the solution? Try to look for more nutritious options to boost your serotonin levels. Healthy foods that include tryptophan are:
- Bananas
- Milk
- Yogurt
- Varieties of cheese like Swiss and Cheddar
- Legumes
- Nuts
- Eggs
- Fish
- Turkey
- Meat

A bowl of steaming hot khichdi is also a healthier option than junk food. Make a whole wheat turkey sandwich or a triple egg-white omelette with vegetables. Put cheese once in a while. It's fine to have a cheat meal even when you are watching your weight. Sometimes, your body needs it. But go about it the right way.

Once you have rebalanced your energies through all above mentioned solutions all the pieces of your master plan will fall into place. Now you know it's not just about the calories consumed, it's also about managing stress, eliminating certain foods, regularizing sleep patterns, and relaxing more often.

Third Commandment: Eat Right

Most health and diet books put you on specific programmes without even delving deep into your personal history. No book talks about the importance of cleansing or what toxicity does to your body. But eating isn't 'One Size Fits All'. Every individual is different—from body types and inherited genes to the foods that one grew up with, one's profession and accordingly, one's stress levels. Now you know it goes beyond the food on your plate, the calorie counting, and the number of hours you exercise.

A holistic diet is not a fad diet; it's not something new. In fact, it is the way our ancestors ate. It's about eating foods which are as close to the natural state as possible, boosting your vitamin intake with certain super foods and most importantly, learning to eat in balance and moderation.

A holistic diet does not advocate any one food group in particular. If you are vegetarian by religion or choice, it's great as long as you stick to healthy, nutritious options, and remember to add a variety of colours of fruits and vegetables to your diet. Similarly, if you opt to be vegan because you are an animal lover or for health reasons, make sure you get your calcium from green leafy vegetables and that you monitor your protein intake. And if you have always eaten meat, opt for leaner cuts because the saturated fats in animal products will harm your heart and body. There's no rule that you have to be one or the other. The emphasis is on Clean Eating and Living—about eliminating slowly and surely all the processed and chemically-injected food from your plate.

From my own experience, I still have people telling me that I have baby skin. Many times, when I do a tough workout in a gym, they marvel at my energy levels. They think that I am showing off. But you just need to open your eyes to see that it is a very easy, enjoyable process of eating holistically. Start eliminating one trouble food at a time and see the difference.

Put it down in your detox journal. Don't try doing it all at once because the more stressed you are, the less your body will respond while the more relaxed you are about making the changes, the faster your body will start functioning at its most optimal level.

If you're serious about losing weight permanently, don't rush in. Your chances of staying leaner and healthier are much better with a slower diet. Plus it's a lot kinder to your body. Crash diets upset your body's equilibrium and ruin your organs.

What you eat, when you eat, and how much you eat is the key to a successful holistic diet.

Carbohydrates: Nothing to be Scared Of!

One of the main dietary components, carbohydrates are also one of the most misunderstood food groups. They include starches, sugars, and dietary fibre. An enzyme called amylase helps break down carbohydrates into glucose, which is used as fuel for the brain and the nervous system.

Now here's what you need to understand about carbohydrates—You want your body to take its time to break down the carbohydrates and releases glucose into your blood stream in a slow and steady manner. The faster the glucose is released in the blood stream, the higher the insulin spike which leads to fat storage. It also makes you feel hungry quite often.

So imagine good carbohydrates as slow burning wood in a bonfire, rather than dry hay. You don't want a raging inferno; you want the fire to burn slowly and for a longer period of time. This leads us to:

Simple Carbohydrates: are the ones you don't want too much of in your body. They have one or two sugar units and include table sugar, sugar found in candy, processed and baked goods like cakes, pastries, and most junk food, white rice, pasta and white bread, fructose found in fruits, and lactose found in dairy products. While processed sugar is a no-no, fruits and milk products contain several vitamins and minerals, making it a better carbohydrate as it is a more natural option.

Complex Carbohydrates: have three or more sugar units. It takes a longer time to break this down into glucose. They are starches found in whole grains, legumes, non-starchy vegetables and nuts, and dairy products that are not sweetened with sugar.

Dietary Fibre: is similar to starches and sugars; the only difference is that the body cannot digest this kind of carbohydrate. These are of two kinds—soluble fibres which dissolve in water and insoluble fibres which do not dissolve. They help in keeping our digestive system running smoothly. Top fibre-rich foods include oats, bran, beans and lentils, whole grains, berries, vegetables—especially the dark green variety—and squashes, potatoes, and nuts.

✓ **Boost your fibre intake; choose the right carbohydrates**

Imagine fibre to be a broomstick which is working inside your system—it helps keep it clean and sweeps away all the toxins and impurities.

Around 1/3rd of your fibre should be in the form of insoluble fibre. You should include whole wheat foods like oats, bran, nuts, and seeds in your diet. It helps in the bowel movement and is vital in preventing conditions like diarrhoea and constipation. Soluble fibre found in fruits, vegetables and flaxseeds, acts differently because it becomes gel-like and absorbs the liquid in the body. Soluble fibre helps hydrate stool, a key in preventing digestive disorders. Sweet potato and celery are excellent forms of soluble fibre.

The effect of fibre is that you feel satiated longer because of slower, steadier increases in blood glucose levels. Increased fibre consumption lowers the circulation of bad cholesterol in the blood. They've been found to promote the production of immune cells and antibodies, potentially boosting immune function. Fibre is also strongly linked to reducing risk of heart disease.

The key is to practise moderation. Don't go on a fibre overdrive; you will feel gassy and bloated. Slowly incorporate fibre by adding sunflower and flaxseeds in your salad, parathas, and boosting your fruit intake.

THE STARCH THAT HEALS THE COLON, EASES IBS, AND MAY EVEN PREVENT CANCER

Everybody is talking about 'resistant starch' and its miraculous properties. Resistant starch is found in the outer skins of seeds, parts of corns and legumes, and room-temperature pasta and rice. It is a certain kind of carbohydrate that does not get digested in the small intestine and enters the large intestine in its original form in which it was put in your mouth.

These starches then ferment in the colon and promote the 'good' bacteria formation in the gut. Among its other benefits, it can kill cancerous compounds in the colon, prevent diabetes by improving insulin sensitivity, and help prevent and treat irritable bowel syndrome.

Best Sources of Resistant Starch:
Room temperature sushi rice and pasta salads
Whole grains like bulgur and brown rice
Black eyed peas and legumes
Bananas
Sweet Potato
Potatoes
Oats
Barley
High-maize cornstarch

Holistic Diet Recommendation: Most people should get between 30 percent–40 percent of total calories from complex carbo-hydrates and natural sugars like fruits and honey.

✓ Eat more whole-grains:

Traditional Options	My Options
White Rice	Brown rice, red rice, wild rice
White Bread	Whole-wheat roti, phulkas, multi-grain bread, rye bread, whole wheat bread, bread with seeds (flaxseeds/etc), bran bread, any bread which is made with organic flour at home
Pasta + Couscous	Quinoa (red or white), dalia/lapsi (broken wheat), amaranth, buckwheat (soba) noodles
White flour	Whole-wheat flour, jowar (sorghum) flour, bajra (millet) flour, nachni/ragi flour (finger millet)

Antioxidants: The Weapon Against Wrinkles and Ageing

Antioxidants are molecules that inhibit the oxidation of other molecules, thus slowing the oxidative damage to our body's tissues. On a very basic level, everything that you eat and drink has an impact on your cells. The antioxidants in colourful vegetables and fruits such as leafy greens, deep red tomatoes, blueberries, and carrots help stop unstable molecules from damaging healthy cells. You cannot feel it when some cells are damaged or dying, but you can see it in the signs of ageing, such as wrinkles.

BENEFITS OF ANTIOXIDANTS

- They clean free radicals out of your bloodstream
- They minimize wrinkles and reduce other signs of ageing
- They protect your skin from sun damage
- They reduce the risk of many diseases like cancer, cardiovascular diseases, cataract, and Alzheimer's

- ✓ Berries
- ✓ Dark chocolate (organic) and raw cacao powder
- ✓ Beans and lentils
- ✓ Fish varieties like salmon and tuna
- ✓ Colourful, varied vegetables (mixed of cooked, steamed, and raw)
- ✓ Nuts and seeds
- ✓ Whole grains
- ✓ Garlic
- ✓ Avocado
- ✓ Safflower and olive oil
- ✓ Green tea
- ✓ Aloe vera juice

Eat these super fruits to get more nutrition in each bite. They are high in vitamins, antioxidants, and prevent diseases in the long run.

Acai Berries: The antioxidant levels in acai berries are higher than other super fruits. It is not so easy to find them fresh. You can buy it in the powder form from medical shops. This powder can be added in protein shakes or fruit juices.

Apples: The special fibre (pectin) in apples protects the body against pollution and relieves indigestion, gout, rheumatism, arthritis, and hangovers. Two apples a day can lower cholesterol by almost 10 percent.

Avocado: These are an excellent source of vitamin E, which helps keep the heart healthy by preventing the oxidation of the LDL or 'bad' cholesterol. One small avocado provides over half the RDA of vitamin B6—essential for a healthy nervous system.

Bananas: This fruit is loaded with potassium, which can lower your blood pressure. Bananas are also one of the best sources of resistant starch, a healthy carbohydrate that fills you up and helps to boost your metabolism.

Blackberries: They are rich in polyphenols, the same family of antioxidants found in green tea, which may help prevent cardiovascular disease, cancers, and osteoporosis.

Blueberries: Blueberries help improve brain function and memory. They are high in anitoxidants and also rich in manganese, which plays an important role in your metabolism, helping to keep you slim and energized.

Cantaloupe: This fruit is good for the skin because it has tonnes of Vitamin A and its derivatives, which boosts cell reproduction, making it a natural exfoliator.

Cherries: The deep red colour in cherries is due to an antioxidant called anthocyanin, which can reduce inflammation, lower triglyceride, and cholesterol levels

Citrus fruits: All citrus fruits—from limes to tangerines—are rich in Vitamin C and fibre. They play an important role in cancer prevention, regulate oil glands, and prevent age spots.

Cranberries: These are super fruits, especially for women. They may prevent urinary tract infections, and help fight ovarian cancer.

Dragon Fruit: Seeds of this fruits are made up of an essential fatty acid, oleic acid, which helps lower bad cholesterol and raise good cholesterol.

Grapes: They have a powerful antioxidant called resveratrol, which promotes a healthy heart. Compounds found in grape seed extract help slow down Alzheimer's disease.

Grapefruit: My favourite is the ruby variety. It helps keep heart diseases at bay by lowering the cholesterol level. The redder it is, the higher the antioxidants.

Kiwi: If you have digestive gripes or IBS, kiwi is your super fruit. It has twice the vitamin C of an orange and as much potassium as a banana, but it's the lutein level that sets it apart. Lutein is an antioxidant that protects against macular degeneration, the leading cause of impaired vision.

Maca Berries: Maca grows at an elevation of 11,000–14,000 feet making it likely the highest altitude food-herb crop in the world. This super-food is considered to be a storehouse of vitamins and minerals that ease hormone imbalances and nourish the body.

Maqui Berries: These berries are not just sweet and bursting with flavour, they also have diverse health benefits. Maqui berries are very rich in anthocyanins, which are purple pigments with very high antioxidant activity. Intake of maqui berries can lead to an increase of insulin in the body, helping to suppress blood glucose, and thereby controlling the formation of new fat cells.

Oranges: Have vitamin C and other key nutrients such as beta-carotene and folic acid. It contains more than 170 different phytochemicals and 60 flavonoids, many of which have disease fighting properties.

Plums: They contain high level of potassium, a mineral that helps manage high blood pressure and reduce stroke risk. The reddish-blue pigment in some plums, called anthocyanins, may protect against cancer by mopping up harmful free radicals.

Pomegranate: It contains high levels of antioxidants. Compounds found only in pomegranates called punicalagins are shown to benefit the heart and blood vessels. Pomegranate also lowers cholesterol and blood pressure.

Papaya: Rich in fibre and lowers cholesterol levels. It contains enzymes that help prevent oxidization of cholesterol, which in return helps to prevent heart attacks. The juice of papaya helps in cleansing the colon.

Pineapple: It contain Vitamin A, vitamin C, calcium, phosphorus, potassium and an enzyme called bromelain which helps breaks down protein. It also aids in digestion and reduces bloating.

Pumpkin: It's a fruit filled with beta-carotene which, combined with potassium, may help prevent high blood pressure. It is a storehouse of many antioxidants and vitamins A, C and E. Pumpkin seeds help boost serotonin levels which ensure good sleep. It is also high in Omega-3s.

Raspberries: help speed elimination and possibly promote weight loss; their natural sweetness may also satisfy food cravings.

Strawberries: High in vitamin C, a cupful of strawberries and you have reached your daily recommendation. They also protect your heart and are full of antioxidants. They keep wrinkles at bay and help to naturally whiten your teeth. Baking soda and strawberries is a good teeth whitener.

Tomato: This fruit is the richest source of the super nutrient lycopene, which is known to protect against breast and prostate cancers and is essential for avoiding vision loss in old age. It is also high in vitamin C, fibre, potassium.

Watermelon: Deeper colour varieties have more lycopene than tomatoes. A daily serving of watermelon has shown to boost energy levels by up to 23 percent. This is because watermelon contains vitamin B6. It is also high in vitamin C.

Sugars: The Good, The Bad, The Ugly

First, the Good Stuff

- ✓ **Sugars Found in Vegetables and Fruits:** Fructose are the most natural form.
- ✓ **Rock Sugar (Misri) or Jaggery (Gud):** Organic form of Indian sugar found in most grocery stores.
- ✓ **Honey:** Since honey has a low glycemic index, it is an ideal option for those who want to lose weight. Rich

in antioxidants. It can also treat insomnia, beautify the skin, help wounds heal, and promote digestion. Always buy the organic varieties.
- ✓ **Demerara Sugar:** It is a mild-tasting, pale coloured, raw cane sugar. The name comes from its lace of origin—Demerara in Guyana. This sugar has more nutritional value and mineral content than its white counterpart.

I have listed some more natural sweetener options below. However, research is still being done on its benefits.

- ✓ **Stevia:** Is a sweet-tasting natural herb found in a variety of foods. Though it is not available as a sweetener, it can be bought as a dietary supplement. It can be safely used in tea, coffee, sweets, and other foods. Since its low in calories, it's the ideal option for those who want to lose weight
- ✓ **Agave Nectar:** It doesn't have the same blood glucose impact as sugar. And because it's derived from a plant, it is also suitable as a vegan sweetener and as a replacement for honey.
- ✓ **Pure Maple Syrup:** About 50–50 glucose and fructose (depending on grade), it contains small amounts of polyphenols—antioxidants that help quell inflammation. It also helps in maintaining the health of the heart, boosting the immune system, and lowering the risk of prostate cancer.
- ✓ **Date Sugar:** Made from ground dates, it delivers all the nutrients in dates—including potassium and calcium—and is similar in antioxidants to molasses.

THE BAD STUFF

- ✓ **Table Sugar:** To be used sparingly. Extracted from sugarcane and sugar-beet plants.
- ✓ **Corn Syrup:** Mostly used in baking. It's virtually all glucose and is made by extracting and breaking down starch from corn.

The Way We Eat

- ✓ **High Fructose Corn Syrup:** Used by commercial food manufacturers, it is a man-made sweetener made by converting some of corn syrup's glucose into fructose. Usually found in sodas and a variety of processed foods, HFCS may encourage overeating to a greater degree than glucose.

THE UGLY STUFF

- ✓ **Artificial Sweeteners:** I see a lot of people adding these chemical substitutes to their tea and coffee. They feel they have saved themselves of empty calories by avoiding table sugar. They have, but at the cost of adding chemicals to their body.

Researchers are still struggling to find evidence which shows the long-term effects of consumption of artificial sweeteners. But people who are sensitive to aspartame have reported headache, fatigue, gastrointestinal problems, and more pronounced symptoms of premenstrual syndrome (PMS).

Sweetener	Times Sweeter than Sugar
Saccharin	200–700
Aspartame	60–200
Acesulfame-K	200
Sucralose	600
Neotame	7,000–13,000

Artificial sweeteners have few, if any, calories, and therefore are non-nutritive because they do not provide energy.

Simple Ways to Curb the Sugar Monster Within You!

Always Read the Ingredients List: Keep an eye out for these on the product label—sugar, white sugar, brown sugar, cane sugar, confectioner's sugar, corn syrup, crystallized fructose, dextrin, honey, invert sugar, maple syrup, raw sugar, beet sugar, corn sweeteners, evaporated cane juice, glucose-fructose, granulated fructose, high fructose corn syrup, fructose, malt, molasses, and turbinado sugar. At best, try to limit foods that have any of these as one of the first three ingredients.

Trick Your Brain: Cut the sugar you take in your coffee or tea into half and try adding a fresh cinnamon stick or a vanilla bean when you make your brew. The sweet smell helps reduce the need for sugar.

It's not as Sweet but it's Still Good: When baking or making any Indian sweet, experiment by cutting the amount of sugar by one-third. Many a time, you will find that your dish tastes as good!

Fruit Puree Works Too: Substitute this for sugar and syrups in recipes. Try adding applesauce in baking recipes instead of sugar in muffins and cakes.

Sugar and Spice, Twice as Nice!: When baking, try adding vanilla extract. Natural spices like cinnamon, nutmeg, cloves, and allspice can naturally sweeten a recipe.

Waffle and Fruit: Chopped strawberries or bananas with walnuts make an excellent substitute for maple syrup on pancakes.

Stay away from Sodas and Sweet Beverages: They are empty calories which provide you with no minerals or nutrients. They also increase food cravings because of the high amount of sugar that they contain. The all-time healthiest beverage is water. You can always flavour your water with a slice of lemon or even herbs like basil or mint. Have natural fruit juices or coconut water when the summer heat gets to you.

Fancy Yogurts are not Always the Best Snack Option: Most yogurts are loaded with sugar. Look out for ingredients like fruit juice concentrate, syrup, HFCS, or corn syrup. Instead buy plain yogurt or have homemade yogurt with fresh fruits or canned fruit. If you're buying yogurt from outside, make sure the label says 'live and active culture', which basically means it contains bacteria that will help cut body fat.

Cereals: Go for select brands of cereals which have less than 5 grams of sugar per serving. Opt for unsweetened cereals and add sliced fruit like bananas, berries, pineapple, and nuts instead.

Are Diet Sodas Bad for You?

You need to ask yourself if you have really lost weight after switching to diet colas. If the answer is no, then just stay away from the chemical-laden bottles. Diet sodas are filled with artificial sweeteners. Sip on these side-effects of diet soda:

- **Drink Yourself to Obesity:** Downing two or more cans daily increased waistlines by 500 percent. Artificial sweeteners can disrupt the body's natural ability to feel satiated. So you start craving for foods and sugary snacks.
- **Higher Risk of Metabolic Syndrome:** Just one can a day is linked to a 34 percent higher risk. Symptoms include belly fat and high cholesterol.
- **It may Harm Your Kidneys:** In an 11-year-long Harvard Medical School study of more than 3,000 women, researchers found that diet cola is associated with a two-fold risk for kidney decline.
- **It's a Can of Acidity:** Diet soda has a pH value of 3.2. The pH of a battery acid is 1 while that of water is 7. So you can imagine how extremely acidic diet soda is! If you drink a lot of acidic beverages, it can cause irreversible damage to the protective enamel coating on your teeth, making your teeth more vulnerable to cavities and more sensitive to pain.
- **My Head Hurts! Horrible Hangover:** Cocktails made with diet soda makes you drunk faster. Before you say that's great, consider this. The sugar-free mixers allow alcohol to enter your bloodstream at a lightning speed, leaving your brain fuzzy—not to mention a terrible hair-splitting headache the day after!

Proteins: The Master Building Blocks

How many times have you heard people fretting about your protein intake? There are so many myths out there about the amount of protein one should intake. Every other day, there seems to be new research on whether high protein intake is good for you or not.

A holistic diet takes into account that the needs of every individual differ. Protein intake depends on your age, your activity level, and also on how your body processes it. One rule does not apply for all.

Let's understand the basics—proteins are the main building blocks of every cell in our body. You need protein to help your body repair cells and make new ones. The primary function is growth and development.

Proteins are made up of amino acids. Now there are many different kinds, but 22 of these amino acids are extremely important for health. The body can produce 13 of these amino acids but the 9 others are derived from the food we eat. These 9 amino acids are called essential amino acids because they are not produced in the body.

Proteins from animal sources such as meats, fish, eggs, and milk are called complete because they contain all the 9 of the essential amino acids. Most vegetable proteins such as soy, legumes, nut butters, and some grains like wheat germ, is considered incomplete because it lacks one or more of the essential amino acids.

This can be a concern for someone who doesn't eat meat or milk products. But people who eat a vegetarian diet can still get all their essential amino acids by eating a wide variety of protein-rich vegetarian foods. For instance, you can't get all the amino acids you need from peanuts alone, but if you have peanut butter on whole-grain bread you're set. Likewise, rajma won't give you everything you need, but rajma-chawal will do the trick. Cut down on the portion of rice if it's white, or have brown rice. That's all there is to it.

The good news is that you don't have to get all the essential amino acids in every meal. As long as you have a variety of protein sources throughout the day, your body will absorb what it needs from each meal. You also do not need to eat animal products to get all the protein you need in your diet. A nutritionally balanced diet provides enough protein. Healthy people rarely need protein supplements. Yes, protein can help you shed those unwanted pounds and keep your belly full. But it's important to eat the right amount and the right kind of protein to get the health benefits.

Holistic Diet Recommendation: You should aim to get 10 percent–35 percent of your day's calories from protein foods. For an adult woman, that's about 46 grams of protein and for an adult man, about 56 grams of protein. For an easier estimation, aim for 1/3rd of your plate to be a protein-rich food. It's not hard to get this amount if you eat two to three servings of protein-rich foods a day.

Protein servings of poultry or fish should be the size and thickness of the palm of your hand. That's about a 90 gram portion. Non-vegetarians should not eat more than two palm-sized servings of meat a day.

✓ Choose your protein choices wisely

VEGETARIAN PLANT-BASED SOURCES:

Good Old Dal: Beans and lentils like garbanzo beans (chole), black beans, kidney beans (rajma), all kinds of dal, and chickpea hummus are a great protein fix—pick one and watch the protein grams add up.

Protein-rich Grains like Quinoa, Spelt, and Amaranth: Whole grains are a great source of protein, but the queen of whole grains when it comes to protein content is quinoa. Quinoa is actually the edible seeds of the goosefoot plant and is mistakenly considered a grain by most people because it is cooked like one. Unlike many sources of vegetarian protein, quinoa contains all of the essential amino acids, making it a 'complete protein'.

Go Nutty!: All nuts including peanuts, cashews, almonds, and walnuts contain protein, as do seeds such as sesame and sunflower. Because most nuts and seeds are high in fat, you don't want to make them your primary source of protein. But they're great as a post-workout or occasional snack. Nut butters are delicious as well—peanut butter is an excellent source of protein. Try almond butter, soy nut butter, or cashewnut butter for a little variety if you're bored of peanut butter.

Soy it Up with Tofu. Tempeh, and Other Soy Protein products: Try adding tofu to your mixed sabzis or enjoy a tofu scramble for breakfast. Opt for soy milk (unsweetened) varieties for a change. Tempeh is made from cooked and slightly fermented soybeans and forms into a patty. You can have it as a veggie burger option. Edamame (green soybeans) and roasted soy nuts are another option. Nowadays, a lot of people add soya flour to their atta to make chappatis—this is an excellent way to boost protein content.

Low-fat Dairy Products are a Good Option: Milk, cheese, and yogurt are all excellent sources of protein. They also contain calcium and help keep bones and teeth strong. Low-fat paneer is another excellent source of protein.

Non-vegetarian Sources

Don't be Chicken—Stick to Lean Cuts of Poultry: Buy skinless chicken parts, or take off the skin before cooking. Boneless, skinless chicken breasts and turkey are the leanest poultry choices.

Eggs: The Complete Protein: Two eggs contain more than twelve grams of protein, just over half in the white and the rest in the yolk. So don't throw away the yolk! I have two eggs a day and I include 1 yolk too. Eggs contain many essential nutrients, including significant amounts of vitamins A, D, E, B1, B2, B6, folic acid, and vitamin B12. Eggs also contain important minerals including calcium, magnesium, potassium, zinc, and iron. Nutrients like choline and biotin, also important for energy and regulation of stress, are present in large amounts in eggs.

Nothing's Fishy About it: Fish is high in protein content and is a storehouse of Omega-3s which is excellent for anti-ageing. Fish is leaner than meat, has lower fat, and contains amino acids and minerals that are vital for the body. There is anywhere from 15gm–30gm of protein in fish depending on the type of fish and how it is cooked. There are a varieties of ways to cook fish—steamed, baked, grilled, or lightly fried (don't pile on the oil!).

SOME PROTEIN CHOICES TO AVOID COMPLETELY

Why is Red Meat Bad for You? It's not Just Fat!: Yes, we all know by now that red meat like beef and mutton has saturated fat and high cholesterol. But recent studies have found yet another reason to stay away from this fatty meat. Beef, lamb, duck, and pork contain a compound called carnitine. Scientists found that when people consume carnitine, certain microbes in the gut step in and metabolize the compound, creating another chemical known as trimethylamine-N-oxide, or TMAO, which, in turn, seems to play a key role in promoting cardiovascular diseases by altering the way the body processes cholesterol.

Stay Away from Processed Meat: Don't trick yourself into believing that deli meats or luncheon meats are healthy. Nowadays a lot of supermarkets stock the most expensive deli meat from all over the world and most of them are laden with fat and salt. The preservatives in salami are carcinogenic compounds that are found in bacon and tobacco products.

Sausages and frankfurters top my list of unhealthiest meats because they are loaded with bad fats and preservatives. Most of the time you do not even know what is in the meat. You are better off sticking to good old chicken.

Vegetarians! Plant-based Proteins to Choose From:

Food	Portion Size	Approximate Protein (gms)
Hempseeds	3 tbsps	10
Flaxseeds (powder)	2 tbsps	3
Almonds	15 almonds	6
Quinoa (raw)	1 cup / 150 grams	5
Tempeh	100 grams	19
Tofu	100 grams	8
Miso	3 tbsps	6
Soya Nuggets (dry, unsoaked)	1 cup / 50 grams	27
Almond Butter	2 tbsps	7
Peanut Butter	2 tbsps	7
Cashew Butter	2 tbsps	4
Wheatgrass (powder)	3 tbsps	6
Wheatgrass (juice)	150 ml	5
Alfalfa Sprouts	1 cup	8
Spirullina	2 tbsps	14
Sprouts	1 cup	3
Green Leafy Vegetables (raw)	2 cups	2
Amaranth Grain	½ cup / 100 grams	14
Pulses & Dals / Lentils (raw)	½ cup	25

Fats: Choose Wisely!

We all know that too much cholesterol and fats can lead to obesity and all sorts of lifestyle diseases. The first day that we start a diet, we first monitor the spoon of oil that goes into every meal like our life depends on it! However, we must understand that our bodies need a certain amount of healthy fats to function.

The cycle of making, breaking, storing, and mobilizing fats is at the core of how you regulate your energy levels. Any sort of imbalance in energy release can result in disease, including heart disease and diabetes. This is the reason why if you have too many triglycerides in your bloodstream, the risk of clogged arteries is increased which can lead to heart attack and stroke is increased. Fats help the body store nutrients as well.

Knowing the different types of fats or fatty acids can make a huge difference in your overall health and weight management.

Saturated Fats: These are the most controversial of fats and oils. But they are still critical to certain body functions, if consumed in less quantity. Saturated fats tend to be solid at room temperature but they also include liquid tropical oils. Oils become unhealthy solid fats when they're hydrogenated.

They're linked to heart diseases and play an important role in the obesity epidemic, too. Examples include butter, stick margarine, the shortening (solid fat made from vegetable oils) used in cakes and other baked goods, and animal fats. Foods that contain solid fat include many cheeses, cream, fatty cuts of meat, bacon, and chicken skin.

There are also a few tropical plant foods like avocados, coconuts, and clarified butter (ghee) which are naturally high in saturated fats. These foods are good for you and can be consumed in small portions without worry.

Why we need saturated fats:

- They form at least 50 percent of the cell membranes and give cells their necessary stiffness
- Play a vital role in the health of bones; necessary for calcium absorption (that's why our grandmothers insist ongiving ghee to toddlers)
- Lower lipoprotein (a)—a substance in the blood that can cause heart disease
- Protect liver from alcohol and other toxins
- Boost immunity levels

Holistic Diet Recommendation: Keep to a minimum. Include a small amount of natural products in your diet. Buy the leanest cuts of meat. Include a little ghee and pure coconut oil in your diet.

Unsaturated Fats: Help decrease inflammation, reduce heart disease and blood clotting, and help regulate blood pressure. Unsaturated fats also lower the bad cholesterol (LDL) and increase the good cholesterol (HDL). HDL is manufactured by the liver to repair blood vessels and help transport fat-soluble vitamins to the cells of the body.

There are two types of unsaturated fats: monounsaturated and polyunsaturated fats.

Monounsaturated Fats: are the healthy fats. They can help reduce bad cholesterol levels in your blood and lower your risk of heart disease and stroke. They also provide nutrients to help develop and maintain body cells. Sources include olives, olive oil, sesame and sunflower oil, nuts, and all kinds of nut oils. Seeds of all kinds also contain monounsaturated fats.

Holistic Diet Recommendation: These are the best oils to have. Consume extra virgin oil as it retains the nutritious qualities. To get the full benefits, experiment with different kinds of oils while cooking. Choose organic whenever possible.

Polyunsaturated Fats (also known as Essential Fats): Are essential for the human body. They are the ones which our bodies cannot naturally make. They are of two kinds:

- *Omega-3 Essential Fatty Acids*: It helps organs function properly and aids in cell activity. It helps in oxygen circulation throughout the body. To ensure you get your Omega-3s, try to include more foods with flaxseed oil into your diet. Walnuts, sesame seeds, spinach, salmon, and tuna are some other foods that will help increase your Omega-3 levels.
- *Omega-6 Essential Fatty Acids*: The main Omega-6 essential fatty acids that your body requires is linoleic acid. Omega-6 essential fatty acids help the body cure skin diseases, fight cancer cells, and treat arthritis. Try to include flaxseed oil, pistachios, chicken, and olive oil into your diet to raise your Omega-6 levels.

Holistic Diet Recommendation: High temperatures can actually strip foods of their essential fatty acids. So if you're using nuts, for example, to raise the levels of your essential fatty acids, eat them raw instead of roasting them. Try sprinkling flaxseed oil (a great source of essential fatty acids) or olive oil onto vegetables instead of using butter or ghee. Dribble olive oil on your salads. These are some simple ways to deliver more essential fatty acids to your diet.

AT THE SEED OF IT ALL!

Seeds are a vital part of our diet. High in fibre, vitamin E, and monounsaturated fats, they help keep our heart healthy and our body disease free. Healthy seeds are also a great source of protein, minerals, zinc, and other life-enhancing nutrients. Numerous studies have shown that different types of seeds and nuts can actually prevent weight gain.

- Flaxseed is high in most of the vitamin B, magnesium, and manganese; rich in Omega-3 fatty acids, and high in fibre.
  Side Effects: Cramping and laxative effect.

- *Fenugreek Seeds:* A very good source of soluble dietary fibre, they lower blood LDLS-cholesterol levels. Bind to toxins in the food and help to protect the colon mucus membrane from cancers. Rich in thiamine, pyridoxine (vitamin B6), folic acid, riboflavin, niacin, vitamin A, and vitamin C
  Side Effects: Excess intake of fenugreek seeds by pregnant mothers can put them at the risk of premature childbirth.

- *Chia Seeds (Subja/kalonji):* It's gluten-free and a good source of all eight essential amino acids, Omega-3 fatty acids, and fibre
  Side Effects: Cramping and laxative effect.

- *Pumpkin Seeds:* Is a very good source of the antioxidant vitamin E; also an excellent source of B-complex. They contain high levels of essential minerals like copper, manganese, potassium, calcium, iron, magnesium, zinc, and selenium.
  Side Effects: Rare cases of allergic reaction.

- *Sesame Seeds:* The seeds are especially rich in mono-unsaturated fatty acids which help lower LDL and increase HDL in the blood stream. Prevents coronary artery disease and stroke. Very valuable source of dietary proteins with fine quality amino acids. Also a good source of B complex.
  Side Effects: Allergic reaction can cause hives, dermatitis, and itching.

- *Sunflower Seeds:* Helps lower LDL and increases HDL in the blood. Prevents coronary artery disease and stroke by favouring healthy lipid profile; it is good source of protein with fine quality amino acids.

Side Effects: Can cause allergic reaction like itchiness of the skin, sneezing, itchiness in the eyes, gastritis, vomiting, etc.

Super Foods: Your Guide to the Best Foods for Your Body

Super foods are those which have incredibly high nutritional values. They are considered to be the healthiest foods you can eat because they contain a much higher nutrient-to-calorie ratio than other foods. A healthy diet incorporating a variety of the following super foods will help you maintain your weight, fight diseases, and live longer. They all have one thing in common—they are all natural, unprocessed foods. Shop for them consciously and add them to your daily diet of salads, meals, and soups.

Almonds and Almond Butter: High in monounsaturated fats, they are the same type of health promoting fats that are found in olive oil, which has been associated with sreduced risk of heart diseases. They also have vitamin E which is considered the best vitamin to fight wrinkles. One of my all-time favourite foods is almond butter. It's simply made by pressing raw or roasted almonds into a paste, like peanut butter. Almonds and almond butter are nutritional powerhouses that contain significant amounts of protein, calcium, fibre, magnesium, folic acid, and potassium. Almond butter has extremely low saturated fat content and is rich in monounsaturated fats, making it a heart-healthy choice. Of course, almonds have no trans-fat.

Alfalfa: Is called the 'king of sprouts'. It is highly rich in minerals like manganese and is also a rich source of vitamins A, B, C, E, and K. It also contains all the essential amino acids. Alfalfa has a higher concentration of calcium than milk.

Avocado: Is high in oleic acid, which has been shown to prevent breast cancer. Toss this super fruit in your salad more often and ensure you get a glowing skin! They are the best fruit source of vitamin E, an essential vitamin that protects against many diseases and helps maintains overall health. The high levels of folic acid in avocado can prevent strokes.

Apples: There are several reasons why this fruit keeps the doctor away. One medium-sized apple contains 4 grams of fibre—some of it called 'pectin'. Pectin is a type of soluble fibre that has been linked to lower levels of LDL or 'bad' cholesterol. It also boosts burning of calories and increases muscle. The wealth of fibre an apple provides keep you feeling full for longer without costing you a lot of calories—there are about 95 in a medium-sized piece of fruit.

Bananas: Are naturally fat and cholesterol free. Bananas are known for their high potassium content, with over 400 mg potassium in a single medium-size banana. The potassium in bananas can help prevent muscle cramps after exercise. Bananas have their share of electrolytes like magnesium, potassium, and calcium which are important for maintaining the body's fluid level and preventing dehydration. This fruit also contains vitamin A and B. If you feel particularly low on energy, banana is the perfect fruit to have.

Barley: Is a cereal grain which can be eaten for breakfast and used in both stews and soups. It has all eight essential amino acids which can actually control your blood sugar levels. The dietary insoluble fibre in barley absorbs water and expands in your stomach which helps you feel full for a longer period of time. It also contains zinc which helps to speed up healing after an injury.

Beans and Legumes: Such as kidney, black, white, chick peas, and all the different kinds of lentils (dals) are high in antioxidants, fibre, protein, B vitamins, iron, magnesium, potassium, copper, and zinc. Eating beans regularly may decrease the risk of diabetes, heart disease, colorectal cancer, and can help with weight management. Beans are hearty, helping you feel full so you tend to eat less. Try innovative dals with vegetables as soup options for lunch, toss boiled channa into your salads, and mash it to make veggie burgers.

Berries: Are a great source of fibre packed with antioxidants that help keep you youthful and fit. Strawberries contain more vitamin C in a one cup serving than one orange and are particularly high in folic acid. Blueberries are packed with antioxidants called anthocyanins that may help keep memory sharp as you age, and raspberries contain ellagic acid, a compound with anti-cancer properties.

Broccoli: It's most noteworthy nutrients include vitamin C, vitamin A (mostly as beta-carotene), folic acid, calcium, and fibre. While the calcium content of one serving doesn't equal that of a glass of milk, broccoli is an important calcium source for those who don't consume dairy products. Broccoli is a rich source of fibre and it keeps you satiated longer.

Brown Rice and Red Rice: Is a whole grain whose outer hull provides 'natural wholeness' which is rich in protein, thiamine, calcium, magnesium, potassium, and fibre. If you are trying to lose weight, brown rice is an excellent resistant starch—which means it digests more slowly and helps keep your appetite at bay. This also helps to reduce insulin spikes, which is extremely beneficial for diabetics.

Cantaloupe and Muskmelons: Are very low in calories and fats. Melons are rich in numerous health promoting plant-derived polyphenolic compounds, vitamins, and minerals that are absolute for optimum health. They are an excellent source of vitamin A and antioxidants which have the ability to help protect cells and other structures in the body from oxygen-free radicals and offer protection against colon, prostate, breast, endometrial, lung, and pancreatic cancers.

Celery: Contains blood pressure reducing properties. This green stalky vegetable contains active compounds called pthalides which relax the muscles of the arteries that regulate blood pressure, allowing these vessels to dilate. Pthalides also reduce stress hormones which can cause blood vessels to constrict. Celery is an excellent source of vitamin C. Drinking celery juice frequently throughout the day helps curb sweet cravings. .

Cheese: Cheese like Cheddar also contains a large amount of other essential nutrients besides calcium such as phosphorous for strong teeth and bones, zinc for healthy skin, a strong immune system, and fertility, riboflavin and vitamin B12 for energy, and vitamin A for healthy skin and eyes. Moderation is the key since the fat content is high in cheese. Low-fat cottage cheese (paneer) is the perfect food for getting casein protein, a slow-digesting protein which keeps you satiated longer and keeps your energy levels balanced.

Chia Seeds: Are an excellent sources of Omega-3 fatty acids. They are a great alternative to flaxseeds in green smoothies. Simply soak them for about 10 minutes prior to blending in a high speed blender.

Coconut Water: It is widely known for being able to replace the minerals and fluids the human body loses during physical activities. It's an excellent post-workout drink. It minimizes ageing, balances pH levels, and keeps the connective tissues hydrated and strong.

Coconut Oil: We've always looked down upon coconut oil. Turns out we were wrong! Coconut oil contains medium chain triglycerides which contribute to lower calories than other fats. They are minimally stored in your body as fat and stimulate your body to burn more calories. The medium chain triglycerides in coconut oil provide 8.3 calories per gram, whereas most dietary fats contain long chain fatty acids that contribute 9 calories per gram. Humans quickly metabolize medium chain triglycerides into energy, whereas the body stores long chain fatty acids for future use, causing you to gain fat and weight. Coconut oil can boost thyroid function, helping to increase metabolism, energy, and endurance. It increases digestion and helps to absorb fat-soluble vitamins.

Dark Green Leafy Vegetables: Are perhaps the most concentrated source of nutrition in any food. They are a rich source of minerals; including iron, calcium, potassium, and magnesium. They also contain vitamins K, C, E, and many of the B vitamins, especially folate. They also provide a variety of phytonutrients including beta-carotene, lutein, and zeaxanthin, which protect our cells from damage, etc. Dark green leaves even contain small amounts of Omega-3 fats. So include spinach, mustard greens (methi), amaranth leaves, kale, chard varieties, turnip and carrot greens, collard, chickweed and sorrel greens, arugula, watercress, red and green romaine lettuce, and iceberg lettuce in your salads. The darker your salad greens, the better it is for your health.

Eggs: It's an excellent source of protein. It's also a good source of choline. Choline is an important nutrient that helps regulate the brain, nervous system, and cardiovascular system. It's an important dietary source of vitamin D and could significantly help to boost daily intake of it. Just one egg provides more than 20 percent of the recommended daily allowance.

Fish: It is a high-protein, low-fat food that provides a range of health benefits. White-fleshed fish, in particular, is lower in fat than any other source of animal protein, and oily fish are high in Omega-3 fatty acids or the 'good' fats. Since the human body can't make significant amounts of these essential nutrients, fish are an important part of the diet. Also, fish are low in the 'bad' fats commonly found in red meat, called Omega-6 fatty acids.

Ginger: It is used to treat nausea, diarrhoea, upper respiratory infections, hair loss, and burns—among other ailments.

Eating ginger might ease sore muscles and potentially help alleviate symptoms of arthritis. Research suggests that certain antioxidants in ginger could also be effective in slowing the growth of cancer cells.

Grapefruit: It is one of the best super foods for losing weight. A compound in this tangy fruit can lower insulin, a fat-storage hormone, and that can lead to weight loss. It's also a good source of protein, and because it's at least 90 percent water, it fills you up, so you eat less.

Green Tea: A steamy cup hydrates like water, which can help fill you up and shed weight. Plus, the antioxidants in green tea help burn fat and calories.

Miso: It is a traditional Japanese seasoning produced by fermenting rice, barley, and soybeans with salt and the fungus koji, the most typical miso being made with soy. The result is a thick paste which is a staple in Japanese cooking. Miso contains all the essential amino acids, making it a complete protein. It stimulates the secretion of digestive fluids in the stomach and restores beneficial probiotics to the intestines. It is a good vegetable-quality source of B vitamins (especially B12). Miso is known to reduce the risk of breast, prostate, lung, and colon cancers.

Nuts and Seeds: Roasted, toasted, or raw, nuts and seeds are a delicious source of protein and fibre. They pack a nutritious punch with heart-healthy monounsaturated oils, vitamins, and minerals. The lingams in seeds have been demonstrated to reduce cholesterol levels.

Oats: It provides a good source of complex carbohydrates. Soluble fibre from oats as a part of a diet low in saturated fat and cholesterol, may reduce the risk of heart disease. A half-cup serving of oats supplies about nine grams of fibre. Have it in your breakfast with almonds or berries, and you can ensure a super start for your day!

Olives and Olive Oil: Rich and fruity, olive oil stands out as a culinary staple in Mediterranean cultures. A good source of monounsaturated fat, adding two tablespoons of olive oil per day to your diet may support cardiovascular health. Toss whole olives into your salad, slice it up and put in your omelette, or use as an ingredient for a sandwich filling.

Organic Dark Chocolate: A nibble of dark chocolate here and there can slow down digestion so you feel full for longer time and eat less. Dark chocolate is full of healthy fats and can rev your metabolism to burn fat and calories. It may also help curb cravings for salt, sweet, or fatty foods.

Oranges: They are low in calories and contain no saturated fats or cholesterol. Like apples, they are rich in the dietary fibre pectin which helps get rid of excess body weight. Pectin, by its action as a bulk laxative, helps to protect the mucous membrane. And oranges are an excellent source of vitamin C, which is a powerful natural antioxidant.

Parsley: It is high in vitamin A, beta-carotene, and vitamin C. As a wholesome organic food, it is also a good choice for bone health with vitamin K. Parsley juice is an excellent tonic for the blood vessels. But remember that raw parsley juice is a potent juice and should never be taken alone—it should be mixed with other vegetables.

Pear: It provides a very good source of fibre and is also a good source of vitamin B2, C, E, copper, and potassium. It also contains a significant amount of pectin, which is a water soluble fibre. Pears have antioxidant and anti-carcinogen glutathione which help prevent high blood pressure and stroke.

Pomegranate: Rich in powerful, free-radical fighting antioxidants called polyphenols, an eight ounce serving of pomegranate juice enjoyed daily may support normal levels of cholesterol and healthy coronary artery function.

Quinoa: Most people mistake quinoa to be a whole grain when it is in fact a seed. It includes all of the eight essential amino acids that are needed for tissue growth and repair. Quinoa is protein packed; it presents vegetarians with an awesome alternative to the proteins found in meat. Additionally, quinoa provides an alternative to those who are allergic to wheat and are suffering from Celiac disease. This is because the super seed is entirely gluten free. It's also an excellent combination of protein and complex carbohydrates which can make you feel fuller for a longer period of time.

These days, kale is being hailed as the new nutritional superhouse. To be honest, I prefer quinoa over kale because it has a range of health benefits. It is not just high in protein, it is also a high source of riboflavin which helps to reduce the frequency attacks in migraine sufferers by improving the energy metabolism within the brain and muscle cells. It is gluten-free, and also has a low glycemic index which is good for weight management.

Salmon: It is one of the best sources of Omega-3 fatty acids, particularly EPA and DHA, which are nature's heart medicines. Salmon is considered an oily fish, which provides more of the fish oil to fight any kind of coronary heart disease. Omega-3s in salmon lowers cholesterol, acts as an anti-cancer agents staves off arthritis, and serves as natural anti-inflammatory.

Spinach: Helps protect against inflammatory problems, oxidative stress-related problems, cardiovascular problems, bone problems, and cancers—at the same time. There are more than a dozen different flavonoid compounds in spinach that function as anti-inflammatory and anti-cancer agents. Spinach is an excellent source of bone-healthy vitamin K, magnesium, manganese, and calcium; heart-healthy folate, potassium, and vitamin B6; energy-producing iron and vitamin B2; and free radical-scavenging vitamin A (through its concentration of beta-carotene), vitamin C, and vitamin E.

Sprouts: Are the cheapest and most convenient sources of complete nourishment. In addition to providing the highest amount of vitamins, minerals, proteins, and enzymes of any food per unit of calorie, sprouts deliver them in a form which is easily assimilated and digested. In fact, sprouts improve the efficiency of digestion. They can be added to your salads and green smoothies, eaten alone, used in curries, or as a filling for sandwiches.

Sweet Potato: It has a high vitamin A and C content which helps to get rid of free radicals and toxins in the body. This in turn helps prevent cell damage, cancer, and various diseases. Eating sweet potatoes on a regular basis helps in stress management. Because sweet potatoes are rich in potassium, blood pressure is regulated and heart rate is normalized. When you go shopping for sweet potatoes, choose the darkest ones. The darker the sweet potato, the higher its beta-carotene content will be.

Tomato: It is a cancer-fighting super food. Not only do tomatoes contain lycopene, the antioxidant phytochemical that also helps prevent heart disease, but they're also a good source of vitamins A, C, and E—all enemies of cancer-friendly free radicals.

Tuna: Is a healthy protein source and packed with essential fats. It also helps prevent strokes, Alzheimer's, kidney and breast cancers, and macular degeneration. Tuna also relieves rheumatoid arthritis and lowers blood pressure. Canned tuna is a wonder food for bodybuilders and fitness lovers, but always buy the salt-free version.

Turmeric: Is a true super food shown to have remarkable healing and anti-inflammatory properties. It is extraordinarily rich in curcuminoid polyphenol anti-oxidants that give it a classic yellow-orange colour. Turmeric has been shown to stabilize blood sugar and reverse cellular insulin resistance.

Walnuts: Among all nuts, walnuts pack significantly higher amounts of Omega-3 fatty acids! They are rich in fibre, B vitamins, magnesium, and antioxidants such as Vitamin E. Walnuts are one of the best plant sources of protein. Add it to your oats in the morning, have it as a snack, or toss it in your salad.

Watermelon: It contains huge dose of antioxidants—about 80 percent of your daily vitamin C and 30 percent of your vitamin A or beta carotene. Watermelon also contains lycopene, the famous cancer-fighting substance found in tomatoes. So put watermelon chunks in your salad or eat it just as it is.

Wheat Germ: It is the most vitamin and mineral-rich part of the wheat kernel. In fact, the germ is actually the embryo of the wheat plant. This embryo will eventually nourish the new wheat plant. Because it is meant to feed the new plant, wheat germ is packed with good nutrients like important B vitamins such as folate, vitamin B1 (thiamine), and vitamin B6. Wheat germ contains lots of fibre which is necessary for good blood sugar balance, cholesterol control, intestinal health, and detoxification.

Yogurt and Buttermilk: Contains probiotics which support the intestinal tract and the immune system. Maintain the overall health of your immune system and enjoy a cup of fruit yogurt or a glass of buttermilk, spiked with chillies and herbs.

My Pixie Dust: Some Extra-Special Nutrition Superstars

There are certain foods that I believe we must try and include in our daily diets, either in salads, smoothies, or juices. I

The Way We Eat

call them my pixie dust—super foods which make me look and feel good. In the raw food and natural health world, super foods are major focal points within the diet. These are available mainly in supplement form. Always include these foods after consulting your doctor or sports dietician because the amount of ingredients to be used has to be carefully monitored. I have listed them in alphabetical order, not in the order of importance.

Acai berry: Packed with antioxidants, it builds strength, promotes weight loss, and supports cardiovascular functions. Available in supplement and powder form.

Adzuki beans: They are sweet red beans, which, when used in the dried form instead of sprouted, may lower your risk of cancer, diabetes, and heart disease. They are a low-fat protein source that is rich in vitamins and minerals.

Algae: Don't turn up your nose! Algae is one of the best super foods for weight watchers. This marine plant sucks up all the toxins in our bodies. Two of the most well-known super foods derived from algae are spirulina and chlorella. Algae have high concentration of beta-carotene that helps fight some types of cancer and cardiovascular diseases. As it is organic in nature and full of enzymes, it is easily digestible and light on the stomach. It is known to facilitate smooth bowel movement and is extraordinarily rich in protein. Chlorella is full of chlorophyll, providing the richest food source of the healthful green pigment, which the body can use to cleanse and heal its organs.

Almond Milk: (Recipe on Pg 148) Almond milk is widely used as a substitute for cow's milk by vegans and people who have problems digesting lactose. High in protein, almond milk is great for your skin because almonds are full of Vitamin E which is important because it protects your skin from sun damage, moisturizes your skin, and gives you an anti-ageing boost. Almond milk also has great cholesterol-lowering effects.

Aloe Vera: We all know that this superior plant is antibacterial, antiviral, antifungal, and an excellent antioxidant. The juice of this plant is a natural medicine for cancer, cholesterol, diabetes, inflammation, and IBS. It's a vitamin superstar—it has vitamins A, B1, B2, B6, B12, C and E, folic acid, and niacin. Drinking a daily dose of this juice can enhance the body's defence system against any kind of oxidative stress. It also supports digestion by naturally cleaning the digestive system and is excellent for people who suffer from constipation.

Artichokes: It's a thistle-like plant whose leaves have a high degree of medicinal properties. It is useful for curing mild indigestion, reduce nausea, abdominal pain, constipation, and flatulence. It also lowers cholesterol, thus diminishing the risk for coronary heart disease. Artichoke leaf extract has proved helpful for patients with functional dyspepsia, and may ameliorate symptoms of irritable bowel syndrome.

Bee Pollen: It contains vitamins, minerals, carbohydrates, lipids, and protein. Bee pollen may also include bee saliva. It's important to avoid confusing bee pollen with natural honey. Bee pollen is also recommended by some herbalists to enhance athletic performance, reduce side effects of chemotherapy, and improve allergies, and asthma.

Black Garlic: It is a form of fermented garlic which is fast becoming a favourite with chefs all over the world due to its complex sweet-sour flavour. It is packed with twice as many oxidants as your regular garlic. Created by a careful ageing process, this garlic fights colds, reduces sugar cravings by helping your body to process glucose, and also has a compound with cancer-fighting properties.

Chywanprash: It is an ancient Ayurvedic remedy now being touted by the West as a 'youth elixir'. It is beneficial in activating the immune system, dissipating stress, depression, and chronic fatigue syndrome. It makes blood, liver, intestines, and pancreas get rid of toxins. It also improves the functioning of the gastrointestinal tract, normalizes the endocrine system, improves sexual function, and is recommended for impotence and frigidity. Chywanprash contains ghee and sugar—so make sure you don't have more than one tablespoon daily.

Cupuacu: Native to the South American rainforests, the cupuacu is a melon-sized fruit with a creamy pulp. The fruit is loaded with antioxidants and other powerful nutrients.

Gojiberry: It's been used for thousands of years in Chinese medicine to boost life-force or 'chi' energy. It's highly nutritious, containing 18 amino acids, including all the essential amino acids. Gojiberries have high protein content and are rich in minerals, vitamins, especially vitamin C, and carotenoids. Eat them straight from the packet as a snack or add a handful to your favourite trail mix, cereal, juice, or smoothie. You can also soak them in hot water to make a nutritious tea.

Hemp Foods like Oil, Milk, and Seeds: is a high quality protein source for vegans and vegetarians. It can provide you with a complete protein, and a balanced ratio of Omega-3 and Omega-6 essential fatty acids. It also contains many B vitamins, vitamins A, D, and E, calcium, sodium, iron, and dietary fibre.

Kale: It is a green leafy vegetable which is abundantly available in the US. Many Indian grocers have started selling it too. It's a nutritional powerhouse and a boon for weight watchers. One cup of kale has zero fat and only 36 calories and is high in vitamins and antioxidants. You can eat this green raw or cooked. Enjoy in salads, soups, stews, stir-fries, and smoothies. The fibre (5 grams in one cup) in kale aids with digestion and liver health. The vitamin C it contains hydrates your body and increases your metabolism, leading to weight loss and healthy blood sugar levels. The fibre in kale also lowers cholesterol and can be helpful in preventing various cancers such as colon, prostate, and ovarian. Its abundant vitamin K content is important for bone health, forestalling the effects of osteoporosis.

Kukicha: It is a traditional form of Japanese tea made not from the leaves but from the stems and twigs of the tree plant. Besides being rich in vitamins and minerals, it is also said to balance the acidity levels in the body.

Maca: It is a root vegetable that is grown and eaten in Peru. It is sold in the US and other countries as a nutritional supplement and a super food. Maca is often taken to boost libido and enhance sexual well-being. It is also said to increase energy and stamina. You can add it to your smoothies.

Phytoplankton: These are microscopic single-cell plants that are the most abundant vegetation in the ocean. They are the richest source of chlorophyll. They provide a complete source of cellular nutrition because they contain many phytonutrients, amino acids, minerals, trace elements, vitamins, enzymes, and cellular material not found in any other food source. They aid weight loss, stabilize energy and blood sugar levels, and help in the detoxification process. This marine plant also eases joint aches and inflammations.

Raw Organic Cacao (Raw Chocolate): It has been an important food in South America for thousands of years. It is high in antioxidants and abundant in vitamins and minerals such as magnesium, chromium, zinc, copper, iron, and manganese. It plays an important role in the prevention of degenerative diseases, particularly cardiovascular diseases and cancers. You can add the powder to your smoothie or have it with milk as a warm drink.

Spirulina: It is a type of algae. Spirulina is the richest beta carotene food, with a full spectrum of ten mixed carotenoids. It's an ideal anti-ageing food; concentrated nutrient value, easily digested, and loaded with antioxidants. It contains a rich supply of many important nutrients, including protein, complex carbohydrates, iron, and vitamins A, K, and B complex. Spirulina is now commercially available in tablet or powder form.

Seaweed: A staple in Asian diets since ancient times, seaweeds are among the healthiest foods on the planet, packed with vitamins, minerals, and antioxidants. And now we know they're great for the waistline too. A 2010 study found that the algae can reduce our rate of fat absorption by 75 percent. Different types of seaweed are wakame, nori, kombu, kelp, hijiki, and arame. They can be tossed into salads or added to stir-fries.

Wheatgrass: A wheatgrass shot—a tiny cup—is equivalent in nutritional value to 1 kg of leafy green vegetables. Wheatgrass contains over 90 minerals, including high concentrations of the most alkaline minerals: potassium, calcium, magnesium, and sodium. It is seen to clear stagnation in the liver and spleen.

> I am not a big wheat eater. Being raised in the south, I am more of a rice eater—that's my weakness. So I have learnt how to substitute. Even in my rotis, now I eat nachni and amaranth. Amaranth is far more economical and healthier than quinoa—so if you can get it, nothing like it. I do eat a lot of vegetables—lentil intake is limited. Sometimes you have to go digging for recipes when you are vegetarian because you can get stuck into a rut, but it's fun. I love being a vegetarian.
>
> LARA DUTTA, ACTOR

The Yin and Yang of Acid/Alkaline Diets

Every part of the body, like the stomach or the blood, has its own pH level which measures how acidic or alkaline it is. A pH of 0 means something is completely acidic while a pH of 14 means something is completely alkaline.

Your body is naturally alkaline. When you put it under stress, eat a lot of greasy, processed food, drink excessive alcohol, have an excess of salt and sugar, or loads of caffeine through endless cups of coffee or tea, your body goes into overdrive producing acid. This is the reason why many of you suffer from heartburn, acid reflux, and ulcers.

Going alkaline is the fastest way to restoring your body's natural balance and being more energetic, having a toned tummy, as well radiant skin. We have to ensure that we eat enough alkaline foods. Acid-forming foods can cause weight gain, bloated stomach, and lethargy among other things.

If you have been feeling tired, bloated, and suffering from acidity problems, here's how to eat the alkaline way:

- Eat food which is predominantly vegetarian. Vegetables tend to be the most alkaline, so include a variety of colours in your food everyday

- Lemons and lime are acidic to taste. But they become alkaline once digested. Include lime-flavoured water in your diet. Make a lemon juice dressing for your salads.
- Choose whole grains like brown rice, millet, quinoa, oats, etc to avoid sudden insulin spikes
- Avoid any kind of alcohol, fizzy drinks, meat, poultry, and dairy products.
- Instead of milk, you can try having almond milk
- Coconut water is one of the things to have to increase the alkaline levels in your body

Highly Alkaline Forming Foods

Lemons, limes, watermelon, muskmelon, cantaloupe, cucumber, sea salt, pumpkin seed, sprouted lentils, seaweed, onion, ginger (fresh), garlic, all kinds of yam, sweet potato, nectarine, dates, figs, papaya, parsley, raspberry, tangerine, pineapple, celery, and seedless grapes (sweet).

Highly Acid Forming Foods

Artificial sweeteners, meats, pork, poultry, fish, seafood, beer, wine, liquor, processed cheese, fried foods, breads, sugar, carbonated soft drinks, cereals (refined), cigarettes, tobacco, coffee, tea (black), flour (white, wheat), jams, jellies, maple syrup (processed), molasses (sulphured), pasta (white), pastries and cakes made from white flour, pickles (commercial), white bread, vinegar, and yogurt(sweetened).

Holistic diet recommendation: If you are trying to restore health, your diet should consist of 80 percent alkaline forming foods and 20 percent acid forming foods. Always consult your doctor before making changes to your diet.

RECIPES

(The quantities provided serve one person)

P=Protein (g)
C=Carbohydrate (g)
FB=Fibre (g)
FT=Fat (g)

Breakfast

Veg

SPIRUCHIA PORRIDGE (236.5 CALORIES)

P=6.7 • C=10.5 • FB=4.2 • FT=19.2

- 1 cup any nut milk you like
- 1 tsp chia seeds
- 1 tsp goji berries
- 2 tsp coconut flakes
- 1 tsp coconut oil
- 1 tsp spirulina powder
- 1 tsp hempseeds

Mix the nut milk with the coconut flakes, coconut oil, and spirulina powder in a blender and then add the chia seeds. Keep it for 10 minutes until the mix becomes thicker and at last, add goji berries and hempseeds.

TOFU SCRAMBLE (416.9 CALORIES)

P=44.3 • C=20.8 • FB=8.5 • FT=20.5

- 2 cups crumbled tofu
- ½ cup spring onion
- ½ cup red peppers
- 1 cup zucchini
- 1 tsp coriander
- 1 tsp nutritional yeast

1 tsp tamari

1 tsp cumin, chilli powder, smoked paprika, turmeric, sea salt

Take the block of firm tofu and scramble it. Put olive oil in a pan on low flame and add the spring onions. Then add the finely chopped red peppers and zucchini. When fragrant, add tofu and mix for about 5 minutes. Add the rest of the ingredients and mix it for another 5 minutes. It's ready to go.

OATS PORRIDGE WITH SEEDS (443.5 CALORIES)

P=25 C=34.5 FB=8 FT=24

½ cup oats

½ cup soy milk (unsweetened)

¼ cup almonds

Cook the oats in water. Transfer in a bowl. Add the seeds just before serving.

Non Veg

GREEN EGGS (BOILED EGGS WITH AVOCADO FILLING INSTEAD OF YOLKS) (384 CALORIES)

P=26 C=28.7 FB=9.5 FT=21

5 egg whites

½ cup avocado

1 tsp olive oil

1 tsp spirulina powder

1 slice whole grain bread

Boil the eggs. Cut the eggs in half. Discard the yolks and replace with the avocado dip.

SALMON SANDWICH (390 CALORIES)

P=33 C=44 FB=4 FT=13

2 slices whole grain bread

- 1 cup smoked salmon
- 1 tsp olive oil
- 1 tbsp mustard sauce

Take slices of smoked salmon, layer it on whole wheat bread with mustard, olive oil, and a dash of lemon juice. Toast, grill, or have the yummy sandwich as it is.

CHICKEN CREPES (405.5 CALORIES)

P=26.2   C=15.4   FB=5.1   FT=10.5

- ½ cup buckwheat or multigrain flour
- ½ cup shredded chicken
- ½ cup mushroom
- ½ cup tomatoes
- 1 tsp tobasco sauce
- 1 tsp olive oil

Mix buckwheat with salt until well combined. Pour the water into the bowl. Again mix until well combined and there are no lumps in the batter. Cover and set aside for at least 30 minutes or an hour or two.

To cook the crepes:

Add the olive oil in the pan, making sure to coat the entire pan. Pour a saddle of rested batter onto the pan. Quickly swirling it around until it forms a circular crepe shape. Allow to cook for about 3 minutes, after which it should be very easy to lift the crepe and flip over. Cook for another 2 minutes & then remove from pan. Continue cooking the crepes until all of the batter has been used up.

To cook the filling:

Take olive oil and added the shredded chicken, along with the mushrooms. Cook until golden brown.

To serve:

Stuff the crepe with chicken and rest of the ingredients.

Bars

ENERGIE BAR (518 CALORIES)

P=13.5 · C=73 · FB=19 · FT=17

2 cups your favourite muesli
1 spoon flaxseed
2 dates

Mix all the ingredients in a food processor. Place for baking on a large pan, make them as thick as you like and give them shape and size. Preheat oven and then put it in for about 30 minutes. Enjoy a small cube of sweetness.

CHOCOLATE ENERGY BAR (353 CALORIES)

P=12 · C=45.5 · FB=11 · FT=9.5

½ cup cooked chickpeas
1 spoon peanut butter
2 dates
1 spoon cacao
8–10 nuts

Mix all the ingredients in a food processor. Place for baking on a large pan, make them as thick as you like and give them shape and size. Preheat oven and then put it in for about 30 minutes.

TAHINI DATE OATBARS (593 CALORIES)

P=6.5 · C=90.5 · FB=7.5 · FT=32

¼ cup medjool dates, pitted
½ cup rolled oats
¼ cup brown rice flour
1 tbsp coconut oil
1 tbsp sesame tahini
1 vanilla bean or tsp vanilla extract
½ tsp a pinch of sea salt
Water

Preheat the oven to 350F. In a food processor, combine the dates, vanilla, and just enough water to blend into a smooth paste. Put this aside. In a large bowl, combine the remaining ingredients. If necessary, add a little water to form a dry dough. Knead the dough with your hands to be sure the ingredients are thoroughly mixed. Lightly oil a small baking pan with coconut oil and spread a layer of ½ the dough on the bottom, then spread all the date paste on top of that. Use the remaining oat mixture to form a third layer on top. You may want to wet your hands with water or a bit of the coconut oil to spread the dough. Press flat. Bake at 350 F for about 30 minutes, until fragrant and lightly browned.

Juices

ABC Juice (102 calories)

P=2 • C=25 • FB=4 • FT=0

½ cup apple
½ cup beetroot
1 cup carrot
1 tsp ginger

Peel all ingredients. Put all in a juicer and then blend it with ginger.

Minty Basil Cooler (139 calories)

P=0 • C=34 • FB=3 • FT=0

1 cup cucumber
½ cup apple
½ cup banana
2 tsp basil
1 tsp mint
½ cup ice cubes

Blend all together in a mixer. If you like it thin texture, blend the apple separately in a juicer.

DEANNE'S GREEN DETOX JUICE (705 CALORIES)

P=21.5 • C=66 • FB=24.5 • FT=44

½ cup parsley
½ cup celery
1 cup coriander
2 tsp spinach
1 tsp mint
1 cup kale
¼ cup seeds
½ cup nuts
1 whole coconut water
Seasonal fruits
Blend all together in a mixer.

PROTEIN PUNCH (408 CALORIES)

P=24.1 • C=57 • FB=24.3 • FT=13

1 cup yellow-green moong dal (soaked & boiled)
½ cup bottle gourd
¼ cup flaxseeds

Soak moong dal in water overnight. Boil moong dal and bottle gourd. Blend together with flaxseeds. Filter this through a clean, thin cloth in a tall glass. Ready to serve. Enjoy!

Smoothies

VEGAN SHAKE (581 CLORIES)

P=31 • C=42.5 • FB=23.5 • FT=34.5

½ cup soy milk (unsweetened)
½ cup flaxseeds
¼ cup dry fig
1 tsp coffee

Blend together flaxseeds, coffee, and figs in unsweetened soy milk. Serve cold with ice cubes.

Protein Power (468 calories)

P=12   C=36   FB=14.5   FT=23.5

½ cup almond milk
1 spoon flaxseeds
1 spoon peanut butter
½ cup banana

Mix all the ingredients in a blender. Serve cold.

Almond Smoothie (436 calories)

P=14   C=35   FB=12   FT=30

1 cup almonds soaked overnight
1 cup carrots
½ cup nectarine
½ cup dates
1 tsp cinnamon

Put a cup of almonds with 2 cups of purified water overnight. Blend until it is well combined. Filter this through a clean, thin cloth. Mix it with a juice of the other ingredients and add a dash of cinnamon. Enjoy!

Tropgreen Smoothie (235 calories)

P=5   C=24.5   FB=11   FT=15

2 cups green leafy vegetables (spinach, kale, romaine lettuce, etc)
1 cup fruit of your choice (apple, mango, orange)
½ cup water or nut milk
½ cup avocado, if you want it creamy
1 tsp sweetener if necessary (jaggery, dates)
1 tsp herbs (basil, parsley, coriander)
1 tsp extras (vanilla, ginger, lemon, cayenne)

Blend and mix together.

Soups

Veg

THAI PUMPKIN SOUP (378 CALORIES)

P=10.85 • C=18.6 • FB=3.7 • FT=26.5

1 cup pumpkin
1 cup shitake
Water or veg stock
½ cup coconut milk
¼ cup tofu (optional)
1 tsp tamari

Heat coconut or sunflower oil in a pan. Add pumpkin in small pieces, sauté with shitake. Add tamari to the mix and close with a lid for 10 minutes on low heat. Add water or stock and coconut milk. Keep the heat low for 10 more minutes.

CARROT GINGER SOUP (447 CALORIES)

P=4.75 • C=37.5 • FB=6 • FT=42

1 cup carrots
1 cup sweet potatoes
water or veg stock
¼ cup coconut milk
1 tbsp coconut oil
1 tsp nutritional yeast
Salt, cumin and black pepper (to sprinkle)

Boil sweet potatoes with skin without chopping them till they are soft, for about 15–20 minutes. Take out of the water and let them cool down. Heat coconut oil in a pan, add carrots and sauté for 10 minutes. Meanwhile, peel the sweet potatoes and cut them in pieces to add to the mixture. Add water or veg stock and bring it to a boil for 5 minutes. Make sure that the carrot is soft and add coconut milk on low heat. Add the rest of the ingredients and blend all until almost smooth.

Green Peas Cream Soup (454.5 calories)

1 cup carrots
1 cup sweet potatoes
2 cups water or veg stock
¼ cup coconut milk
1 tbsp coconut oil
1 tbsp yeast
1 small spring onion
½ tbsp garlic
Salt, cumin, black pepper (to taste)

Chop spring onions and garlic finely and place in a pan with olive oil, on low flame. Add small chunks of potatoes, carrots, and mix together for 10 minutes. Add water or veg stock. Then add coconut milk and coconut oil. Boil for 20 minutes with the lid closed. Let it cool and blend until smooth. Add salt, cumin, and black pepper.

Red Pepper Energy Soup (467 calories)

P=16 • C=56.5 • FB=24.5 • FT=20.5

3 red peppers (seeded and chopped)
1 yellow pepper (seeded and chopped)
1 cucumber (peeled and chopped)
1 small avocado
Handful green sprouts such as alfalfa or sunflower
Juice of 1 lemon
¼ cup soaked sunflower seeds
1 tsp extra virgin olive oil
1 tsp cold-pressed flax oil
A pinch of sea salt
A tiny pinch of cumin
A pinch of black pepper
Handful chopped fresh herbs such as coriander, parsley, or mint
Water

Combine all ingredients in a food processor and blend. Add water to reach desired consistency. Top with a sprinkle of seeds.

GREEN GODDESS SOUP (240.5 CALORIES)

P=18 • C=24.6 • FB=6.2 • FT=7

Bunch of spinach or chard
Handful of kale leaves (stems removed)
Handful of green sprouts such as alfalfa or sunflower
1 small tomato (diced)
2 stalks celery (chopped)
1 cucumber (peeled and chopped)
Juice of 1–2 lemons
1 tsp spirulina
1 small hass avocado
1 clove garlic (minced)
Handful fresh herbs—basil, coriander, mint, parsley, dill
1 tbsp olive oil
A pinch of sea salt
A pinch of cayenne

Combine all the ingredients in a blender or food processor. Sprinkle with chopped fresh herbs, cucumber, or a handful of sunflower seeds.

Non Veg

THAI CHICKEN SOUP (497 CALORIES)

P=31.35 • C=19.6 • FB=3.7 • FT=29

1 cup pumpkin
½ cup carrot
½ cup coconut milk
¼ cup tofu
1 tsp tamari
½ cup shredded chicken
Ginger, lemongrass, coriander, lime juice

Heat water in a pan. Add small pieces of pumpkin with shredded chicken, carrot, ginger, and lemongrass. Add tamari to the mix and close with a lid for 10 minutes on low heat. Add coconut milk and tofu. Keep the heat low for 10 more minutes. Finally, add lime juice.

SPICY TURKEY SOUP (275.9 CALORIES)

P=35 C=25.6 FB=2.2 FT=13

½ cup turkey
1 cup shitakey
1 cup tomatoes
2 cups chicken stock
Thyme, bayleaf, pepper, parsely, lime juice

Dice turkey pieces and boil them in chicken stock. On a non-stick pan, spray oil once and mildly cook all the other ingredients. Add all the spices to the turkey and chicken stock. Cook for 10 mins on low heat. Serve with grinding fresh pepper corns.

Salads

Veg

SPROUTS SALAD (564.5 CALORIES)

P=21 C=20.8 FB=8.2 FT=51

½ cup any type of sprouts
1 cup lettuce of your choice, baby greens and basil leaves
¼ cup red and yellow pepper
¼ cup beetroot and carrot
¼ cup avocado (optional)
Mix all together. Add the dressing of your choice.

<u>Ginger Miso Dressing</u>
1 tbsp olive oil
1 tbsp sesame oil
1 tsp sesame seeds
1 tbsp white miso

1 tbsp apple cider vinegar
pinch of ginger (minced)

Mix and blend. Add water as necessary.

Love Salad (357 calories)

P=8 • C=33.5 • FB=11.5 • FT=25

1 cup lettuce of your choice
¼ cup beetroot shredded
½ cup peach
½ cup avocado
2 tbsp walnuts
Gomasio, black sesame (sprinkle)

Mix all together. Add the dressing of your choice.

Apricot Dressing (426 calories)

P=4 • C=43 • FB=5.5 • FT=29.5

½ cup dried apricot
½ cup fresh mint and dill
pinch of ginger (minced)
1 tbsp flaxseed oil
1 tbsp olive oil
1 tbsp white miso
1 tbsp lemon
Mix and blend.

Seeds Dream (568.5 calories)

P=10 • C=54 • FB=13.5 • FT=38

1 cup lettuce of your choice
½ cup cucumber
2 tbsp sunflower, pumpkin, and flaxseeds
1 tbsp currants
Mix all together. Add the dressing of your choice.

Caesar Dressing

¼ cup cashew nuts
1 tbsp olive oil
1 tbsp apple cider vinegar
1 tsp lemon juice
½ tsp nutritional yeast
½ tsp Dijon mustard
½ tsp garlic, black pepper
Mix and blend.

MANGO COLESLAW (439 CALORIES)

P=12.5　C=63.7　FB=19.5　FT=17.1

2 cups white cabbage
2 cups red cabbage
2 cups carrot
1 cup mango
½ cup onion (optional)

Cut the cabbage into thin, long slices. Cube the mango and julienne the carrot. Mix and add dressing.

AVO DRESSING

¼ cup avocado
¼ cup cashew
2 tsp lemon juice
2 tsp coriander
1/2 tsp sea salt

Mix and blend well.

LIVING GREEN DRESSING (343 CALORIES)

P=4　C=12.2　FB=7　FT=31.5

2 cups zucchini
1 tsp flaxseed oil

1 tbsp olive oil
¼ cup avocado
Apple cider vinegar (to taste)

Clove, ginger, spirulina, lemon, basil, dill, cilantro, parsley, sea salt (to taste)

Mix and blend well.

Non Veg

LEAN SALAD (418 CALORIES)

P=43.7 • C=31 • FB=4.1 • FT=14.3

1 cup turkey
½ cup celery
½ cup green onion
½ cup red bell pepper
1 tbsp mustard sauce
Apple cider vinegar (to taste)
Salt (to taste)

Use shredded turkey pieces. Mix all together. Add vinegar and salt to taste.

ASIAN CHICKEN SALAD (399 CALORIES)

P=47 • C=8.5 • FB=2.5 • FT=19.1

1 cup chicken
1 tbsp sesame seed oil
½ cup green onions
1 cup iceberg
1 tbsp soy sauce
apple cider vinegar
Salt (to taste)
Mix all together. Serve cold.

Greek Salad (433.5 calories)

P=30 • C=24.6 • FB=9.2 • FT=23

1 cup spinach
1 cup tofu (marinated)
1 cup cucumber
1 cup tomato
4–5 chopped black olives
1 tbsp apple cider vinegar
½ cup onion, baby spinach, fresh mint leaves, fresh basil leaves

Marinate tofu overnight in a bowl with olive oil, tamari, and lemon depending on your taste. Cut tomato and cucumber in big pieces and slice onion long and thin. Mix the rest of the ingredients and serve.

Balsamic Dressing

½ cup olive oil
3 tsp balsamic vinegar
2 tsp maple syrup
2 tsp lemon
Mix and blend.

Mango Pineapple Salsa (354.5 calories)

P=22.8 • C=41.6 • FB=8.7 • FT=11

1 cup mango
½ cup pineapple
1 cup red pepper
1 cup tomato
¼ cup fresh cilantro (finely chopped)
1 green onions (finely chopped)
Juice of 1 lime
½ small jalapeno (deseeded and minced)
A pinch of sea salt
A pinch of cayenne

Combine all the ingredients together in a bowl, allowing flavours to mingle for 30 minutes before serving. This tropical salsa makes a great topping for leafy greens. You can also add some chopped avocado for a filling meal.

VEGAN PAELLA (490.5 CALORIES)

P=13.7 · C=91.6 · FB=19.2 · FT=2.4

1 cup whole rice
1 cup onion
½ cup red pepper
½ cup tomato
1 cup green beans (boiled for 10 minutes)
½ cup green peas (boiled for 10 minutes)
¼ cup azuki beans (soaked overnight)
Coriander for garnish

Take a big flat pan and heat olive oil, Add minced onions. Sauté for 5 minutes, add fresh tomatoes, and a few minutes later add pepper. Add green beans and peas. Sauté for 15 minutes. Add azukis. Then add a bit more oil, spread the rice all over the pan and sauté for 5 minutes until it is all well mixed. Add the veg stock, bring to a boil for 15 minutes. Put off the flame and wrap it with aluminium foil for 10 more minutes. Add a bit of lemon if you like.

Lunch

Veg

BROWN/RED RICE TABBOULEH (434.5 CALORIES)

P=4.75 · C=37.5 · FB=6 · FT=42

1 cup brown rice
1 cup tomatoes
1 cup cucumber
¼ cup parsley
½ cup mint

1 tbsp sunflower seeds

2 tbsp pomegranate

2 tbsp onions

Salt, cumin, black pepper (to taste)

Take brown rice or red rice in a bowl and pour boiling hot water to it. Then cover the bowl tightly with plastic wrap and let it stand for 15 minutes. Drain in a sieve, pressing on rice to remove any excess liquid. Transfer the rice in a dry bowl and toss with all the other ingredients.

Curry Tofu Salad (524.5 calories)

P=23.5 • C=27.5 • FB=7.5 • FT=31.5

1/2 cup tofu

½ cup carrot (grated)

¼ cup celery (diced)

8–10 almonds

½ tbsp chive

Salt and dried basil (sprinkle)

Take a block of firm tofu and scramble it or cut it in square pieces if you prefer. Blend almond until it is chopped finely. Mix all ingredients and add dressing.

Curry Mustard Dressing

½ cup tofu

1 tbsp olive oil

½ tbsp cumin

½ tbsp Dijon mustard

½ tbsp apple cider vinegar

½ tbsp maple syrup

½ tbsp black pepper

Mix and blend well.

SPAGHETTI IN VEGAN PESTO SAUCE (440 CALORIES)

P=5 • C=53.5 • FB=6.2 • FT=22

2 cups basil
1 cup coriander
¼ cup olive oil
1 tbsp garlic minced
2 tbsp dried tomatoes
1 cup spaghetti

Put everything in a blender and it's ready. You can garnish with little olive oil on top. Boil whole wheat pasta and add.

SPAGHETTI IN SUNDRIED TOMATO SAUCE (514.5 CALORIES)

P=9.2 • C=57.6 • FB=11.3 • FT=20.2

½ cup sundried tomatoes
1 cup fresh tomatoes
½ cup red bell pepper
8–10 walnuts
1 tsp brown miso
1 tbsp olive oil
1 cup spaghetti
dried oregano, dried basil, smoked paprika, cumin (to sprinkle)
1/2 tsp garlic, minced (optional)

Soak dried tomatoes in water for 1 hour until they soften. Blend all ingredients together and add water if necessary, then garnish with oregano. Add whole wheat pasta to this.

SUNNY FAJITA (454 CALORIES)

P=25.25 • C=71 • FB=24.7 • FT=9.6

1 cup black beans (soaked overnight)
½ cup water
½ cup onion

1 cup carrot
1 cup pumpkin
1 cup kale
1 tbsp guacamole
2 tbsp tofu
Salt, cumin, garlic, chilli (to taste)

Boil the beans in water until they get soft. Put oil in a pan and sauté the onions until they get translucent. Add carrot and pumpkin in small squares. Close the lid and simmer for 5–10 minutes. Sauté with kale or spinach or both and add beans. Sauté for 10 minutes. Then serve this mix in a fajita with guacamole and tofu.

Polenta Curry with Coconut (655 calories)

P=13.5 C=66.7 FB=18.4 FT=2.3

1 cup polenta chunks
½ cup chickpeas (soaked overnight)
½ cup coconut milk
1 tbsp coconut oil
1 cup broccoli
½ cup green peas
¼ cup onion
¼ cup fresh coriander
1 tsp tamari and lime juice
Salt, curry, cumin (sprinkle)

For making the polenta chunks, you need to boil 4 cups of water and then add 2 cups of polenta and a bit of oil. Keep moving the mixture for 5 minutes. Put off the flame and place it in a large pan to cool. Then cut into small pieces. For the sauce, sauté the onions in coconut oil, then add the green peas and the broccoli. After 10 minutes, add chickpeas tamari and lime, sauté for 5 minutes. Add the coconut milk and the rest of the ingredients. Gently move the mixture and simmer for 10 more minutes.

Raw Sushi (488.5 calories)

P=16 • C=53.7 • FB=9.5 • FT=26.7

2 nori sheets
½ cup cauliflower
¼ cup cashews
¼ cup red bell pepper
¼ cup avocado
¼ cup carrots
1 cup onion
½ cup rice
1 tsp sesame & sunflower oil
½ tbsp alfalfa sprouts

For the rice, mix cauliflower and cashew nuts in a food processor. Add a mixture of apple cider vinegar, jaggery, and salt. For the 'tuna pate' mix almonds, sunflower seeds, minced ginger, sesame oil, sunflower oil, wakame or nori sheets, and black pepper. Add all as per your taste.

Turkish Millet (345 calories)

P=13.5 • C=66.7 • FB=18.4 • FT=2.3

1 cup millet
2 cups tomatoes
1 cup zucchini
1 cup asparagus
1 cup aubergine
½ cup spring onion
salt, dried rosemary, oregano (sprinkle)
black pepper, cayenne (optional)

Heat olive oil in a wok or pan. Sauté spring onions for 5 minutes. Add fresh tomatoes and 1 tsp of salt, oregano, rosemary, and cayenne. Mix for 5 more minutes and add aubergines and asparagus, sauté for 5 minutes and add zucchini mix and place the millet. Sauté all together and slowly add water or stock and keep stirring the mixture. Close

Non Veg

Egg and Bean Salad (454 calories)

> P=37.5 • C=62.2 • FB=22.5 • FT=7.1

1 cup sprouts
½ cup onion
1 cup beetroot
1 cup spinach
1 tbsp avocado cubes
5 boiled egg whites
Salt, garlic, chilli (to taste)

Boil the egg whites. Discard the yolk. Make sprouts or you can buy readymade sprouts. Boil or steam the sprouts before using. Toss all the ingredients together.

Chicken Noodles (504 calories)

> P=31.7 • C=36.3 • FB=5.4 • FT=34

½ cup noodles
¼ cup spring onions
¼ cup red pepper
½ cup zucchini
¼ cup olive oil
1 tsp sesame seed
½ cup shredded chicken

Boil the noodles and coat them with olive oil after discarding the water. Sauté chicken with rest of the ingredients in the pan. Add the noodles to the pan along with the vegetables. After a quick toss it's ready to eat.

Steamed Fish and Veggies with Peanut Sauce (631.5 calories)

P=25.5 • C=31.7 • FB=11.9 • FT=59.8

1 cup steamed fish
½ cup spring onions
1 cup tomatoes
½ cup asparagus
¼ cup olive oil
2 tsp sesame seed

Peanut Sauce

1 tbsp peanuts
1 tsp brown sugar
1 tbsp sesame oil

Steam the fish on a steaming rack. Add the spring onions and the asparagus in the boiling water of the steamer. Once the fish and vegetables are steamed, add freshly cut tomatoes, sprinkle sesame seeds, and lightly toss all ingredients with olive oil.

For the sauce:

Take all the ingredients and blend together. Make a smooth or coarse paste as per preference of texture. Serve alongside the fish.

Herb Turkey Filled with Fresh Greens (556 calories)

P=30.5 • C=20.7 • FB=14 • FT=40

½ cup turkey
¼ cup olive oil
½ cup herbs
1 spoon flaxseeds
1 cup fresh green leaves (spinach, rocket, lettuce)

Arrange turkey slices in a baking dish. Pour lemon juice over it. Cover and refrigerate for 1 hour.

Preheat oven to 450°F. Add olive oil in small saucepan over medium heat. Mix finely chopped herbs, green leaves and spices and add it in pie dish. Brush turkey on both sides with olive oil. Coat turkey slices on both sides with herb mixture. Place slices on baking sheet. Bake until turkey is cooked through and is golden for about 20 minutes. Transfer to plates. Serve hot.

Snacks

Veg

CARROT DIP (355 CALORIES)

P=1.5   C=26   FB=4   FT=28

½ cup carrot
1 tbsp olive oil
1 tbsp sesame oil
2 tbsp parsley
pinch of cumin powder
pinch of salt

Steam or boil carrots until they are soft enough to blend. Put all ingredients and blend until smooth. Slowly add water if necessary. I like to have this with sesame crackers.

GUACAMOLE (183.5 CALORIES)

P=2   C=12.1   FB=8.7   FT=15

½ cup avocado
1 cup fresh tomatoes
1 tsp lemon juice
½ cup coriander
½ tbsp. garlic, minced
salt and cayenne for taste

Make a small cut at the bottom of the tomatoes and place them in a bowl of hot water for a minute. Then peel them and mix all ingredients in a food processor.

Baba Ganoush (440.5 calories)

P=2.2 • C=76.2 • FB=3 • FT=14

2 tbsp tahini paste
1 cup aubergine roasted
½ cup water
1 tsp lemon juice
4 tsp tamari
1 tbsp olive oil
½ tbsp garlic minced

Make two long cuts on the aubergines (choose big ones) and put them under a grill, placing them very close to the fire. Grill them until the skin is burnt and then turn to the other side. When ready, put them to cool. Peel off the skin and keep aside.

For the sauce, mix the rest of the ingredients in a food processor and add more water if necessary. Add more lemon if desired. Then add the aubergine.

Coconut Alioli (637 calories)

P=13 • C=20.5 • FB=3.5 • FT=66

½ cup cashews soaked for 6 hours
½ cup coconut milk
2 tsp coconut oil
1 tsp sesame seeds
½ tsp lime juice
½ tsp garlic
½ tsp sea salt

Put together in a blender and enjoy.

Black Tapernade (352 calories)

P=0 • C=10 • FB=0.5 • FT=35.5

½ cup black olives
2 tbsp olive oil

½ cup fresh parsley
½ tsp dried oregano
½ tsp garlic, minced (optional)
½ tsp spring onion (optional)

Put all together in a blender and it's ready.

BROCCOLI CAKE (1172 CALORIES)

P=23.5 C=198 FB=19 FT=54.5

1 cup rice flour
1 tbsp flaxseeds
2 tbsp olive oil
½ tsp salt, oregano, rosemary
1 cup water
3 cups spinach
1 cup broccoli steamed or boiled
1 tbsp garlic
1 tbsp chia seeds
¼ cup almond flour
Salt, nutmeg, black pepper (to taste)

For the pastry:

Take the flour and mix with flaxseeds, salt, oregano, and rosemary. Make a hole in the middle and add olive oil and water. Combine all until you get a sticky paste. Place in the fridge for 10 minutes. Then spread it and put it in a mould.

For the filling:

Heat oil in a pain and add the garlic minced. Stir for few minutes and add broccoli and spinach and then sauté for 5 minutes. Blend all and add the rest of ingredients. It should be a thick consistency – if not add more almond flour and chia seeds. Then fill in a mould and bake in a pre-heated oven for 20 minutes on 180 C.

Non Veg

Tuna on Brown Bread (363 calories)

P=31 • C=44.5 • FB=8.5 • FT=7.5

½ cup tuna
1 cup whole wheat bread cubes
½ cup white beans
1 tsp olive oil
Salt, black pepper, organo, rosemary, lemon juice (mixture to taste)

Whisk lemon juice with all the other ingredients. Add beans and tuna to the mixture. Toss and coat well. Make cube shapes of the bread. Spread tuna mixture on the bread cubes. Enjoy a healthy, yummy snack.

Shredded Chicken with Chickpea (492 calories)

1 cup shredded chicken
½ cup tomatoes
1 cup chickpeas
½ cup green bell pepper
½ cup carrot
Salt, coriander, lemon juice (to taste)

Cook the chickpeas in a pressure cooker after soaking overnight, drain the excess water. Add all the ingredients along with shredded chicken. A filling, tasty, high protein snack is ready to eat.

Salmon Paste on Whole wheat Bread (387 calories)

P=54.7 • C=7.5 • FB=1.6 • FT=13.2

2 cups salmon
½ cup feta cheese
2 tsp mustard

Spring onion greens, pepper, salt, lemon juice (mixture to taste)

Whole wheat bread cubes (2 thin slices)

Puree feta cheese and lemon juice into a fine paste in a food processor. Add salmon and other ingredients to blend. Serve chilled with whole wheat bread.

Dessert

Desserts are to be tasted, not eaten in large quantities. Healthy desserts provide some nutritious benefits other than just empty calories. The following section has a few such recipes. Because they are healthy, they are not low on calories. So enjoy the goodness in small bites. Relish it. And make the most of these yummy desserts.

CHOCOLATE BLISSBALL (446 CALORIES)

P=13.5　C=52　FB=20.5　FT=26

¼ cup walnuts
½ cup cacao powder
¼ cup dates
1 tsp salt

Mix all in a food processor, adding dates one by one until you get a sticky texture for making the balls. You can place them in a freezer for a few minutes before serving.

RAW CARROT CAKE (1122 CALORIES)

P=12　C=163.5　FB=18　FT=43.5

½ cups carrot (shredded)
¼ cup fresh coconut (shredded)
8–10 walnuts
¼ cup green raisins
¼ cup dates
2 tbsp maple syrup
Sea salt (to taste)
Cinnamon nutmeg (to taste)

The Way We Eat

For frosting:

- 1/4 cup cashew nuts (soaked 6 hours)
- 1/4 cup dates
- 2 tbsp maple syrup or jaggery
- 1/2 tsp vanilla
- 1/4 cup water

For frosting:

Mix cashew nuts, lemon, jaggery, and vanilla. Add a bit of water at a time until you get a thick, creamy sauce. Put in the freezer for 10–15 minutes before placing it on top of the cake.

For cake:

Mix all the ingredients in a food processor and add dates one by one until it gets sticky. Leave it in the freezer for 15 minutes. For garnish, use walnuts and cinnamon.

For semi-raw version:

Bake the cake for 20 minutes at 180 C.

MANGO CHEESECAKE (789 CALORIES)

P=11.75 · C=87 · FB=2 · FT=49.5

For crust:

- 1 cup your favourite biscuit (crumbled)
- 1 tbsp coconut oil
- 1/2 tsp sea salt

For filling:

- 1/4 cup firm tofu
- 1/2 cup mango
- 1/4 cup coconut milk
- 2 tbsp maple syrup
- 1/2 tsp lemon juice
- 1/2 tsp coconut oil

For crust:

Mix cookies, coconut oil, and salt in a food processor. Place in a mold and keep it in the fridge.

For filling:

Blend together the rest of the ingredients until smooth. Place into the crust and set in the fridge for a few hours.

RAW STRAWBERRY TART (645 CALORIES)

P=8.2 C=108.5 FB=17 FT=15.4

½ cup dried figs
¼ cup pecan nuts
1 tbsp cacao powder
½ tbsp sea salt
1 cup strawberries
8–10 almonds (soaked for 8 hours)
2 tbsp coconut flakes
2 tbsp maple syrup
½ tbsp soya lecitine

For crust:

Mix dried figs, cacao powder, pinch of salt in food processor and add dates one by one until you get a sticky paste. Place in mold and freeze for 15 minutes.

For filling: mix rest of ingredients in a high speed blender until you get a smooth cream. Add more almonds if needed. Then freeze for 5 minutes. Place cream on top of crust and let in freezer for ten more minutes. Use strawberries for garnish.

LIME TART (753 CALORIES)

P=5.5 C=72.2 FB=11 FT=50

¼ cup shredded coconut
1 tbsp walnuts

¼ cup pitted dates
Sea salt (to sprinkle)
¼ cup avocados
2 tbsp maple syrup
1 tsp lime juice
¼ tsp soya lecitine
Kiwi for garnish (optional)

For the crust:

Put coconut, macadamia, and salt in food processor and then add dates one by one till you get a sticky paste. Place it in a mold and put it in the freezer for 15 minutes.

For the filling:

Blend all the ingredients until smooth and then place in freezer for 15 minutes separately from the crust. Then fill the mold with the cream. Garnish with kiwi slices.

VEGAN CHOCOLATE MUFFIN (737 CALORIES)

P=1355 • C=119 • FB=19 • FT=41.5

1 cup whole flour
½ cup cacao powder
½ cup ripe banana mashed
1 tbsp coconut oil
½ cup nut milk
2 tbsp maple syrup
½ tsp baking soda
½ tsp sea salt, cinnamon

Preheat the oven and prepare the mould with a little bit of oil on it. Mix all the dry ingredients in one bowl and all the wet ones in another. Combine both and stir well. Bake around 30–45 minutes until toothpick inserted in the centre of the muffin comes out clean.

Ginger Apple Crumble (652 calories)

P=2.3 • C=121 • FB=8.5 • FT=30

1 cup apple chunks
2 tbsp maple syrup
1 tsp cup lemon juice
½ tsps shredded fresh ginger

Mix both the ingredients in a bowl and place in a pan on low fire, with lid. The apple should become soft, add little bit of water if necessary.

For the crumble:

¼ cup rolled oats
1 tbsp coconut oil
2 tbsp maple syrup

Mix all the ingredients together and bake in a pre-heated oven for 20 minutes at 180 C. Place the crumble over the apple and enjoy.

Soups

Veg

Unsweetened Almond Milk (1 Cup) (30 calories)

P=1 • C=1 • FB=1 • FT=3

Almonds
Water
Honey/Maple/Coconut Sugar/Stevia/Dates/Agave
Cinnamon/Vanilla/Cardamom

Nut milks are quite flexible and wonderful on their own or when used in recipes. Fresh homemade 'nutmilks', made from soaked or sprouted nuts, are infinitely superior in taste and nutrition to packaged, factory-made milks.

First, it is ideal to soak the almonds in fresh water and a pinch of sea salt for 8 hours or overnight. This soaking neutralizes the compounds in nuts which can make them more difficult to digest, and also makes the nutrients in the nuts more bio-available. When making nutmilk, simply rinse the nuts in clean water after soaking, then place the wet nuts in the blender with water. The amounts can vary according to how rich you like your milk—a good starting point is 1 part nuts to 4 parts water, although a richer milk is definitely yummy.

If you like your milk plain or intend to use it to cook non-sweet dishes, you can make it with only those two ingredients. If you want to drink it alone or make dessert, it is nice to add a bit of the sweetener and spices of your choice—a spoonful of honey and a dash of cinnamon are a good option.

Simply blend all ingredients on high until the nuts are finely ground, then strain through some layers of cheesecloth or a nutmylk bag, and enjoy.

The leftover nut pulp can be reserved to make dehydrated raw crackers, and will keep in the freezer.

Nut milks are quite flexible and wonderful on their own or when used in recipes. Fresh homemade 'nutmilks', made from soaked or sprouted nuts, are infinitely superior in taste and nutrition to packaged, factory-made milks.

First it is ideal to soak the almonds in fresh water and a pinch of sea-salt for 8 hours or overnight. This soaking neutralizes the compounds in nuts which can make them more difficult to digest, and also makes the nutrients in the nuts more bio-available. When making nut milk, simply rinse the nuts in clean water after soaking the, then place the wet nuts in the blender with water. The amounts can vary according to how rich you would like your milk—a good starting point is 1 part nuts to 4 parts water, although a richer milk is definitely yummy.

If you like your milk plain or intend to use it to cook non-sweet dishes, you can make it with only those two ingredients. If you want to drink it alone or make a dessert, it is nice to add a bit of the sweetener and spices of your choice—a spoonful of honey and a dash of cinnamon would be a good option.

Simply blend all ingredients on high speed until the nuts are finely ground, then strain the through some layers of cheesecloth or a nutmilk bag, and enjoy.

The leftover nut pulp can be reserved to make dehydrated raw crackers, and you can keep it in the freezer.

It's a fact that there are more general illnesses today's than there were in the past simply because we have let ourselves go. We are forever chasing more and more complicated lifestyles in the pursuit of happiness. You need to detox your body once in a while to create more balance in your life. A sensible approach in your diet is important to help you chage your lifestyle to a more healthy and rewarding balance, providing better energy, more satisfying sleep, and faster repair of the cells in your body.

Now you know that every macronutrient has a particular role to play and that all foods have different strengths. Find a full spectrum of organic foods, try and include the super foods that have been mentioned in the chapter into your diet to help the liver to neutralize the toxins in your body, and whip up a mango cheesecake with the help of the recipe I have given.

Don't be scared of eating rice or bananas or avocados just because someone says they are fattening. I don't believe in putting oneself on ridiculous diets that make you feel guilty when you fall off the wagon. I don't want you to deprive yourself of anything, provided you know it has to be eaten in moderation. Don't get disheartened if you see the carbs or fats are on the higher side in the recipes. Understand these complex carbs and essential fats are needed for your body. But don't get obsessed with food either—it could lead to serious health conditions like anorexia and bulimia. As I said earlier, balance is the key.

Someone has rightly said, 'The food you eat can either be the safest and most powerful form of medicine or the slowest form of poison.' Think and act sensibly as far as your diet is concerned for it has far-reaching effects on your long-term health.

CELLULITE

The Miracle Cure for Cellulite

That got your attention, didn't it? Described by so many names—dimpled derrieres, orange peel syndrome, cottage cheese thighs—cellulite is the dreaded fat which all women love to hate. It has given rise to a million dollar cosmetic industry promising you quick fix-it solutions.

Your body is exposed to a variety of toxins—processed foods, refined salts, pesticides, and preservatives—the list is endless. Such foods are loaded with grease, chemicals, and preservatives which our body finds very difficult to break down. All these 'poisons' make our fat-producing hormones go out of whack! Smoking and consumption of alcohol adds to the build-up of toxic waste inside your body. The dimples and pockets of your cellulite store these toxins in your fat.

Other causes of cellulite are poor diet, sedentary lifestyle, fluid retention, and bad blood circulation.

Cellulite Formation in Skin

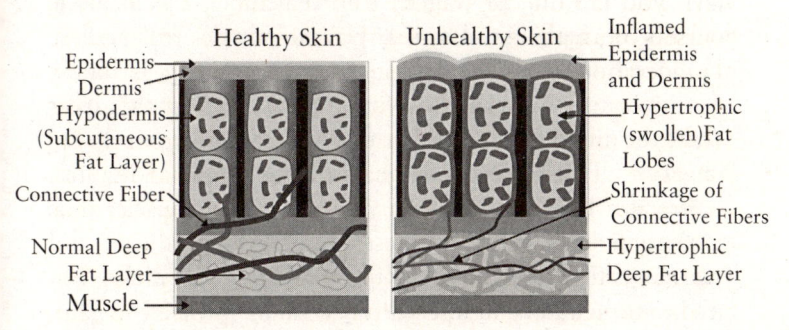

Healthy Skin — Epidermis, Dermis, Hypodermis (Subcutaneous Fat Layer), Connective Fiber, Normal Deep Fat Layer, Muscle

Unhealthy Skin — Inflamed Epidermis and Dermis, Hypertrophic (swollen) Fat Lobes, Shrinkage of Connective Fibers, Hypertrophic Deep Fat Layer

Photo credit: www.antiageingsavantess.com

With age, the strands of connective tissue that connect the fat tissue to the skin gets thicker while our skin gets thinner. Also, as one gets older, muscles get replaced with fat. It affects women more than men because the layers of skin and fat are structured differently in men. In women, the subcutaneous fat layer has large upright chambers while in men, there are smaller slanting chambers. It's not a disease or an illness—it's just an additional layer of fat, most commonly found in the form of bumps or ugly dimples on the buttocks and thighs. It is caused due to poor elasticity of the skin. When fat cells become too big for the natural fibre chambers of the skin, it forms a bulge and uneven layers of fat underneath.

As upsetting as this may sound to the samosa and French fries lovers, junk food is one of the worst offenders. The other red flag to look out for when you suffer from cellulite is weak glutes. If you have a desk job, or a lower back or hip pain, you are most probably suffering from weak glutes. Poor posture, long periods of sitting and wrong exercise routines can cause weak glutes and the result is an unappealing, saggy butt with a lot of cellulite!

The miracle cure is simple: clean eating, weight training with compound moves, and high intensity cardio with interval training. There is no other cure—no massage, no cream, no oil, no hope in a jar. If there was one, believe me, I would have sold it to all my clients! But remember, cardio alone will not decrease the dimples. Flaccid muscle can increase the appearance of cellulite, so strength training is highly recommended. You should work the muscles in the areas where the dimpling is occurring two to three times a week. Do lunges in all directions and squats for the thighs and glutes.

Strength training will help you regain lost muscle, thus preventing cellulite. All these expensive products and treatments that lure you in are just marketing gimmicks. You need to train and be fit internally. The more muscle you gain, the less will be the chances of cellulite striking on your body.

Some other methods of reducing cellulite formation in the body are:

1. Detoxify and cleanse your system by eating healthy, nutritious, fibrous food, adding greens and various coloured fruits and vegetables.
2. Boost your metabolism with high intensity interval training.
3. Lift weights! You must do a resistance training programme because you need to build muscle mass and tone. If the muscle is weak and flaccid, the subcutaneous fat will rest on top of the muscle and give the lumpy look that we all detest!
4. Stimulate the lymphatic system (the lymph sits just underneath the surface of your skin) through dry bristle skin brushing and massage. This helps toxins to circulate into the elimination channels for release. Swap your refined salt (table salt) for celtic sea salt or Himalayan crystal salt.
5. Drink enough pure, clean water and get organic hydration from fresh fruits and vegetables to flush out the toxins. Water is essential for life and it is also essential for reducing and preventing further cellulite.
6. It has been seen that hormones play a major role in cellulite formation (that is probably why women typically get it and men don't). So working towards proper hormone balance can help reduce cellulite.
7. Flaxseed supports estrogen levels and boosts collagen growth. Collagen is the main component of connective tissue; by strengthening the skin, it helps reduce the appearance of cellulite. Sprinkle 2 tablespoons on oatmeal cereal and yogurt every day, or you can eat the seeds alone to prevent the formation of cellulite.
8. Avoid crash dieting; it can make cellulite worse. When you lose weight quickly, you lose muscle tissue—the stuff that makes your legs and butt look toned and smooth.

It's time to stop feeling ashamed of the cellulite on your body and doing something about it. Don't think that you're alone in your struggle against cellulite because almost 90 percent of women face this problem at one time or another in their lives. Try the solutions listed in the chapter and see the results for yourself. And don't forget the benefits of incorporating weight training in your exercise programme to tone your underlying muscles and reducing the appearance of cellulite.

Part Two

1

History of Bodybuilding

THE BODYBUILDER VS THE ATHLETE

Bodybuilding and power lifting are beautiful sports, and while bodybuilding is done more for aesthetic reasons, power lifting is a strength-based sport. Bodybuilding is an art—each muscle is well-defined and the body is so chiselled that the body looks like it's straight out of an anatomy book. If you compare a bodybuilder's physique to an Olympian-class athlete, there is a world of a difference. Sportspeople build their bodies to maximize their performance in specific sports. On the other hand, bodybuilders aspire to develop an aesthetically pleasing body and balanced physique. But functionally they will not be able to move as smoothly as world-class sportspeople.

I am not against bodybuilding. In fact, I have great respect for bodybuilders like Eugen Sandow who built a Grecian-style physique in the mid-19th century, without an ounce of supplements or any kind of steroid injections. The world has been inspired by the stellar physiques of Arnold Schwarzenegger or Sylvester Stallone in *Rambo*, to mention a few. Bodybuilders inspired millions to take up fitness and push their potential. In India, in the 11th century, Indians would lift primitive dumbbell weights made of stone and it has been reported that in the 16th century, weightlifting had become quite popular in the country.

The point that I want to highlight here is that if you take up bodybuilding, know that it is a sport aimed to win tournaments of a different kind. It is not the most efficient way to train if you are living a daily, routine life. For that, it would be ideal if your training programme leaned towards the athlete's program because it is functional—your muscles then get conditioned and strengthened to do daily tasks of walking, running, pushing, pulling, lifting, squatting and holding. Aiming for size is pleasing to the ego, but does the giant size help you functionally?

DOING IT THE RIGHT WAY

I am most inspired by Eugen Sandow, also known as the 'Father of Bodybuilding'. Born in Germany in 1867 as Friedrich Wilhelm Muller, he changed the way the world looked at bodies in 1890s. Sandow was the first superstar of physical fitness who promoted bodybuilding and weightlifting through his travels across Europe and America. He also wrote fitness books, and starred in short films on bodybuilding. He had muscle quality and aesthetics comparable to that of a modern day bodybuilder, which he developed by studying how the muscles worked and by using his self-made dumbbells. His legacy still lives on—the winner of the most prestigious bodybuilding competition in the world, 'Mr Olympia', is awarded a statuette known as the 'Sandow'. What I find most fascinating about Sandow is that he never used any artificial supplements or steroids to build his perfect body.

Take raspberry ketones for example. Made popular by a leading doctor in America who has his own health show on primetime television, raspberry ketones are all the rage these days because they 'supposedly' help you lose weight

History of Bodybuilding

without you having to move a muscle. Made from the natural phenolic compound found in red raspberries, they give the fruit its signature smell. Most people believe that they assist you in losing weight because they help your body break down fat more efficiently. Now before you rush to your nearest chemist and buy these supplements, keep in mind that there has been no scientific study to support such a claim. So be cautious before blindly popping the pill. All fat burners have dangerous side effects.

Nowadays, I see people on television and fitness magazines, feed consumers garbage about supplements and steroids. Big stars endorse it and make you feel like it's a normal thing to pump your body with unnatural foods. They are taking you for a ride; you do not need it! Don't judge people by appearances 99 percent of them are building their physiques in an unnatural way and it will take a toll on their health eventually. If your trainer tells you he will make you look like a certain actor, and that you need to have supplements, show him the door. All this hype and hysteria around protein supplements, protein shakes, health bars, fat-burners, and steroids has fuelled a multi-billion dollar industry but they have produced marginal effects on people. In fact, if you closely look at the lives of the people who use these products, they suffer from severe side effects.

Have you ever been to an 'akhada'? It's an old-fashioned wrestling centre where men wrestle, perform squats, push-ups, lunges, and build muscle bulk with old-fashioned weights. Their philosophy is that everything in the world—food, activities, and people—are divided into three gunas or tendencies: *sattva* (calm), *rajas* (active), and *tamas* (dull/lethargic). Since they weight train vigorously, the rajas tendencies are high. This is the reason why they consume sattvic foods like milk and ghee to increase the sattva qualities.

WHERE IT ALL WENT HAYWIRE

Protein supplements and steroids were not used by our akhada men; they were not used by Sandow or by Clancy Ross (Mr America, 1945), Steve Reeves (Mr America, 1947), and George Eiferman (Mr America, 1948). These champions built their god-like physiques before the invention of protein powders! Instead they ate high-protein diets by drinking lots of milk, drinks made of soy powder, and raw eggs. If you take a huge step back in time, the ancient Greeks ingested testicles of animals before they competed in any kind of performance sport because this would help increase the testosterone levels in their bodies. They even ate plant-based diuretics and meat to keep fit. Natural was the way to go.

So when did it all change for the worse? In the 1960s, steroids started becoming popular as the bodybuilding craze caught on. It was all about getting bigger faster. It was the era when Arnold Schwarzenegger was promoting steroids and it became the 'in' thing to do. In the West, protein supplement companies had started building research and spending billions on advertising. It started going downhill from there as bodybuilding supplements became the next few fad in the 1980s. In more recent years, fat burners and creatine have come to the scene. Several high-profile diets which glamourized protein came into the picture, making it sound as if it was the only food group we needed. In spite of many deaths due to high cholesterol problems which have been linked to excess protein intake, people still continue to believe this information without doing any research.

From what began as a beautiful sport, bodybuilding had now become all about abusing the body with steroids and surgeries. Anabolic steroids had been used during the 60s and their use increased as the bodybuilding mania soared. The darker side of fitness emerged—the Sandows of the world were forgotten.

Yes, if you are a bodybuilder or a professional athlete, you need to monitor your protein intake and boost it over regular requirements. But if you are a gym goer, or exercising for health reasons, there is no need to increase your protein intake with processed products like supplements, shakes, or health bars. It's not needed.

Harmful steroids have been banned in athletic events, and even now there are sports superstars who have fallen out of grace after failing their doping tests. While I am glad that the rules are becoming more stringent in world-class events, I worry about the local gyms and personal trainers who are still peddling and pushing these protein supplements and steroids onto their clients. Most of them have half-baked knowledge about them. You can't ban people from buying processed protein supplements and steroids over the counter. In my own way, I want to raise awareness that this is absolutely not needed. You are just carving a lifetime of health troubles for yourself.

THE TRUTH ABOUT ANABOLIC STEROIDS

Anabolic steroids are just 'steroids' in the fitness world. Anabolic steroids mimic the ability of testosterone in our body and this leads to increase in muscle mass at a fast rate. Steroids or anabolic-androgen steroids are synthetic and man-made. Steroids have been linked to various health problems which make them extremely risky to take. They need to be taken on medical advice only.

Now you may think that how much of a health risk is it? To shock you out of your dream world, I want you to read a real-life conversation between a well-known trainer based abroad called Mike (named changed to protect identity) and his psychiatrist friend. I have been given permission to use part of the conversation. Mike, a good looking man in his late 20s, who is a well-known trainer internationally, has risked his health and family life by injecting himself with steroids to build muscle mass.

Mike (M): Is that you on the magazine cover? Omg! Wow. I think I'm in love!

Psychiatrist friend (P): Thank you :)

M: You are beautiful. (<3) Sure you know that already?

P: How's your training going?

M: Good. Pumping a lot of iron.

P: With your lifestyle, it's so hard for u to dedicate time for this great body that u have. How do you manage it?

M: I have been training for 15 years now and steroids help me out a lot.

P: Have you got any injuries because of steroids or anger outbursts or mood swings?

M: Side effects are bad.

P: ☹

M: I am very sexual when I'm on steroids. I need sex regularly. And then I have bad aggression and a short temper.

P: The sex is a plus point but the aggression is bad.

M: And it makes me more violent.

P: Go on...

M: Hair loss has begun.

P: Do u know this can damage your heart?

M: I feel it sometimes in the heart. But it's not so bad as I do a lot of cardio. What is bad is my sexual lust when I am on steroids. Because if I don't get sex, it makes me even more out of control.

P: Just to look good, you don't have to do this.

M: And I can't focus on anything. Worse thing is an erection without knowing it. But when there is a high, there is a low.

History of Bodybuilding

P: That is bad.

M: When I'm off the steroids...my body has a breakdown.

P: Go on...

M: That I lose all my sexual desires. And then I don't want or need sex. It's bad for relationships as it always affects partners.

P: So that is fine right? For a while you will feel like that; then you will be okay.

M: It's ruined a lot of my special moments in life. Yes...

P: No you need to stop the steroids ASAP!

M: You take HCG (human chorionic gonadotropin steroid) to balance hormones out. Let me show you a picture. With and without steroids. It will help you understand why I do it.

(Sends pic with and without steroids.)

P: Stop taking them. You are perfect without them. Start having natural supplements.

M: I'm not confident without them. Like now I'm so sexual.

P: It's all in your mind.

M: Amazing in bed. And really ripped. Strong. And I feel amazing.

P: It's an obsession and the feelings that you go through are temporary.

M: XXX (A common friend) and I stopped talking.

P: Why?

M: Because he couldn't handle my mood swings. And I get very depressed.

P: That's a fact as it will make your relationships suffer.

M: And I get really low. ☹

P: Stop the steroids.

M: Problem is that I can't stop.

P: When you here, come visit me. I will help you get off it.

M: It's too hard.

P: It's my work. It's all in your mind.

M: I can't. I look ugly without them. Women love me because of my body.

P: It's all in your mind. Stop it. It's all fake love, they want you for your body and not for you.

M: True…I feel powerful.

P: Your natural physique is much better. The steroid body is too big.

M: And because I'm aggressive when I'm on it, I feel in control. You found me big in this picture I sent you? I'm even bigger now! ☺

P: You need an entire lifestyle change for long-term health, the pure holistic organic way. Steroid and supplement abuse has to stop.

M: Worse thing is…it makes me very, very, very down.

P: It is going to.

M: And negative.

P: I know.

M: But I need to keep doing it. It makes think I'm in love. And then I get hurt.

P: You are going to harm yourself badly. You know that. Stop the steroids now.

M: I did a test. And they said my heart has irregular beats. I have to do a follow-up ECG scan. They say the steroids I do are making my heart pump too hard. It's hard to explain, not over the phone. I will come and see you again. I need to

History of Bodybuilding

talk to you (cuts off and starts off on another note again). Then I'll tell you all. I like the feeling I'm sexy…I only get this feeling with steroids…when I'm off I feel ugly (keeps repeating his problems).

P: Ok. But I am disturbed at how your mind thinks and I want to help u. How about Monday 4.30 pm?

M: I am already taking 50 mg of Anavar (one of the more popular steroids). I'm too far gone. I don't think I can be helped.

P: Stop it. We will discuss it on Monday. You gonna kill yourself one day. I will help you.

M: Huh—it's not that simple. Almost every top actor takes it. They all do it. I have only been doing it for 5 yrs.

P: You have a wife right?

M: Yes and 2 kids.

P: Do it for your kids.

(*M sends pic of wife and kids*)

P: Wouldn't you want a long life to see them grow? Your wife is so beautiful. Such beautiful kids.

M: Yes she is. But that's another problem. I need to discuss with you. I don't wanna be near my wife when I am on drugs.

P: Think about them. Put yourself last for once.

M: Besides getting low, I am a nightmare to be around. And I am uncontrollable. But I have a dark past.

P: Go on…

M: I just finished my last case.

P: Case?

M: I was arrested for beating someone an inch of their life. Yes for GBH Section 18. I was found not guilty as it was self-defence.

P: You have to stop all this. It's taking you too far to destruction. It's affecting your kids, wife and career. Once you lose all of this, what is the use of the steroids? You need to understand that you are on a self-destructive path and you need to stop it right now.

M: But with steroids, it makes you very strong and also angry. It feels I don't have much going for me.

P: What's the use?? You wanna die?

M: I failed as a model. Couldn't make it as an actor. So all I have is a body. Sorry, I shouldn't say this. Let's leave it at this.

P: If your work is as good as a fitness expert, it will take you places.

M: I'm hired a lot in the UK as a trainer. I wanna do it worldwide.

P: I will see you on Monday. Be on time for your consulting.

(He goes back into negative thinking)

M: You can't help someone who doesn't believe in being helped. When you are on that road it's hard to come off it. It's very personal and it's very dark. Another thing, I want a divorce. Wanted it for years. And steroids keep my mind away from my other life.

P: (Sighs) ☹ Think about your kids…

M: That's why I am not divorcing. I will only do it when they are older. I have a dark side which u may not like.

P: We will discuss it on Monday.

M: Actually I'm just really screwed in the head.

P: We'll meet and we'll talk soon. Take care.

End of conversation

When I read this conversation, it made me feel really sad for Mike because he insists that he can't maintain his ripped, muscular physique without steroids. His heart-health is not good, his moods are aggressive, he is sexually violent, he is losing hair, and more than anything, he is not mentally stable. He has also done umpteen surgeries on his face and body because he felt he wanted to look 'perfect' in his training videos. How sad to not be able to look at your own body in the mirror!

There are thousands of such people that are going through substance abuse—it could be for a job, for power, for aesthetic reasons, for lack of confidence, or just for fame.

Magazines and supplements make you believe that it's very easy to lose the kilos by popping those fat burning pills. It is human nature—it's hard to resist a quick-fix. At the end of the day, you would rather go for these products than put in effort. It's interesting how we start explaining it to ourselves, let's drink a highly-caffeinated drink or pop the fat burners just to jump-start the weight loss. You may get your instant fix but remember you are doing much harm to your body. You may suddenly bloat up, your immune system may crash, and your skin and hair will start looking dull. Additionally, you get emotionally unbalanced because your hormones are out of whack. It's like injecting yourself with slow poison.

The last time I was in New York, I was conversing with this well-known American fitness expert. He had recently read an article in the *New York Times* about how the latest obsession in Bollywood is getting the coveted six-pack. Suddenly all the trainers were putting the actors through the wringer so that they could all have a cookie-cutter bodybuilder's physique. He was in shock and asked me, 'Does this really happen?' New York, considered the fitness capital of the world, has moved beyond the concept of a six-pack—fitness trainers there believe in having a natural, lean, organic physique. The trainer was shocked that this sort of obsession still exists in

Bollywood because abroad, the training is focussed on the kind of role the actors have to play. For example, Brad Pitt trained for seven months to play the Greek warrior Achilles in *Troy*. But over here, even if the actor is an office-goer or a simpleton, or even if it's just a dance sequence, every trainer worth his salt makes sure the biceps show, the six-pack is there, and the chest is bulky.

Insecurity leads people to have fat burners, unnatural supplements, and surgeries because it is not possible to sustain that body for long. Surgeries are meant to be done when you have a valid reason—like an accident which has disfigured your face or your body. It shouldn't be misused. Instead, everybody is trying to outdo the other and look better—it's a vicious cycle.

STEROIDS: THE BRIGHT SIDE

Steroids have been used successfully by doctors for medicinal purposes. These include:

- **Stimulates Appetite:** People with digestive problems or those who are unable to eat the right amounts of food due to healthy issues are recommended steroids because it triggers hunger. Usually people who suffer from cancer and AIDS are given these steroids. That it increases muscle mass is an added benefit.
- **Libido Enhancement:** Since steroids manage to copy the ability of testosterone, it is used to boost virility in older men. Testosterone replacements are not recommended in huge doses like the kind bodybuilders take—they are usually prescribed in smaller amounts by physicians.
- **Bone Marrow:** Steroids were used to treat people with hypoplastic anemia in order to stimulate the bone marrow to produce the elements required to boost the immunity system. However, other medicines are used instead of steroids now.

STEROIDS: THE DARK SIDE

You can see how in Mike's case, the constant use of steroids had completely thrown his emotional system out of gear. He was in severe depression and admitted that he was extremely aggressive in bed. These are pretty common symptoms after taking steroids. Let's take a look at the negative effects of steroids:

- **Sex Hormones Play Havoc:** Anabolic steroids are believed to boost estrogen—the main sex hormone in females—in the body. This is often linked to the development of female-like tissues in male users. This condition is called 'gynecomastia'. On the other hand, women who use these steroids may experience acne problems, deepening of the voice, and an increase in body hair.
- **Reproduction Functions Thrown Out of Gear:** Steroid use is linked to shrinking of the testicles, reduced sperm count, and infertility in men. In women, the side effects include decrease in menstrual blood flow, enlargement of the clitoris, and infertility. Research has shown that it may affect foetal development too. For youngsters, it is particularly dangerous as it can cause stunted growth because it may stop the lengthening of bones. It also increases the frequency and duration of erections, and cause premature sexual development in adolescent users.
- **Negatively Impacts the Brain:** Studies show that steroid use affects the neurological pathways of the brain. People who take steroids in high doses may get dependent on it. They experience severe withdrawal symptoms when they try to discontinue its usage.
- **Violent Behaviour or 'Roid Rage':** Steroid users show signs of very violent behaviour, which is termed as 'roid rage'. The higher levels of testosterone cause increase

in aggressiveness, hostility, paranoia, mood swings, irritability, and stress. Steroids use has also been linked to depression and suicide.

- **Hypertension and Cholesterol Levels get Impacted:** Steroids users are more likely to develop hypertension and high blood pressure. What's more, steroids increase LDL, the bad cholesterol and decreases HDL, the good cholesterol. It also causes changes in the structure of the heart, which can cause a heart attack or other cardiovascular diseases.
- **Liver Damage:** Steroids that are orally taken can cause damage to the liver. They can also cause tumours and blood-filled cysts to form in the liver. When such a tumour or cyst ruptures, the individual suffers from internal bleeding.

Impact of Steroids

In Male:	**In Females:**
➤ Reduced Sperm Production	➤ Decreased Breast Size
➤ Infertility	➤ Deepening of the Voice
➤ Shrinking of the Testicles	➤ Growth of Excessive Body Hair
➤ Impotence	➤ Loss of Scalp Hair
➤ Irreversible Breast Enlargement	➤ Changes in or Cessation of the Menstrual Cycle
➤ Hair Loss	➤ Infertility
➤ Insomnia	➤ Acne
	➤ Insomnia

If you overhear your trainer talking about cycles and stacks, know the he is discussing steroids. The period of time that a person takes steroids is called a cycle. When more than one type of steroid is used in a cycle, it is called stack. The more steroids you stack into your cycle, the more side effects your body faces. The different steroid cycles include beginner cycles, three-week blitz, double mini cycle, inverted pyramid, and diamond cycle.

Ten of the most popular steroids include:

1. Clenbuterol
2. Winstrol
3. Anavar
4. Dianabol
5. Deca Durabolin
6. Primobolan
7. Anadrol
8. Sustanon 250
9. Testosterone Cypionate
10. Testosterone Enanthate

THE TRUTH ABOUT PROTEIN SUPPLEMENTS: CREATINE & GLUTAMINE

The Curious Case of Creatine

It is a substance made in the liver and it plays an important role in producing energy in the body at a fast rate. It does this by creating adenosine triphospate, or ATP, the main energy molecule our cells use for activity. Creatine is one of the most popular protein supplements and is also one of the most researched. It's often taken by sportspeople and bodybuilders to build muscle mass and to improve athletic performance. Studies show that creatine is most effective in high-intensity training and explosive activities like power lifting or sports like sprinting, football, and baseball that requires power and short bursts of effort. There is less support to show that creatine improves endurance performance and aerobic exercises. So what does this prove again? A normal gym-goer does NOT need to take creatine. The jury is still out there on whether it is legal for sportspeople to take creatine.

While there has been no study which proves that creatine is bad for the body, there have been anecdotal cases of kidney damage, heart problems, diarrhoea and muscle cramps among others. Kidneys excrete creatinine, a breakdown product of creatine, and it has been a concern if kidneys can handle excess creatine.

One thing that everybody agrees on—creatine causes weight gain. The initial weight gain of a kilo or more is due to water retention and subsequently it leads to muscle mass gain. But you can build muscle only if you are weight training vigorously. Again, please understand that it is not a miracle powder which just makes your muscles pop out. You need to work out like a maniac, only then can creatine be of any help to you.

Glutamine: What's all the Fuss About?

Glutamine is an amino acid found naturally in the body. Amino acids are the building blocks of protein. Glutamine is produced in the muscles and is distributed by the blood to the organs that need it. Do you need to take glutamine supplements? NO! It is easily found in cabbage, beets, beans, milk, dairy products, fish, chicken, and eggs. If you have an excess of glutamine in the body, it just goes to waste because it can't be stored for an extended period of time.

Glutamine has potential side-effects—it can worsen severe liver disease. If you are sensitive to monosodium glutamate (MSG), you could be allergic to glutamine because the body converts glutamine to glutamate. There have been concerns that glutamine could increase the likelihood of seizures.

THE TRUTH ABOUT FAT BURNERS

Come on, admit it—you have been so tempted to try the fat burners advertised in newspapers and magazines, haven't you? Pop a fat burner, sit on the couch, watch TV, and yet lose the weight. Now who wouldn't want to do that? But hold on, let's use a little logic here—if fat burners really worked and if they didn't have deadly side-effects, don't you think every big conglomerate worth their salt would be selling this over the counter? The reason why you see shady advertisements and have equally shady doctors and trainers peddle these fat burners is because they are either absolutely ineffective or downright unhealthy. Most companies who have sold fat burners have been sued for false claims and misleading advertisements.

The reason why fat burners sell is that they probably work for a very short period of time. There may be a slight thermogenic effect—they produce heat which increases the metabolism rate. Some products may suppress appetite. But reports show that fat burners lead to a range of medical problems—from high blood pressure, irregular heart-rate, insomnia, nervousness, tremors and headaches, to seizures, heart attacks, strokes, and even death.

Instead of taking fat burners, you could just eat less and raise your metabolism rate by taking your dog out for a walk, running, joining a gym, or taking up a yoga class. Think about it—do you want to harm your body by putting in fat burners and letting it rot without exercise? It's really not an option.

THE TRUTH ABOUT LAXATIVES AND DIURETICS

Laxatives and diuretics were meant to be used for medical reasons, but now they have become the most abused drug for weight loss. And of course, this is extremely dangerous for your health! Laxatives are meant to be taken to stimulate the bowels by stimulating the nerve endings in the large intestine. It is meant to be used when you suffer from constipation, and not to lose weight. Remember the calories from the food have already been absorbed by the small intestine. On the other hand, diuretics are meant to remove excess water from the body and are prescribed for, among other problems, high blood pressure. Since diuretics remove water from the body, causing dehydration, this makes people feel thin. But soon enough, the body recovers and retains water to make up for the loss of water. This makes a person feel fat and then the vicious cycle of diuretic addiction begins.

You are in a lot of trouble if you are addicted to laxatives and diuretics. It's not a problem you can flush away, no pun intended! Among other things, you upset the balance of electrolytes and minerals in your body since the fluid is removed. Your muscles and nerves start feeling the negative impact. Overuse of laxatives can cause liver damage, infections, as well as irritable bowel syndrome. You can also experience dizziness spells, muscle cramps, and blurry vision when you have excess of laxatives and diuretics.

SO WHAT'S THE DEAL ON PROTEIN?

Protein is the building block of every cell and tissue in your body, including muscle tissue. So only if you meet your body's demand for protein, will you be able to build lean muscle mass. An increase in muscle mass raises the metabolism rate and helps burn fat faster. So protein is definitely good, but excess is not necessary. How much protein does your body need? This depends on your body weight and physical activity level.

Are you blindly taking protein powders on your trainer's recommendation? Or do you down a protein shake every time you complete your gym session or use it as a meal replacement, without checking if your body needs it in the first place? Have you run your diet through with your dietician or sports nutritionist to check if it is deficient in protein? You need to stop and take a hard look at the way you train and eat. Consult an expert—a sports nutritionist.

If you have a healthy, varied diet filled with animal- and plant-based protein, nuts, seeds, berries, cheese, and different types of grains, you are probably meeting your daily protein requirements.

According to the ACSM (American College of Sports Medicine), the protein requirement for a sedentary person is 0.8–1 gram per kilogram of body weight. So if you are an 80 kg man, you would need about 64 to 80 grams of protein each day. Here is a sample menu—both vegetarian and non vegetarian meals—which shows how the 80 kg man can get his protein in the form of natural foods.

Non Veg Diet Plan

Meals	Suggested Diet
Meal 1	Any 1 fruit
Meal 2	2 Eggs + 3 slices of multigrain bread
Meal 3	1 fruit
Meal 4	2 chicken rolls in wheat roti with salad
Meal 5	1 katori of kurmura
Meal 6	milk (skimmed, plain) or salted lassi
Meal 7	grilled fish (4–5 pieces fish) + vegetables + brown rice (1 bowl)

Veg Diet Plan

Meals	Suggested Diet
Meal 1	Any 1 fruit
Meal 2	250 ml milk (skimmed, plain) + 4–5 tbsps wheatflakes
Meal 3	1 glass fruit smoothie
Meal 4	1 katori sprouts + tofu 7–8 cube dice pieces + 1–2 wheat rotis and salad
Meal 5	1 slice multigrain bread + 1 tbsp peanut butter
Meal 6	Almonds (8–10)
Meal 7	Paneer (100 gms =8–10 dice cube pieces) + vegetables + brown rice (1 bowl)

PROTEIN CONTENT IN DIFFERENT FOODS

Chicken	**Protein**
Chicken breast	30 gms
Chicken thigh (average size)	10 gms
Chicken wing	6 gms
Fish	
Fillets or steaks (approximately 100 gms)	22 gms
Eggs and Dairy	
Large egg	6 gms
Milk (1 cup)	8 gms
Paneer (½ cup)	15 gms
Yogurt (1 cup)	8–12 gms
Cheese (1.5 to 2 slices)	6–9 gms
Beans (Including Soy)	
Tofu (½ cup)	20 gms
Soy milk (1 cup)	6–10 gms
Beans (black lentils ½ cup cooked)	7–10 gms
Soy beans (½ cup cooked)	14 gms
Nuts and Seeds	
Peanut butter (2 tbsp)	8 gms
Almonds (¼ cup)	8 gms
Peanuts (¼ cup)	9 gms
Sunflower seeds (¼ cup)	6 gms
Pumpkin seeds (¼ cup)	8 gms
Flaxseeds (¼ cup)	8 gms

(For more details on plant-based protein sources, refer to the chapter titled 'The Way We Eat', pg 93.)

EXCESS PROTEIN = FAT!

If you are vigorously strength training, you will need far more protein to build good quality muscle. But remember—the most important word here is 'vigorously'. Too much protein through supplements and shakes can help you maintain your muscle tissue, but it can also lead to increased body fat. That's why it is important that you take advice from a sports nutritionist or your doctor before you take any sort of protein supplement. It has to be tailored to the kind of workout you do.

Here are some of the options for natural, pure protein supplements. But do understand that powders do have side effects and they must be taken under medical supervision only. Protein powders are available in a variety of flavours. I still prefer that you stick to natural protein products. (For natural protein shakes, bars and meal options, refer to the chapter titled 'The Way We Eat', pg 121) But I am including the natural protein powders for information.

#*Whey Protein Powder:* One of the most common supplements used by bodybuilders and athletes today. Whey protein is made from whey, the liquid which remains when you make cheese or paneer. Milk is made of two main protein components—whey and casein. When the casein is removed to make cheese, whey is the by-product. This is then purified and made into powder form. It is a complete protein because it contains all the essential amino acids.

There are three types of whey protein powders available in the market:

- **Whey Protein Concentrate (WPC):** Low level of fat and comparatively higher levels of carbohydrates; have 29 percent–89 percent protein by weight
- **Whey Protein Isolate (WPI):** Processed to remove fat; have 90 percent+ protein by weight
- **Whey Protein Hydrolysates (WPH):** Pre-digested and therefore, easily absorbed by the body; costlier than WPC and WPI

Organic whey options are the newer supplements claiming to have been made from milk of the cows fed organically. For example, The Organic Whey, Tera's Organic Whey, and Source Organic Whey are all the best options available abroad. You can either buy it when you holiday abroad or ask someone to get it for you when they go for a holiday.

#*Casein Protein Powder:* It is the dehydrated, supplemental form of casein. Caseins are phosphorus-containing proteins and they make up 80 percent of the protein in cow's milk. The other 20 percent of protein is made up of whey proteins. Casein powder moves through the digestive tract slower than whey protein and can take several hours to fully digest. It is preferred for its ability to form a gel or clot in the stomach, which makes it very efficient in nutrient supply. The clot is able to provide a sustained slow release of amino acids into the blood stream, sometimes lasting for several hours.

#*Egg-white Protein Powder:* It is made from egg white. It's fat-free, very high in protein, and is considered a perfect source for protein because of its complete makeup of essential amino acids, branch chain amino acids, and glutamic acid. Egg protein is completely absorbed by your body. It is an option for people with lactose intolerance.

VEGETARIAN OPTIONS

Soy Protein Powder: It is a plant-based protein that comes from soy beans. Like whey, it is considered a complete protein and contains all the essential amino acids. Soy protein helps in muscle formation. Soy has a slower absorption rate than whey which means it takes the body longer to digest the protein. So while it is less helpful in rebuilding muscle, it aids in forming new muscle tissue. Because soy is plant-based, it is an alternative for people who are lactose-intolerant. There are some concerns about the isoflavones found in soy. Studies suggest that isoflavones can disrupt the body's hormonal balance.

Hemp Protein Powder: Hemp protein is a protein found in the seed of the cannabis sativa plant. Despite its origin, hempseed does not contain psychoactive compounds and is an excellent source of protein, essential fatty acids, and various nutrients. Hemp has many benefits over other protein sources—it has a wide range of amino acids, easier digestibility, and a more balanced ratio of essential fatty acids. Hemp protein has a rich, nutty flavour and can be added to a number of dishes for its health-promoting properties. Protein powders made from hempseed can be added to smoothies, yogurt, or even eaten plain. Hempseed oil—also a good source of protein—can be used for cooking or added to salads.

#*Pea Protein Powder:* It is a relatively new form of protein powder. It is a gluten-free and vegan option and it is less allergenic than soy. It is valued for its high digestibility and low price. Pea protein powder is also mixed with a small amount of water and used as a jam or a spread.

#*Rice Protein Powder:* It is a protein supplement in powder form made from brown rice. The rice is treated with enzymes that cause the carbohydrates to separate from proteins. This resulting protein powder has a very distinct taste and can be added to smoothies or health shakes. Rice protein powder is easily digested and can be used as a gluten-free and vegan option. It is commonly mixed with pea protein powder because this combination offers a superior amino acid profile that is comparable to dairy or egg protein powders.

Excessive consumption of protein can have unwanted side-effects on an already compromised kidney. In any situation and for any food, too much is always bad for our health. Similarly, taking too much protein will harm you too. Supplements are usually heavily processed foods and have added sweeteners. So always check with a dietician or a sports nutritionist before you have any protein supplements.

GOING THE NATURAL WAY

Is it possible to achieve a bodybuilder's physique without pumping your body with steroids or supplements? Of course it is. Yes, the alternatives to steroids may take more hard work but it is a more holistic approach to becoming healthy. What's the use of getting a perfect physique if you have liver and heart problems and if you are an emotional wreck most of the time? Think long-term. Don't do something just because your favourite star or cricketer is doing it. It may cost you your life. Try and understand that they have crores of rupees riding on them to look and play a certain way These stars probably know what they are getting into and the risks that are involved. As a regular gym goer, you need to focus more on improving your strength and flexibility to enable you to do regular tasks with ease.

Remember, it will take a lot of hard work, focus, effort and dedication, but in the end you will be rewarded with a fit body and mind. So if you are willing to stand up to the hype and hysteria and put your head down and train in a holistic way, get ready to see big results. You will be amazed to see that what the mind can conceive, the body will achieve.

| How Bodybuilders And Athletes Train Differently ||
Bodybuilders	**Athletes**
Do longer duration workouts	Do shorter duration workouts
Lower intensity	Higher intensity
Have to make a longer time commitment	Have to make a shorter time commitment
Often opt for isolation exercises	Focus on more on functional exercises
Use a slower rep speed to increase muscle tension period	Accelerate the concentric portion of the rep
Exercises of choice: stationary biking, stair stepping	Exercises of choice: sprinting and jumping

History of Bodybuilding

The choice between bodybuilding and athletic training depends upon your fitness goals. But I will still advise you to go for the latter because the modern man is not a bodybuilder. He requires more of a functional body, workouts that don't take too much time and shows them quicker results. I don't have anything personal against bodybuilding. I feel he can benefit more greatly with athletic training than bodybuilding. It's a real pity that what started off as a great sport has been defamed over the years by the use of unnatural supplements, steroids, and fat burners being peddled in the market. If you really want to be a bodybuilder, use Eugene Sandow as your idol because he is the greatest example of how one can build one's body the natural way. That is why it is so important to understand the history of bodybuilding so that you understand how it all began. Closer home, use Mihir Jogh's case study as an inspiration to build a fab body, naturally—the young, 23-year-old boy who has been training for 3 months without any supplements.

When I was 19, I was only obsessed about getting a six-pack. It was all about the biceps, the aesthetics of it. About a couple of years ago, I started reading up on fitness and started speaking to people. Everyone has an opinion, everyone knows everything about fitness. But it was always about looking good, about being the guy who had the best body.

Yes, there were supplements available and I was very much aware of it. I know how it works and I have talked to people about it, read books on how to use them. I have seen people take supplements and transform their body in 3 months; but I also saw them give in and then go back to how they were before they took supplements. But I choose to go the natural way—and I have stayed consistent with my health and fitness levels and my looks. It did take me longer, but it never made me feel frustrated. I made it a lifestyle change. People always told me, 'Oh, you are so dedicated!', and I said, it's not about being dedicated, it's about finding a balance, about making it a lifestyle change.

I never tell people I am dieting. When you say diet, it sounds like I am starving myself. Then they say you are so boring because you are always eating healthy. And I tell them I don't think it's boring—I genuinely enjoy my whole foods, my organic khana, and raw vegetables, I never consider it as a diet. When you enjoy it and when you see results, you get really motivated. Within the first 6 months to a year, I started seeing definition in my body.

I started with working out at a gym before I really took to functional training. I had more of a 'gym body' and I was still a little stiff. My biceps and chest were more defined than the rest of my body. Once I started functional training, my body looked more natural. Yeah, I don't have 15-inch biceps, but I have the same strength as someone who does. Just because someone has a big body doesn't mean he is strong. For me, it's very important to get a balance in my workouts—strength, cardiovascular endurance, flexibility, and balance. It has to have the agility too.

Those who look at the aesthetic aspect of it are not really into fitness. They work out at the gym and look all buff. Then they go on a one month holiday and when they come back, it's back to square one. For me, it's different. Even when I am on a holiday, I will enjoy it. I enjoy activities, walking, explore. I do have cheat meals but I make it up by controlling what I eat the rest of the time. Or I just do a little more cardiovascular activity and keep my body moving. I am not a saint, and I do enjoy my drinks once every other weekend. But again, it's about finding a balance. You can't be working out during the week and then be ruining your health by drinking and eating heavy every weekend. When you go out, enjoy your wine or beers. But then make up for it through your diet or exercise.

History of Bodybuilding

I know the effect that junk food has on my body; I know how it is going to affect me in the long run. I have my burgers once in a while or if I eat dessert, I eat how much I want to. I don't necessarily finish the entire thing.

I am motivated by the high energy levels and how my body has changed. Ever since I started doing functional training, I have become the handyman among my friends and family. If something needs to be fixed, if I need to climb somewhere, I can do it easily because of my training. My body now feels so much more useful.

With my friends, I have noticed that they are fixated on the look aspect of it. They are fixated on getting a six-pack and then they work so hard on it and then fall out of it. When it comes to girls, they just don't eat much. They starve themselves. I feel it works when you are younger, but it starts taking a toll on your body eventually. Their energy levels dip, their skin loses the glow. They are thin but they don't have body definition or muscle tone. Also, once they starve themselves, they put on weight in their mid-section or legs and thighs. Abroad, I see women more fit and doing more adventurous sports.

My diet: I have zero supplements.

Breakfast

A cup of green/black tea (I avoid sugar; may take milk).

Big bowl of fruits with nuts—sunflower seeds, almonds, flaxseeds, sprinkled.

5-6 egg whites—poached, baked, scrambled.

Yogurt (probiotic) with honey.

Post workout: 2 coconut waters.

Small omelet with tuna or chicken tikka/tandoori chicken (I don't have protein shakes—either tuna or chicken).

Lunch

Vegetables + cooked sabzis.

I avoid starch—rice or potatoes—in the afternoon.

I do have light dal in the afternoon, a single chappati or rice.

I divide my plate into three—2 will be colourful veggies—salad, sabzi. The rest is a lean protein—dry chicken, mutton, or fish.

I have healthy fats in the form of fish oil supplements or walnuts or olive oil in salad.

Snack: at around 4–5 in the evening (I repeat lunch in a smaller version).

Light soup or a salad.

A cup of coffee – normal chai and a couple of biscuits

Dinner

Salad with fish—steamed or tuna, tandoori chicken—olive oil.

I also have 2 tbs of chyawanprash, vitamin B supplements.

Workouts: CrossFit for a little less than 2 years, 4–5 times a week.

2 days of weightlifting—squats, dead lifts, and other compound exercises.

Once a week—walk for an hour and a half or swim.

Stretching with gymnastic moves—if I feel sore, I do it a lot more.

Rest day: relaxed walk.

I take massages to relax the muscles.

2
Before You Start Exercising

PART ONE

MEASURE OF SUCCESS!

It's important to educate yourself on the factors below before you know the gym lingo. The first step is to get a fitness journal to keep yourself motivated—it can be an old-fashioned notebook, an excel sheet, a notepad on your phone, or any other fancy app on your computer that you're most comfortable with. Do whatever floats your boat, but keep it simple so that the process is fun and not complicated. Record the following information in your fitness journal before you begin weight training.

Your Height and Weight

Measuring your height and weight is an easy process; you need it to calculate your Body Mass Index (BMI). I believe more in inches that have melted away, rather than the kilos or pounds that you lose. But weight is an important indicator of your health.

Check your weight first thing in the morning, once a week—say every Sunday morning—on an empty stomach or before drinking a glass of water. Don't become one of those obsessive people who check their weight every day.

I have noticed even hotel rooms now have weighing scales in the bathrooms. Stop this vicious cycle of beating yourself up every time you put on even a measly 200 grams. It's a number game you want to stay away from. Also remember that muscle weighs more than fat. When you begin weight training, many a time you may find that your weight is shooting up. Don't fret, it is quite normal.

Body Mass Index (BMI) and Waist Size

How do you know whether you are overweight, underweight, or healthy? From your BMI and waist size.

BMI formula:

BMI = Weight (kg)/ Height^2 (metre)
A note about your height:
1 foot = 12 inches
1 inch = 0.0254 metres.
Let's do the calculation! So if you are 5 feet 4 inches tall, first convert it into inches: 5×12 = 60 + 4 = 64 inches.

Now, convert inches into metres. 64 × 0.0254 = 1.6256 metres

If you are too bored to do the math yourself, use websites like http://www.metric-conversions.org. There's always help at hand!

Calculate your BMI using this formula. How do you fare?

Rating	BMI	
Underweight	<18.5	Low
Normal	18.5–24.9	Healthy
Overweight	25–29.9	High
Obese	30–34.9	Very high
Morbidly obese	35–35.9	Very high
Extreme	>40	Extremely high

While BMI gives you a sense of your healthy weight range, it's not the most accurate way of accessing a healthy individual. In contrast, your waist size is a good indicator of the intra-abdominal fat that you have. Intra-abdominal fat, also known as the visceral fat or more popularly 'belly fat', is located inside the abdominal cavity and is packed between organs like the stomach, liver, intestines, and so on. It differs from subcutaneous fat which lies right below our skin, like the one which gives suppleness to our face.

With a measuring tape, measure your waist. Place the tape at the narrowest part of your waist, approximately half an inch above your belly button. Ideally for a man, the number should be less than 40 inches and for a woman, it should be less than 35 inches.

You certainly don't want intra-abdominal fat because it is linked to cardiovascular diseases. Building strength and developing muscle lessens intra-abdominal fat faster. A high waist size means you need to lose weight ASAP.

Measurements of the Whole Body

Body measurements are a great way of tracking your progress. Do this first thing in the morning to ensure accuracy. Use a simple measuring tape; you can ask somebody else to help you out too. The tape should be firm against your skin. The common measurement sites are:

Chest: Put the tape across your nipples around the largest part of your chest.

Waist: Place the tape at the narrowest part of your waist, approximately half an inch above your belly button.

Hips: Place it on the widest part of your hips.

Buttocks: Wrap the tape around the widest part of your buttocks and make sure the tape is parallel to the ground.

Thighs and Calves: Measure the widest part of each thigh and each calf. Note down measurements of your right and left sides.

Upper Arm and Forearm: Again, measure the widest part of your upper arm (above the elbow) and forearm (below the elbow).

Neck: Measure around the widest part of your neck.

Sometimes, the weighing scale may lie according to the water your body retains. If you've eaten a heavy meal or your food has not been completely digested—it contributes to a number variation. Inches are more dependable. So it is better that you invest in a simple measuring tape than one of those fancy weighing machines.

Body Fat Percentage

You don't want to be 'skinny fat'. You want to be 'slim lean'! This is why it is important to track your body fat percentage. A skinny fat person is one whose body fat percentage is high. A slim lean person will have more muscle mass and a lower fat percentage—basically here, the body is a calorie burning machine. A skinny fat person has absolutely no muscle mass on his body. So while a skinny fat person's body will be spongy, a slim lean person will have a more powerful, toned, tight, and beautiful body. I have seen that women are generally wary of picking up weights than their male counterparts because they fear they will become bulky. They would rather spend crazy amounts of money on dieticians than lift weights. What they fail to understand is that dieting will only help them lose weight, not tone their body. Such people can be 'skinny fat' but will not be 'slim lean'.

To be a tighter version with the same body weight, pick up weights so you have more muscle mass and less fat.

The most accurate way of measuring your body fat is by the skinfold test or pinch test using calipers. Just pinch the fat away from your body and measure it. If you pinch more than

Before You Start Exercising

an inch, then you know it is excess fat and it has to go. You need to measure fat on the:

- Back of your arm (triceps): Take the measurement in a vertical direction directly on the centre of the back of the upper arm
- Front of your arm (biceps): Centre of the front of the upper arm
- Back: Just below the shoulder blade. Note that the skinfold is taken at 45 degrees angle
- Waist: Pinch the fat near the protrusion of the hip bone, a little towards the front from the side of the waist. You can also take a ruler to measure the distance from your belly button so that you can accurately measure the same area every time

You will need somebody else to help you out with these measurements. Just like with body measurements, remember to do it at the same time of the day, preferably early morning. I track this number once in 2 to 4 months for my clients. Sometimes, certain areas of your body will show a higher fat percentage reading than others; so now you know which body parts you need to work out on a lot more. Use this data to calculate overall body fat percentage.

If you are using any other device or test for body fat percentage, then compare the number with the table given below to figure out where you stand.

Body Fat	Men	Women
Essential Fat	2–4 percent	10–12 percent
Athletes	6–13 percent	14–20 percent
Fitness	14–17 percent	21–24 percent
Not Acceptable By Me! Work Harder	18–25 percent	25–31 percent
Obese	26 percent plus	32 percent plus

There are other methods too, like the water displacement method and whole body air displacement plethysmography (ADP). In the water displacement method, the body is completely submerged in water and then the body is calculated based on buoyancy. There are also fancy machines which are overtly expensive. Or you can get a DEXA scan done at a clinic for an accurate analysis.

Medical Tests

Most people think it is a waste of money and time to get medical tests done. For me, it is one of the most crucial indicators of certain problems that a client might not be aware of. I insist that each of my clients first gets a medical test done before we begin talking about an exercise plan. For example, I might find that with one of my clients, osteopenia or osteoporosis is just setting in, which means your body has a low bone density level. This could explain why your wrist or your lower back hurts after a certain exercise. Many a time, a person's thyroid levels are out of whack—and this explains the sudden weight gain.

That's why it is necessary that you get a health check-up done before you begin an exercise programme. You could suffer from sudden dizzy spells, and not know that you are anaemic. Or a client could gain weight and suddenly suffer from acne; she may not have realized that she has developed PCOS (Polycystic Ovary Syndrome) because of her stressful life. PCOS indicates an imbalance of female sex hormones.

Once you do your medical tests, if there is a problem, visit your doctor and work out a strategy. Once my client gets an okay from the doctor, we begin the exercise programme.

I know most of you want to get the six-pack or fit into the tiny bikini or wear that backless choli for a family wedding. But believe me, you have to go beyond superficial factors and appreciate how much good you are doing to your body internally when you regularly exercise. It's a great way to

Before You Start Exercising

boost your self-confidence. Not just that, you have saved so much money by not having to visit a hospital at a later date because you would have caught any possible health problem early on. So don't skip the medical tests!

Recommended Medical Tests:

1. Pathology Test
   CVC/ESR (in CVC, haemoglobin is the main test)

2. Diabetic Profile
   Blood sugar (fasting)
   Blood sugar (post meal)

3. Liver Profile
   SGOT
   SGPT
   GGTP
   Bilirubin (total direct, indirect)
   Alkaline Phosphatase
   Proteins (Albumin, Globulin, A/G ratio)

4. Lipid Profile
   Triglycerides
   Cholesterol
   HDL Cholesterol
   LDL Cholesterol
   VLDL Cholesterol
   LDL/HDL Ratio
   Total Cholesterol/HDL Ratio

5. Renal Profile
   Urea
   Creatinine
   Uric Acid
   Calcium

Shut Up and Train!

6. Thyroid Profile T3, T4, TSH
7. Sonography (PCOS/PCOD)
8. Stress Tests (Electrocardiogram (ECG)
9. DEXA Bone Densitometry (bone mineral test)
10. Pap Smear Test
11. Skin Check
12. Dental Examination
13. Colorectal Cancer Screening
14. Breast Cancer (Mammogram)
15. Abdominal Aortic Aneurysm
16. Sexually Transmitted Infections (STI) Screenings
17. Testes Examination
18. Bmi Assessment
19. Waist Circumference Measurement
20. Eye Check-up
21. ENT Test: Hearing, Nasal and Throat Assessment
22. Faecal Occult Blood Test (FOBT)

Resting Heart Rate

It's the number of times your heartbeats per minute when your body is at rest. RHR can be tested by checking heartbeat by pulse points on wrist and neck in the span of a minute. Preferably, this is done early in the morning. You need to be perfectly still while in bed. Any movement—even getting up from your bed—will not give you the right reading.

A normal RHR for adults is between 60–100 BPM (beats per minute). If you have been exercising regularly, it could be a 50 and if you are an athlete, it may be lower—even as low as 40 BPM. This means your heart is pumping more efficiently.

If your RHR is over 100, you should call your doctor to get it checked. This should worry you all the more if you are exercising. Get your medical tests done, do a stress test, find out why. It could be an indicator that you are overtraining or your trainer is putting you through an extremely rigorous routine.

Sit and Rise Test (SRT)

This test is used to determine your longevity. Sit on the bare floor, without taking the help of a cushion. Try and get up without any support. Award yourself 5 points if you can manage this without losing your balance. Deduct 1 point if you make use of a hand or a knee for support. If you had to use both, subtract two points. If more than two limbs were involved, subtract one point for each additional limb. If you also lost your balance while getting up subtract another half a point. In the end, you will have your final score. Try the same technique with your ankles crossed over each other.

It is seen that people with a lower score have a six times higher chance of dying than people who scored around 8, 9 or 10.

Simple Flexibility Tests

You can do a simple 'sit and reach' test. Sit on a mat with your feet flexed, toes touching the wall. Keep your back straight and lower tummy tucked in. Try and touch your toes. Write down in your diary if you are able to touch your knee, calf, or ankles. If you are easily able to touch your toes, then hurrah for you! But if you are not, then this is a good way to gauge the improvement in your flexibility. This is a sure-shot way of knowing whether you have flexible hamstrings or not.

Many times, you will find that your plump neighbourhood aunty will probably be able to touch her toes while the macho guy on the really cool Harley is able to probably touch just his knees! Most men who are weightlifting do not pay attention to flexibility. One of the primary roles of the hamstring muscle is to stabilize the knee. If the muscle is too tight, you are risking an injury to the knee.

Simple Strength Tests

How many push-ups can you do? If you are a man and you can do 60–100 without losing form, you are strong. For a woman, I would keep it to 20 to 30. This is again a good measure of how much strength you are gaining as you advance through your weightlifting programme.

NUMBER CRUNCHING

At the end of the day, this is how your fitness journal should look like:

My Fitness Journal

- Body Mass Index
- Body Measurements
- Body Fat Percentage
- Medical Tests Including Blood Pressure, Cholesterol levels
- Resting Heart Rate
- Sit and Rise Test
- Simple Flexibility Test
- Strength Test (Push-ups)

All these factors give important metabolic indicators of your overall health. When you do a weight training programme consistently, you will see improvement in three areas:

- Fat Percentage
- Body Mass Index
- Medical History

PUMP IT UP!

It's important to combine cardiovascular activity with weight training to get the best benefits of exercise. Remember that any cardiovascular exercise will help you strengthen your heart and lungs. This in turn helps you improve your overall fitness and it compliments your weight training programme. So what are the numbers that can give you a good indicator that you are on the right track? It's your Maximum Heart Rate (MHR), Target Heart Rate (THR), and VO2 max.

At the Heart of it All: Maximum Heart Rate (MHR) and Target Heart Rate (THR)

Maximum Heart Rate is the highest beats per minute your heart can do without any severe problems through exercise. Your age plays an important factor here.

You can get an accurate analysis of your MHR through a treadmill test done at any medical facility. Or you can use this formula:

Maximum Heart Rate = 220 – Age

Take a 30 year old man, Armaan. His maximum heart rate is 190 Beats Per Minute (BPM) (220-30).

You can now calculate your Target Heart Rate (THR). This is the range you need to exercise within to burn fat and to build muscle, without taxing your heart too much. It can be calculated as a range of 50 percent–85 percent intensity.

How to calculate your target heart rate

Highest Range of THR = 85 percent intensity = MHR × 0.85
Lowest Range of THR = 50 percent intensity = MHR × 0.5

So let's take Armaan's example again. His 85 percent intensity will be (190 × 0.85) = 161.5 BPM. And his lowest range will be (190 × 0.5) = 95 BPM.

Armaan's target heart rate should be between 161 BPM and 95 BPM. If he records a 180 BPM while working out, that means he is doing too much and if he records an 80 BPM, that means he is shooting too below his target.

Smart Tip: True Lies on the Treadmill

When you get onto a treadmill, ski machine, or elliptical cycle, it is important that you enter your right weight and age. The data is used to calculate your target heart rate as you use the treadmill. Don't cheat by entering a lower age, or weight, to impress your cute trainer—remember you are only cheating yourself!

Using a Heart Rate Monitor:

I recommend investing in a good heart rate monitor if you are serious about fitness. The gadget includes a watch to be worn on your wrist and a strap which wraps around your chest near your heart region.

Set up the heart rate monitor by following the manual. You need to punch in your data like height, weight, age, etc. The heart rate monitor then measures your target heart rate. When you exercise, it starts beeping when you go above your target heart rate. So then you know you need to slow down.

Sometimes when you perform a lunge, you will find that the heart rate monitor may beep. This is because when you do the lunge, the leg muscles—which are the largest muscle group in the body—are worked. The heart has to work extra hard to pump in blood to the legs during a lunge. So don't worry if the heart rate monitor beeps once during a lunge. Use your discretion.

As you get fitter, your target rate will not change. But your heart will become more efficient; it will do more work with each stroke. From being able to work out at 60–70 percent of your maximum heart rate, you will soon be able to go up to 80 percent and will find that you are not huffing and puffing as much as before. Your RHR will become better. That's why

I stress on investing in heart rate monitors—they are as good as your weight in gold.

Smart Tip: Know Your Training Zone, Use Your Heart Rate Monitor Efficiently

You can keep increasing the intensity of your workout by adding time or distance. Make it intense. That's how I do my cardio workouts—I do 45 minutes of walk, run, walk—divided to 1 to 2 minutes cycle. Then sometimes, I make it a walk, run, and a short sprint. I never make my workout very comfortable because I enjoy pushing my body a little out of its comfort zone. Slow, gradual changes will help you achieve fat loss and there will be no injuries.

What I mean about different intensities is that you take your heart rate to the maximum level of your target heart rate. This is called interval training. When you do this kind of training with your heart rate monitor on, you know you won't harm your body. You will know exactly which training zone you are in.

Be strategic in your planning. Like a business plan, keep the pace of work slow and steady. Don't expect results in the first week itself.

#Maxing Your Oxygen Intake: VO-Max

VO_2 max is a measure of your aerobic fitness. It is the maximum amount of oxygen you take in when you workout intensely. In technical terms, it's the number that tells you how much oxygen you can take in per millilitre of blood in a minute per kilogram of your body weight (Unit: ml/mnt/kg).

The more oxygen you can pull into your lungs and then in turn into your bloodstream, the harder your body can work. This means the higher your VO_2 max, the better is your aerobic fitness level. VO_2 max is generally largely genetic. But it can be increased when you train hard.

VO2 max levels
Typical male adult: 30–40 ml/mnt/kg
Typical women adult: 25–35 ml/mnt/kg
Elite endurance athletes: > 60 ml/mnt/kg

Most medical centres and hospitals offer a VO2 max test. Some gyms have a facility to test this too. Measuring VO2 max accurately involves a physical effort, usually on a treadmill or a cycle. Tubes are attached to your mouth. For ten minutes, they make you cycle or run and then check with tubes. They fully tax your aerobic energy system. VO2 max is reached when oxygen consumption remains at a steady state despite an increase in your activity load.

YOUR BODY: A FUEL MACHINE

Keep this book down. Jog in place or walk briskly for 30 seconds to a minute, and then pick the book up again. Are you panting or are short of breath?

Have you wondered how your body is able to generate energy to do this movement? Just like a car needs fuel to move, our body too generates energy for our daily activities and workouts. There are three energy systems that our body uses to power our movements—the phosphagen, glycogen, and the oxidative system.

Each of these super three systems works at different times in the body, according to the movement that we perform. Think of the relationship between these three energy systems as something that need each other and are meant to be. Like dal and chawal or Shah Rukh Khan and romance!

First up, the **ATP-based energy system** or **Phosphagen system.**

This system provides energy for high intensity activities such as sprinting for short distances or lifting heavy weights.

For instance, if you have to make a dash for the lift or do a quick sprint to catch a frisbee, this is the system that comes into play. In sports, heavy lifters or cricketers who hit the ball out of the park get power from the ATP-based system. So when Sachin Tendulkar hits that sixer out of the stadium, he has used his ATP system. In weight training, if you do a single barbell dead lift with maximum weight, you are firing up the same system.

ATP stands for adenosine triphosphate—a high energy phosphate stored in our muscles—which is the magic fuel source for all physical activities. The ATP system kicks in the first 10 seconds of a high-powered activity, after which the body switches to the other two systems. That's why heavy lifters and javelin throwers require rest of at least 4–5 minutes before they perform a similar high-powered activity.

Training the ATP-based system helps build power and serious strength. We need this system during a 'fight or flight' situation. In the human 'fight or flight' response in prehistoric times, 'fight' meant aggressive behaviour and 'flight' was when our ancestors fled potentially threatening situations, such as being confronted by a predator.

As we age, our body loses the ability to generate as power for sudden activities. So it is natural for our ATP systems to not fire up as easily as it is meant to be. If somebody steals your wallet and runs, you need to be responsive and run behind the thief as fast as possible. This is why you need your ATP-system in high gear!

How do we train our ATP-based system?

High powered activity lasting 10–15 seconds with rest in between. Examples: heavy lifting, short sprints, jumping jacks.

Glycogen-based system or Glycolysis

This is used in medium intensity activities like running, jogging, cycling for slightly longer distances, and strength training.

Now your glycogen-based system kicks in after the first 10–15 seconds of any activity. The main fuel comes from carbohydrates. The carbohydrates or glucose gets converted into ATP and lasts for about a minute or so. So if you have done a 400 metre run, push-ups, or barbell curls, you have used your glycogen-based system.

Why do we need to train this system?

Training this system is a great way to burn fat because you gain muscle and lose fat in the most efficient way possible. That's why I recommend interval training with weights. This kind of 20 minute workout is more effective for building muscle than a long-drawn 45 minute cardio session on the treadmill.

How do we train this system?

Interval training, sprints of 400 metre, kettlebell training, strength training, HIIT (high intensity interval training).

Oxidative system or Aerobic system

This system gives energy for low intensity activities for a longer duration such as marathon running or any cardiovascular activity done for a long period.

This is the system that comes into play after glycolysis and it is the only one that directly uses oxygen to function. This is why it is also called aerobic system. It's fuelled mainly by fat—the slow burning fuel. So if you are running a marathon, swimming, and cycling for more than half an hour, you are using the oxidative system. Basketball and football players use this system as do any athletes who perform activities for longer durations.

Compare a marathoner to a strength trainer. You will notice the marathoner has a leaner, scrawnier, unhealthy look. His aerobic system is in top shape—his heart and lungs are probably functioning most efficiently. But his muscle mass will be very less and so will his fat levels. On the other hand, people who strength-train in the right way look leaner, have more muscle and less fat, and this is the healthier way to train.

Why do we train this system?

Any aerobic activity done for longer duration helps in making the heart and lungs more efficient. But you will not gain that muscle and the tone that you are aiming for. What I am saying is that you rather be 'slim lean', not 'skinny fat'! It's imperative for any healthy person to train the oxidative system to keep the organs in order, but you don't need to do it for such long durations.

How do we train this system?

Cardio session of 20 minutes, which elevates the heart rate. Examples: Treadmill running, cycling, skipping, leisure swimming.

Why You Need to Train All 3 Systems

There are two kinds of people that you encounter when you enter a gym—the people who do excessive cardio or the ones who do only weight training. The person on the treadmill feels he is better off than the weightlifting guy—either he thinks the weightlifter will become too bulky or that weightlifting is too boring. On the other hand, the weight training people will feel cardio is a waste of time.

But now that I have explained how your body works, you know that any cardiovascular activity will help make your heart and lungs more efficient while weight training helps you build muscle, tone up, and give a big boost to your endurance levels. Both have advantages but you have to get the right mix.

BURNING CALORIES WITHOUT EXERCISING

Did the headline catch your attention? Stop scratching your head. What I am talking about is your Basal Metabolic Rate or BMR. This is the number of calories you will burn in a day, even when you were just snoozing in bed. It is the amount of energy required to maintain the body's vital processes, such as heartbeat, respiration, and maintenance of body temperature, while the body is at the rest.

The higher your BMR, the more likelihood of the calories of the food that you consume will be utilized to provide energy to your body rather than it being stored as fat. So you really want to raise your BMR!

A young child's BMR is much higher than and adult's. So now you know, as you age, your BMR keeps dipping. BMR also depends on your height and weight.

The most common way to calculate your BMR is by using the Harris-Benedict equation, which uses sex, weight, height, and age to predict your energy requirements. Remember 1 kg = 2.2 lbs

Women

BMR = 65.5 + (4.35 × weight in lbs) + (4.7 × height in inches) − (4.7 × age in years)

Men

BMR = (6.23 × weight in lbs) + (12.7 × height in inches) − (6.8 × age in years)

For example, let's take a 40-year-old woman, Reena, who is 64 inches tall and weighs 116 lbs.

BMR = 65.5 + (4.35 × 116) + (4.7 × 64) − (4.7 × 40) = 1272.4

Reena expends 1272 calories by just doing nothing at all. That's the number of calories her body is using to just do the daily vital activities.

Your basal metabolic rate is a good starting point to know how many calories you should consume in a day. To determine the total calories needed to maintain your current weight, multiply your BMR by your activity factor.

YOUR DAILY CALORIE NEEDS

#Sedentary (little or no exercise): BMR × 1.2

#Lightly active (light exercise, one to three times a week): BMR × 1.375

#Moderately active (moderate exercise, three to five times a week): BMR × 1.55

Before You Start Exercising

#Very active (hard exercise six to seven times a week): BMR × 1.725

#Extra active (very hard exercise, sports, physical job): BMR × 1.9

For example, Reena does five days of moderate exercise per week.

BMR × 1.55 = 1272.4 × 1.55 = 1972.2

This is how many calories Reena needs in a day to maintain her current weight.

But if Reena dropped her activity level to light exercise twice a week, her daily calorie requirements to maintain her current weight change would be:

BMR X 1.375 = 1,749.55

So you can see that the calorie requirements drop to almost 1,750 when she does less exercise.

This formula is good for most people but underestimates the energy needs of a highly muscular person, since muscle burns more energy just for cells to function without doing any extra activity. The formula also overestimates the calories of a fat person since fat burns less energy. It is a useful indicator to make sure that you are not too way off in the calories you expend or consume, when you are trying to lose weight.

PART TWO

Now that you have learnt about the different ways of calculating your body fat and BMR, let's get down to the basic gym lingo reps and sets which are the basic building blocks of a weight training programme. Once you have a better understanding of these, I will talk about the number of reps and sets you should do to maximize your training results. Then on the basis of six personal questions, you will be able to chart out a specific training programme for yourself.

I can't tell you how much it bothers me to see a new person at the gym get a white slip by the trainer which will list down 'X' reps with 'Y' sets for 'Z' days. The poor guy has no idea how to lift the weight correctly, forget knowing what the trainer means. If you are one of those lucky ones who have an exceptional trainer, then you know you are blessed; for all the others, it's time to get educated!

START GETTING THE LINGO RIGHT

Remember, just knowing the terms is not enough. You should know how to do a rep in the most efficient and perfect manner.

Repetitions: A repetition (commonly referred to as rep) is a single complete motion of an exercise.

Set: A set is a series of consecutive repetitions.

If your trainer has asked you to do 2 sets of dumbbell curl—10 reps each—it means that you have to do 10 consecutive dumbbell curls, rest, and then do another 10 dumbbell curls. When you complete this, pat yourself on your back—you have just completed 2 sets, 10 reps each!

The Three Components of a Repetition:

- Concentric phase is when you lift the weight (aka the positive movement)
- Isometric contraction is the pause when you hold the weight before you lower it
- Eccentric phase is when you lower the weight (aka the negative movement)

For instance, if you are doing a dumbbell curl, the concentric phase is when you curl your forearm and lift the weight. The isometric contraction occurs when you hold the weight. Then comes the eccentric phase when you finally straighten your arm to lower the weight back to the starting position. Your working muscle here is the bicep.

Before You Start Exercising

Smart Tip 1: How to Maximize Efficiency in a Rep

The longer you hold a muscle in isometric contraction, the more effective the weightlifting is. For example, if you are doing a pull-up, pull yourself towards the bar and hold it for longer. Contract the muscles here. Holding a muscle is better than doing 15 pull-ups in quick succession.

Remember this pause is different than the one you take after you complete one rep. After you complete one rep, you should NOT pause for too long. The longer you hold the pause after one rep, the harder the next rep is going to be. This is because you have neutralized the natural ability of the muscle. The ability to snap back from a stretched position to a flexed position will be tougher. Try to hold the weight till you feel the muscle burn (that's the lactic acid building up) and then, let go in a controlled manner in to the concentric phase. I see people doing repetition after repetition without understanding how to do it properly.

This does not apply when the weight is too heavy. Your pause after you complete one rep with a heavy weight will differ.

HOW HEAVY SHOULD YOU LIFT?

One of the most common questions that I am asked is, 'Deanne, how much weight should I lift to build muscle?'

Smart Tip 2: Always be Armed with Your One-rep Max.

One-rep Max (Or Max Load): It is the maximum weight you can lift with good form. It gives you an indication of your strength. It is usually done with free weights, but I would recommend doing it on a machine so that you don't injure yourself. Progressively increase the weight you are able to lift. If you are just barely able to lift it once, you have reached your maximum load or One-rep Max (1RM).

Calculate your 1RM using these formulas.

For your upper body, find the heaviest weight you can lift 4–6 times and plug it into this equation: (4–6RM × 1.1307) + 0.6998.

For instance, if you can do 5 reps of 60kg, then according to the formula – (60 × 1.1307) + 0.6998 – your 1RM will be 68.5kg.

For lower body use this formula: (4–6RM × 1.09703) + 14.2546. Round up a decimal point.

By knowing 1RM, you can choose the right volume and intensity to train at to suit your training goals.

A word of caution here: Your trainer needs to be very alert and should only focus on monitoring you. Your movements need to be controlled as the chance of injury is high. It's better to do it when you have your trainer around and the gym is not crowded. There should be no distractions, disturbances, and no music. Do it preferably in a quiet corner.

This is how I do the One-rep Max test for my clients. I would rather do the test on a machine. All machine options are safe. Pushing to the max places a lot of stress on your body parts and can cause extreme muscle soreness, even in weightlifters.

If you lift too light a weight, you will not develop good quality muscle and if you lift more than necessary, you will overtrain your muscles and injure yourself.

The biggest problem I see is that most of you don't take the trouble of figuring out One-rep Max for every exercise you are doing. I see many gym-goers lifting the same weights week after week, which is why their body structures do not change very much.

KNOW YOUR REPS AND SETS

One of my favourite activities is to study how people work out at the gym! Most people go to a gym four or five days a week and lift weights the way that they know best. Sometimes they are fascinated by a new trend or a machine and they jump onto that. There is no method to their madness.

Here's what they need—a well-designed programme with a goal set at every stage. The workouts should be varied to keep them motivated and excited. That's how I like to work out and the same rule applies to my clients. If you do the same workout week after week and don't really know when to increase the tempo or intensity, you are surely going to get bored. That's why the gym drop-out rate is so high!

The first stage in a beginner's programme is building endurance, then increasing muscle mass, and finally, strength.

The Number of Reps and Steps you Should do Should Depend on Your Fitness Goal.

WEIGHT TRAINING PROGRAMMES

Programme Goal	Sets	Repetitions	Resistance	Rest Between Sets
Endurance	3	15 to 25	50–65 percent of 1 Rep. Max	30 to 60 seconds
Health/Fitness	1 to 3	8 to 12	60–80 percent of 1 Rep. Max	30 to 60 seconds
Strength	3 to 6	5 to 6	80–88 percent of 1 Rep. Max	3 to 5 minutes
Size	3 to 6	8 to 12	80–85 percent of 1 Rep. Max	30 to 60 seconds
Power	3 to 6	2 to 4	80–90 percent of 1 Rep. Max	3 to 4 minutes

The above chart shows that if your goal is to develop muscle endurance, start with high volume at a lower intensity, which simply means lift lighter weights but have a higher rep range.

For muscle building as your main goal (also called Hypertrophy), start working with heavier weights and fewer reps. The longer you keep a muscle under a lot of tension, the more it will grow. You are not working with maximum weights here.

For strength building, drop reps while increasing weights. At the same time, increase the number of sets. Here, one also lifts faster because the objective is no more to build bigger muscles by keeping them under tension but to build strength.

FACTORS TO KEEP IN MIND BEFORE CHALKING OUT A SPECIFIC TRAINING PROGRAMME:

1. What is your fitness goal?
2. How long have you been working out?
3. What is your fitness level?
4. What is your age?
5. What is your body type?
6. What is your body shape?

What is Your Fitness Goal?

You need to really think about this. If you are trying to lose weight for a family wedding or your birthday bash, this is what I want to say to you—it's great to have a specific goal but trying to build a body and losing kilos in a hurry, only to put it all back in the next three months is a vicious cycle you just don't want to get into. You will only do harm to your body.

Instead, think about whether you want to lose 'x' kilos, so that your body will feel lighter or whether you want to be lean and athletic. Do you want your body to feel strong? Do

Before You Start Exercising

you want to get fit so that you can play cricket with your son without huffing and puffing? That's the kind of fitness goals I am talking about—one that goes beyond the superficial self. It's only when you make a fitness goal for life, that you truly achieve long-lasting results. (Refer to the section on 'Fast-twitch slow-twitch', pg 32 to understand how to train muscles according to your fitness goals.)

When setting a goal, think about it piecemeal. Think about what you want to achieve in the next 30 days. Also think about what you want to aspire for in the next 3 months. So now you have a goal and a sub-goal.

For instance, your sub-goal could be: I want to feel fitter or I want to get my body used to an exercise routine or I want to do 'x' squats with proper form. Your main goal could be more specific: 'x' kg or body measurements.

Losing 1 kg to 3 kg a month is a safe option. If you are trying to gain 5 kg, and have just begun weightlifting, you will need at least 6 months to gain that lean muscle mass. You are more likely to stick to your programme if you keep your goals realistic.

How Long Have You Been Working Out?

Are you the kind who gets up one fine morning and decides, 'From today, I will be really, really good with my fitness programme!'? And then, you put on your running shoes, thump up and down on a concrete road for more than 40 minutes without a proper warm-up only to groan in pain for the next three days. And then, the running shoes stay abandoned for a month or a year!

I have met so many clients who seem dejected and want a quick-fix to achieve their fitness goals. It doesn't work like that. I usually ask them, 'How long have you been working out?' And they say very confidently, 'Over 6 months'. But when we get down to what exactly they have been doing, the answers vary from gym once a week, running twice a week, to 'took a break for my son's exams and then got back to the gym'. I'm sorry but that's not 6 months of training!

If you have been regularly working out for approximately 30–45 minutes at least 3–4 times a week, then you have been training your body regularly—just about! You are still only a beginner to fitness. This is an important point to understand! If you have not been regular, then you haven't been training at all.

Now answer the question—how long have you been working out?

Your answer is the starting point to how you should design the number of sets and reps in your programme. Exercise is a good form of stress to the body to mould it to the form that we want. It is important to progressively increase this stress, so that you are not hurt in the process. I have seen so many trainers pushing beginners in the gym to the point where they can't walk at all, or they feel pain to lift their arms for days. Some muscle burn is good, but excessive soreness is just plain silly and harmful. You have to begin small and take pride and motivate yourself if you want to see big results.

What is Your Fitness Level?

Here's what I like to define fitness level as:
- Exercise Virgin: If you don't exercise for 30–45 minutes three times a week regularly, you are an exercise virgin. You are—in my books—untrained.
- Beginner: If you have been regularly exercising for a while at least thrice a week, you can be labeled a beginner.
- Exercise Enthusiast: If you have been working out for 30–45 minutes at least 5–6 times a week for a while, you are a level above a beginner.
- Advanced: If you exercise for 45 minutes a day to an hour intensely at least 5–6 times a week for months, congratulate yourself! You are someone at an advanced

fitness level. The intensities could vary from moderate to high intensity
- Obsessive Gym Brat: There is also the other end of the spectrum. Are you spending hours at a gym, training for more than 5–6 times a week? Uh oh. You are most likely suffering from an obsessive-compulsive disorder.

What is Your Age?

I have never tried to hide my age. I have been working out for the last 15 years and have a very strong fitness base. But I always use common sense and listen to my body while attempting any new fitness routine.

Recently I signed up for a CrossFit class, which is an intense interval training programme. On the first day itself, I was asked to jump over two blocks. While I could easily do it, I asked the trainer to put me through a beginner's routine first. Now, why did I do that? Because I listened to my body. I know as I age, I need to be careful of sudden jerky movements.

Remember the body tends to lose flexibility and coordination after the age of 35. Most people above 45 years of age have joints problems. In fact, now it starts as early as late 20s and early 30s. That's why I don't believe in group classes that exceed more than 6 to 8 people. It gets tough for the instructor to monitor the person's movements and body alignment.

When you design a programme for yourself, remember that you need to factor in your age. There's no shame in being honest with yourself. Slow and gradual is better than injuring yourself for instant results. It's just stupidity to pick up a heavy weight because the other guy at the gym is doing it!

For exercise virgins, it is better to start with just one set with a light weight and 12–15 reps. Get your form, technique and breathing right. Start with this routine for at least two weeks so that your body is conditioned and then gradually increase the load or intensity.

Children under the age of 18 should not lift over 50 percent of their body weight. They run the risk of stunting their height growth.

What is Your Body Type?

It's imperative that everybody understand their own body type which, simply put, is skinny, plump, or athletic.

Skinny = Ectomorph

Is this you?

- ✓ Small frame and bone structure
- ✓ Find it difficult to put on weight
- ✓ Thin
- ✓ Fast metabolism
- ✓ Small shoulders and flat chest
- ✓ Not very muscular

Ectomorphs are the skinny people who everybody loves to hate. They are the ones who eat the chocolate pastry and say, 'Honestly, I never put on weight!' They can eat and eat and never gain kilos. But here's the thing—they also find it difficult to build muscle.

They need to eat a lot more—not junk food but healthy nutritious food for which they need to consult a good nutritionist. They should not do too much cardio because they are blessed with high metabolism. Cardio will just rev up their metabolism even more. The weight training programme needs to be built around working on their biggest muscle groups and it needs to be intense, where they feel the muscle burn. This helps develop muscle mass. Of course, by now you know that this kind of training has to be done only after taking into account your fitness level and your age. Because of their body type, ectomorphs need to slow down the pace of their activity with de-stressing routines like yoga, Pilates, walking, or leisure swimming. They also need to take naps to relax.

Plump = Endomorph

Is this you?
- ✓ Soft and round body
- ✓ Stocky build
- ✓ Gains fat easily
- ✓ Slow metabolism
- ✓ Finds it difficult to lose fat
- ✓ Don't have well-defined muscles

Endomorphs are easy to spot; they are the ones with short limbs and usually strong upper legs. They are able to do squats effortlessly. They put on weight easily. Unfortunately, they put on fat more easily than muscle. Endomorphs respond well to interval training which involves short bursts of cardio along with weight training. They need to eat small meals frequently during the day to boost their metabolism, which is naturally sluggish.

#ATHLETIC = MESOMORPH

Is this you?
- ✓ Rectangular shaped body
- ✓ Athletic and strong
- ✓ Gains muscle easily
- ✓ Gains fat more easily than ectomorphs (skinny people)
- ✓ Well-defined muscles
- ✓ Hard body, not soft and round

Mesomorphs are the ones who are blessed with a naturally athletic body and they gain muscle easily. Of course, it goes without saying that they respond the best to weight training.

They should keep a lookout for creeping fat gains because they tend to put on the dreaded fat more easily than ectomorphs.

#*Body Combination Types*

All of us are unique and cannot be divided into three neat brackets. There are people who can be a combination of ectomorph and mesomorph or endomorph and mesomorph.

So what body type are you? Depending on the answer, you will have to modify your exercise programme and the number of sets you do.

There are a number of factors that need to be taken into consideration before you decide the number of sets you need to do. Remember, even the skinniest guys or the fattest girls can get a toned, muscular, and fit body. You just have to put in the hard work and be smart about it. There is no glory in just copying your favourite Bollywood actor's workout or doing a routine similar to a size-zero actress. You are unique, your goals should be defined by you and your workout should be customized for you!

EXERCISING ACCORDING TO BODY TYPE

Always remember that each person's body type and shape, fitness levels, and goal is different. Your body is different from your friend's or own sister's body or from the actor you look up to. One may be more flexible than the other; someone could need more shoulder strength while their lower body muscles may be strong; somebody could have had a past knee injury and probably can't do an intensive workout for the lower body. Somebody's endurance and stamina levels could be very high. So first evaluate your body type, shape, and fitness levels before you begin an exercise programme.

Your goal could vary. Some of you may just want to get off the couch. For some, it may be to break a fitness plateau. Yet others may want to lose the kilos or build muscle. You may also just want to tone up, or increase your muscular look or you may want to boost your endurance levels.

Before You Start Exercising

FOR WOMEN: EXERCISE ACCORDING TO YOUR BODY SHAPE

For women, it may be easier to work out according to their body shapes. There are 4 types of body shapes: Apple, Pear, Stick, and Hour-glass.

1. Apple Shape

- Broad shoulders
- Large bust
- Excessive weight around the abdomen area

If you are stuck with an abnormally large tummy, you are battling visceral fat. This is a dangerous kind of fat that is located in the abdominal region which surrounds vital organs. It is more dangerous that the subcutaneous fat which lies just under the skin. Excess visceral fat has been linked to several fatal diseases like heart disease, type-2 diabetes, and cancer.

Apple-shaped people tend to have higher levels of cortisol—the body's key stress hormone (Refer to pg 75 to read more on cortisol). If your body is producing excessive cortisol, you are most likely holding on to your body fat even when you are exercising.

Battle the Bulge: To get rid of the excess fat, you need to practice different forms of interval training. Don't just walk, slowly advance to walk-jog and then walk-jog-run. Apply the same principle to any cardiovascular activity that you take up—alternate sudden bursts of high-intensity movements with low-intensity activity. Strength training is the best way to lean down—make sure you perform compound moves. Add on weights when you have got your form right and you are comfortable with your own body weight. Bring down stress levels by practicing breathing techniques, yoga, leisure walks, or swimming. This combination will help boost both your aerobic and anaerobic systems to speed up metabolism and burn belly fat.

2. Pear Shape

- Narrow shoulders
- Slender upper torso
- Heavy at the bottom; excess weight on hips, thighs, and buttocks

If you look at your bottom every time you try on your jeans or despair that your waist is tiny but your hips seem to belong to some other person, you know you are a pear. The secret to changing your body shape is understanding that you are carrying extra subcutaneous fat, unlike the apple-shaped person. While this fat is actually better than visceral fat, it is much harder to get rid of. It has less blood flow and clings on to calories, which makes it tough to burn it off.

Bust the Bottom: Concentrate on compound moves for the lower body—squats and lunge variations. Try and pump it up to circuit-style training by adding cardio intervals in between. For instance, combine your compound moves with jumping-rope or jogging-in-pace intervals. You can then advance to High Intensity Interval Training (HIIT). This way you will increase your lean muscle mass, boost your metabolism rate, and reduce cellulite.

3. Stick Shape

- Athletic figure
- Slim and straight; lacks curves
- No extra weight on any area

Stick-shaped women are rarely overweight—their real issue is just an overall lack of shape. They usually don't have curves and are stick-straight. There is no need for a drastic

Before You Start Exercising

change of diet or exercise required for this kind of women. You need to give your body frame sexy definition by working out according to your body shape.

Get the Curves: Focus of building your shoulders, buttocks, and core to get a better frame and a more symmetrical body shape. Weightlifting should focus on bench presses and shoulder pressures and combine compound moves with weights. For instance, do squats with dumbbells in hand. If you are athletic, mix it up by taking up river rafting or canoeing—it's an excellent way to improve upper body strength. Go rock-climbing—this will give your glutes a good definition.

4. Hour-glass Shape

- Perfect waist
- Curvy figure
- A bit of flab on bust and hip

This is considered the ideal body shape but if you skip exercising or body-toning exercises with weights, you run this risk of gaining fat around your thighs and upper arms as you age.

Tone it up: To keep your shapely body firm, focus on simple weight training routines with timeless moves like squats, lunges, dead-lifts, push-ups, and planks. Build core strength through twisting moves, yoga, or Pilates. Swimming and walking are the best cardiovascular activities which will not harm your joints.

FORM & TECHNIQUE

I keep coming back to the chapter on biomechanics because it is intrinsically linked to form and technique. The study of biomechanics involves the study of motions, and how one can maximize performance with the right knowledge of how the body (and all that it is made up of) moves and how the muscles work in tandem to facilitate movement.

Be in Control

Every gym has that guy who lifts heavy, grunts, and makes all sorts of noises but his form will be all wrong by the second rep! Enjoy the drama but don't get taken in by the histrionics. When you lift weights, you need to go through a full range of motion (ROM). Avoid jerky movements; instead make it deliberate and controlled. Always be aware of your posture and alignment.

Don't Get Intimidated at the Gym

If you are lifting too much or too little, you have to find your balance through trial and error. You men out there; please understand that it's always better to start with a lighter weight. Get your form right first, then increase the weights. Don't feel shy about lifting light! Remember you have to think about your health first, not your ego. Don't be afraid to ask for help while you are in the gym; remember you have paid for the services!

Get Your Intensity Right

I have seen macho men who will use all the machines, then do a lunge walk on the floor, and some more crazy stuff for hours. They make a khichdi out of their workout routine and then feel very good about working out for a long time. Instead all they need to do is a few squats, lunges, dead lifts, and chin-ups where they put in focused effort. The workout could probably be over in 30–40 minutes. The objective is to get the muscles slightly inflamed. Once the wear and tear happens, the muscle will then grow.

Before You Start Exercising

Spotting

Every weight lifter needs to be acquainted with the term 'spotting'. A spotter stands behind a lifter and assists during lifting as and when required. For example, a spotter may assist you during a bench press if you can't finish the lift. There is a high risk of injury when you lift a heavy weight while in the supine position, and so you should ask for a spotter.

Sometimes, a lifter can become too dependent on a spotter. So be aware of the situation, but always ask for help when you need it. It is better than getting injured.

KEEP YOUSELF MOTIVATED, CHANGE IT UP A BIT!

There are different ways of varying your programme. While your trainer is responsible for adding variety to your programme, I want you to be aware that you can add spice to your training routine by changing the intensity, volume, and frequency of what you do. This is called periodization of a training programme, which is structuring training into phases.

Intensity: It is the percentage of your One-rep Max that you lift for any exercise. High-intensity is a heavy load while low-intensity is a light load.

Volume: It is the amount of work you do during a workout session. Work is calculated as **Sets × Reps × Weight**. You can change the volume of your workout by changing the number of sets, reps, or weight.

Frequency: It is the number of times you work each muscle group per week. A high frequency would mean working out each muscle group 3 times a week while a low frequency could be working it out only once a week. Rest and recovery is required, so frequency depends on the intensity and volume of your routine.

Periodization: It involves varying volume and training intensity and simply means organizing your programme into different themes. For example, one month, you may use weight machines and the next month, you may switch to dumbbells and barbells. Or you can change the number of sets, reps, and exercises you perform from one period to the next.

Smart Tip 4: Beat the Blues, Climb the Plateau!

You need to continually challenge your muscles in order to see results and avoid the dreaded 'plateau'. Use the principle of progression. Overload your muscles by lifting a heavier weight each time. You will reach muscle failure faster which will stimulate your muscles to get stronger. To continue to overload your muscles and keep making progress, you need to find new ways to challenge your muscles. If you are able to do your 12th rep easily, then you know it is time to increase the weight you lift—maybe by 5 percent. Again here, if your goal is building strength or muscle mass, you will do fewer repetitions. In general, wait for 6 to 8 weeks to see visible results from your training when you are new. Internal changes start to occur immediately in response to your first training session.

HOW TO BREATHE WHEN YOU LIFT WEIGHTS

Keeping your breath in sync while weightlifting is very important—always breathe out on exertion. Relaxed breathing is the best. While doing your cardiovascular exercises, if you find yourself getting a little too out of breath, it's because you are starting too fast or doing too much, too quickly. So you need to slow down here and let the breathing be a little more natural.

I usually do the talk test with clients. Do this next time—if you can talk normally when you are on the treadmill or on an elliptical cycle, then you know you need to raise the tempo. On a cycle, you can increase the resistance. If you find yourself completely out of breath, then you need to lower the speed or resistance.

Never hold your breath. Holding on to your breath can cause a condition called latent hypoxia which is the lack of oxygen to the brain. You experience dizzy spells and you might feel giddy.

Inhale through your nose and exhale through your mouth. When you inhale through the nose, the air goes through a natural 4-stage filtration process. If you inhale through the mouth, you skip this process. This makes you vulnerable to tonsillitis, sore throat, and even ear infections. When you exhale through the mouth, you naturally expand the airways in your body, allowing for more efficient usage of air.

Lifting weights temporarily causes your blood pressure to shoot up, which normally isn't a problem. When you hold your breath, your blood pressure shoots up even higher. Holding your breath creates intra-thoracic pressure—pressure in the chest cavity that stops your circulation of blood from your muscles, but can increase blood pressure. When you relax, the muscle relaxes, the blood begins to flow again, and your blood pressure drops. This drastic drop may cause you to pass out and drop the weight you are lifting. And if you have a heart condition, you could be in serious jeopardy.

Smart Tip 5: Breathe like a Yogi to Develop Focus

What does yoga have to do with weightlifting? Everything! The best bodybuilders are the ones who are focused. You can lift more when your movements are controlled and your breathing is in tandem with your movements.

There is a well-known saying in yoga, 'Where attention goes, energy flows'. By controlling the breath, we can control the mind and by controlling the mind, we can control the body. So remember to connect and coordinate your breathing with the weightlifting. Through proper breathing, an intense purification is said to take place. A deep, internal heat is created and through the sweat, and impurities are burnt. It is like the alchemist who turns lead into gold and the body becomes strong.

HYDRATION: GETTING THE H20 FACTOR RIGHT

Muscle is considered an active tissue and water is found in the highest concentration in active tissues. Your muscles are 72 percent water. In order to move your muscles, you need water. Drink at least two 8 ounce glasses of water before starting your weightlifting routine. If your body is even slightly dehydrated, your performance will decline. If you don't have enough water, you perspire at a lower rate and the body temperature rises. You won't be able to cool down properly. Water loss reduces the ability of the body to release heat from the body. It also puts a lot of strain on the heart and kidneys. So it is necessary to hydrate yourself long before, during and after the activity.

Signs of dehydration:

- Dry mouth
- Fatigue
- Loss of appetite
- Headache
- Dry cough
- Dark yellow urine

Always sip on water during workouts, don't gulp! And try and empty your bladder before you workout. Then stay hydrated during your exercise.

If your exercise activity is less than 60 minutes, then sipping on water is enough. If it lasts for a longer time, then you need to have water with electrolytes. Electrolytes are minerals that, when dissolved in water, break into small, electrically charged particles called ions. They mainly create

Before You Start Exercising

the electrical impulses essential to all aspects of physical activity—from basic cell function to complex neuromuscular interactions needed for athletic performance.

Avoid artificial colours in the drink that you choose. Have you noticed that sometimes people have a blue mouth after sipping on water with electrolytes? That's because of the colours that are added to the liquid. Stay away from such drinks.

Sometimes, people do just 45 minutes of exercise—that too in a cool environment—and then sip on electrolytes. This is not needed. Only water is enough. When you go beyond an hour of cardio, you are likely to go into a sodium loss. That's the time you need to replenish and replace sodium loss through electrolytes.

For the people who hate drinking water, come up with solutions for yourself because now you know how important it is to hydrate your body. You can add a slice of lemon or flavour your water with mint, basil, or even add a teaspoon of honey. The other solution is to opt for vitamin water that is available in the market. Go for the ones which don't have any artificial preservatives.

> The only healthy thing that I have consistently done all my life is I hydrate myself. People usually forget that—they don't think it's really important. You know we eat, we have coffee, chai, and all kinds of drinks, and then we think that that's hydration. But it's really not. Even if you drink just 3 litres of water every day, it's very good. It flushes out your toxins, and you feel better. That's the only consistently healthy thing that I do.
>
> PRIYANKA CHOPRA, ACTOR

REST & RECOVERY

Short, smart, and intense workouts are the way to go, that's why less is more when it comes to weight training. Gradual progression is critical to getting the best possible results and avoiding injury.

When you train, you stress or overload your muscles. Microscopic tears occur in the muscle fibre. When you rest, your body repairs these tears and your muscles become stronger. When your muscles reach failure at the end of a set, you need to rest before you can challenge that muscle to work again. You need to allow it to recover for at least a day before you train it again. You have to rest that particular muscle worked on for at least 24–48 hours. This doesn't mean you can't lift weights for two days in a row—you could work on your chest and back one day and then your legs the next day. But if you are doing a full body routine, don't lift weights more than three times a week every alternate day and don't cram your three workouts into one weekend.

AVOID OVERTRAINING

As unbelievable as it may sound to a beginner, many exercisers become only enthusiastic after they start getting results and think that if a little is good, and then more has to be great.

Overtraining typically occurs in the following scenarios:

- Training too many times per week
- Doing too many exercises per session
- Repeating excessive number of reps and sets
- Lifting too heavy a weight over too long a period of time
- Doing split training over a period of time

These are the tell-tale signs if you are overtraining: chronic fatigue, poor sleep, excess muscle soreness, mood changes, loss of interest in training, and increased frequency of illness and injuries.

Before You Start Exercising

PART THREE

VARIETY, VARIETY, VARIETY!

By now you know that being fit can be as fun as you make it. As children, we love to play but as adults, we forget to have fun! Think of the time you climbed walls or trees, remember when you ran the wind in your face or pushed yourself to the limit on the swing. I want you to incorporate the same fun element in your workouts—whether you create a jungle gym, train indoors or outdoors, with accessories or weights, or do CrossFit or cross-train.

Too much of the same form of training leads to boredom, so never be shy of trying out other forms. Keeping in mind that strength should be your base, add variety to it. Your goal should be to sustain fitness lifelong, so look at it as a lifestyle choice instead of temporary fitness.

DIFFERENT FORMS OF TRAINING

I have divided different methods of training into four broad areas: Strength Training, Endurance Training, Flexibility and Balance Training.

You have to make sure that you keep the 4 pillars of fitness (4PF)—strength, endurance, flexibility, and balance—in mind when you workout. If you add variety and 4PF in your workouts, you will never fear the 'dreaded plateau' or bang your head against the 'weight loss wall'!

#Strength Training: Is when you use any kind of resistance to contract your muscles to build strength and anaerobic endurance. It helps increase muscle mass, ligament strength, bone density, and improves cardiac function.

FOR THE EXERCISE VIRGIN

Gym Machines: This is the best option for a person who is new to the gym because you risk injury with free weights.

First find your way through the most basic machines, keep it simple till you get acquainted with the equipment. There is no need to hurry through this stage. Always ask for help at the gym.

Resistance Band Training: Get hold of a resistance band or tube. You can do full body workouts with this magic band.

FOR THE BEGINNER

Using Your Body Weight as Resistance: Why is it that certain exercises like lunges are quite challenging even though you are lifting zero weight? It's because you are lifting your own body weight. With a number of exercises like push-ups, squats and planks, moving your own body weight offers plenty of resistance, especially for beginners. For instance in the push-up, you push-up your entire body weight upward directly against the force of gravity. Yoga and Pilates are excellent examples of body weight training.

Free Weightlifting: 'Free weights' are the most basic gym equipments—they are 'free' because they are not attached to any pulleys, cables, pins, or weight stacks. Dumbbells, barbells, and weight plates are all forms of free weights. All beginners should train on machines first, get their form and technique right, and then go for free weights.

Isotonic Weightlifting (Dynamic Training): It involves the shortening and lengthening of the muscle. Any exercise that involves lifting and lowering weights or opening and closing joints, such as pressing or squatting, are considered isotonic. Examples are dumbbell curls, leg extensions.

Isometric Training: It works your muscles without any joint movement. The length of the muscle remains consistent. For example—in the plank, your core muscles are strengthened while at a fixed length; they are not moving.

For the Exercise Enthusiast

Training Opposing Muscles: It's very simple really—think bicep and tricep in your arm or back and chest. Remember what I told you about agonist and antagonist muscles? When you train opposing muscles, you balance the muscle growth and it helps prevent injury.

❖ Upper Arm	Biceps	Triceps
❖ Upper Torso	Pectorals	Latissimus Dorsi
❖ Shoulder	Anterior Deltoid	Posterior Deltoid
❖ Spine	Abdominals	Erector Spinae
❖ Legs	Quadriceps	Hamstrings
❖ Calf	Gastrocnemius	Tibialis Anterior

Playing With Different Types of Sets

A straightforward set is when you use the same amount of weight for a standard number of sets. But like I said, variety is the name of the game. Change it up when you think it's getting boring!

Pyramid Sets: You change the weight used and reps performed as you progress through your workout. For example, in set one you do 12 reps with 60 pounds; in set two you perform 10 reps with 70 pounds; and in set three you do eight reps with 80 pounds. This warms you up gradually as you increase the intensity. A reverse pyramid is exactly the opposite—when you go from high to low.

Super Sets: You pair two exercises—say lunges and squats—and you do not rest through the pairing. Here you are working the same muscle group. You can also work opposite muscle groups—like say leg extensions and leg curls. Another way to do a superset is to pair upper and lower body muscles, like step-ups and bicep curls.

Tri Set & Giant Sets: If you combine three exercises to do a superset, it's called a tri set. And if you combine four or more, you have a giant set!

Slo' Mo' Training: It involves the combination of very slow speeds of lifting and lowering the weight. So you lift the weight up for about 10 seconds and take 10 seconds to lower it. Only one set is usually performed a challenging weight is used. This is tough because of the tension created in the muscles.

Training to Failure: You know that image of a bodybuilder where he is sweating, his veins are bulging, and his muscles are tense and contracted—that's training to failure. It is repeating a rep to the point of momentary muscular failure.

Training To Time: It is when you do 'x' number of reps in the time you want. So, say as many bicep curls that you can do in a minute. Here the time is the constant.

TRX Training: This is another form of body weight training and involves straps called 'suspension trainers'. You use your own body weight to perform intense movements from different angles and recruit more muscle fibre; so you engage more muscle groups at the same time and working on your core.

FOR THE ADVANCED

Power Lifting: This is what the guy in your gym who's all macho and uses 'brute' strength to lift weights does. It's the best type of training for maximal strength. A power lifter's goal isn't appearance; it's strength. Power lifters lift an extremely heavy amount of weight for only a few repetitions.

Drop Sets: Once you have reached muscular failure, you immediately reduce (or drop) the weight and continue your set using a lighter weight to work your muscles more intensely.

Before You Start Exercising

This technique is used by bodybuilders to increase muscle mass. An example for bicep curls would be performing 10 reps using 40 pounds to failure, then 7 reps using 30 pounds to failure, finishing with 6 reps using 20 pounds to failure.

Bodybuilding: There is a specific goal for this kind of training: to make muscles bigger, but not necessarily stronger. You will notice that many bodybuilders are not as strong as say, Olympic athletes. That's because their goal is aesthetics, not athleticism.

Metabolic Resistance Training (MRT): It is sometimes also called 'madman training' because of the intensity involved. It involves supersets, circuits, compound exercises, and cardio done at high speed and small rest periods.

#***Endurance Training:*** Training which increases stamina and endurance. This kind of training makes sure your muscles can endure a good kind of strain for a longer period of time. It also helps increase your cardiovascular fitness—your heart and lungs get stronger.

Types of endurance sports:

- ✓ Marathon, triathlon
- ✓ Road cycling for long distances
- ✓ Competitive swimming

How do you increase your endurance levels?

For the Exercise Virgin

Continuous Training: It's exactly what the name suggests! You do any aerobic activity continuously for approximately 20 minutes at the lowest level of your Target Heart Rate (50 percent of Maximum Heart Rate). There is no rest period allowed. So this could mean walking on the treadmill, using the elliptical, a power walk in the park, or a swim at a steady pace, without rest.

For the Beginner

Interval Training: Once you have conditioned your body to 20 minutes of continuous training, you can mix it up. I believe that the body needs to be pushed from its comfort zone through interval training. It's a form of physical training which weaves high intensity exercise with low intensity exercise with rest periods in between. You are pushing your body at intervals and progressively increasing the intensity.

The simplest example would be a 60 second jog–90 second walk–60 second jog on the treadmill. Continue this for 20 minutes. If it's too intense, change the walk period to 2 minutes. Once you get used to this workout, gradually advance to the elliptical and then the ski machine. Challenge yourself by then doing the same workout in the neighbourhood park and then, the beach. Interval training in the gym can be done using different machines too—rotate between the treadmill, ski machine, and the elliptical.

Hydrotherapy Training: I would recommend simple water aerobics for the exercise virgin to beginner level. Water helps strengthen muscles by providing resistance. At the same time, the buoyancy ensures minimal pressure on the joints. You can gradually advance to underwater treadmill running and finally, underwater spinning.

For the Exercise Enthusiast

Circuit Training: Kick your metabolism into high gear with circuit training. This is my favourite kind of workout—it's short and smart where you basically target large muscle groups without rest.

You do 6–8 exercises back to back with short rest periods (30–60 seconds) in between. Once you finish the circuit, you start from the top again. Preferably start with a machine circuit in the gym—choose 6–8 machines or 'stations' for your circuit. Once you have mastered this, you can add on free weights.

Challenge yourself further by adding cardio. Finish a circuit, do 10 minutes of cardio (treadmill or elliptical), and then, go back to your second circuit. Want to graduate to a higher level? Make the cardio more intense—do rebounding exercises on a mini trampoline or free-hand exercises like jumping jacks, star jumps, or mountain climbers (basically, anything that shoots up your heart rate).

For the Advanced

Fartlek Training: Fartlek means 'speed play' in Swedish. It blends continuous training with interval training. A session could include a hard sprint of 10 seconds, a power walk of 20 seconds, and then a one minute jog—this set is then repeated continuously. You can try this in the gym by trying it on an incline or decline. This kind of training is usually done by athletes. Sometimes, coaches make it tougher by making athletes run on sand or even run uphill. People who play field sports like cricket, football, badminton, tennis, or hockey benefit from Fartlek training because it mimics the change of pace required in their sport.

Plyometrics: A type of exercise which requires explosive power and involves high-intensity muscular contractions. This kind of training is mainly done by athletes—plyometric exercises mimic the actions in sports such as skiing, football, basketball, and tennis. For instance, they would be asked to jump off a box, rebound off the floor to another higher box. If you don't have the strength, you could twist your ankle. Low-intensity plyometric exercises include star jumps, jumping jacks, and skaters.

CrossFit: It is a fitness company in the US which promotes a strength and conditioning programme, involving high-intensity, functional movements. Workouts are typically short and combine high-intensity cardio like running, jumping, and plyometrics, with weightlifting with equipments like kettlebells, barbells, and dumbbells. The programmes usually demand an all-out physical exertion.

High-intensity Interval training (HIIT): Low intensity exercise (50 percent of Maximum Heart Rate) followed by high-intensity exercise (which means you go all out! Hit your maximum heart rate) and end with a period of cool down exercise or rest. It usually lasts for 9 to 20 minutes. For example, you do a 30 second jog followed by a 30 second hard sprint—which is the maximum you can do—then walk for another 30 seconds. And repeat this cycle for the time that you have set. This is mainly done to improve athletic performance.

High Altitude Training: Elite endurance athletes, such as runners, swimmers, and triathletes, often train at high altitudes for a month or more because the body creates more red blood cells to adapt to the lower oxygen content of the air. This increase in red blood cells then tricks the body into carrying more oxygen to fuel muscles when the athletes compete nearer to sea level. Nowadays, you can simulate altitude training in certain gyms with special equipment like a generator and workout kit that includes a mask. It is also called hypoxic training in which oxygen-reduced air is produced to simulate altitudes of up to 21,000 feet. For instance, you wear the oxygen mask while using an elliptical or treadmill. While you exercise, you breathe normally into the mask which is connected to a generator and pumps oxygen into you.

Before You Start Exercising

> My day is endurance training. I have 20-hour days with no weekends. I don't take holidays. I don't believe in holidays. I think my life is pretty much my endurance training. Now I do endurance training because of my movie (On Mary Kom), because boxing needs that.
>
> PRIYANKA CHOPRA, ACTOR

#Flexibility and Balance Training: Without flexibility and balance exercises, you are sure to end up with a joint problem. While flexibility refers to the range of movement in your joints, balance helps you improve your coordination and athletic performance.

FOR THE EXERCISE VIRGIN

Begin with basic static stretches.

For balance, try this exercise:

Standing On One Leg: Stand on one foot behind a sturdy chair, holding on for balance. Hold position for upto 10 seconds. Repeat 5 times with each leg. You can progress to using no support.

For the Beginner

To improve flexibility, try holding static stretches for a longer period (30 seconds).

For balance training:

Walking Heel To Toe: Put the heel of one foot in front of the toes of the other foot. Your heels and toes should almost touch. Focus on a point in front of you to keep yourself steady as you walk. Now as you take steps, out your heels just in front of the other foot.

For the Exercise Enthusiast

Dynamic stretches: Dynamic stretches involve active movements of muscle that bring forth a stretch but is not held in the end position. The opposite of this is static stretching, consisting of stretching in which the position is held for any given amount of time. Air squats, leg kicks, lunges, and jump squats are examples of dynamic stretching.

Adding Balance Equipment: Add balance equipment to your strength training routine. Nowadays, there are so many options available—BOSU ball (Both Sides Utilized), Swiss ball, wobble boards, balance pads, dyna discs and so on. You strengthen not just your core, but your sense of balance and your neurological system when you incorporate balance equipment into your workouts.

Don't go straight on a BOSU ball or Swiss ball. First, start with the beginner's level of balance pads where the surface is hard. Then, progress to more softer and wobbly unstable surfaces. Always hold on to something when you begin, like your trainer's hand for support. Then, graduate to not holding anything for support.

Advanced

The advanced flexibility routines like isometric stretching are for ballet dancers and gymnasts which involve a lot of flexibility of the spine. For balance, you can do what I do. I practice most of my yoga asanas on a BOSU ball. You can also practice on sand, like at the beach where the surface offers resistance. Don't do it on a Swiss ball, you run the risk of hurting yourself.

HOW TO CHOOSE A PERSONAL TRAINER

I recently came across this article which mentioned that a model was suing her personal trainer on account of negligence. In one of the sessions, the trainer had pushed the model into doing an extreme workout, one that her body was not ready to take, thus causing her a slipped disc. Remember, it takes two hands to clap. Just because your trainer asks you to do something doesn't mean you will blindly hang on to every word of his. With the right knowledge of what is good or bad for your body, you can instantly know when your trainer is going wrong. Continue to educate yourself so you can put your foot down and say NO if the trainer is asking you to do something that is at odds with your body. You should be able to tell the trainer, 'Listen, I haven't rested well and my back hurts, so I won't do leg lifts today.' Don't choose a trainer just because he is responsible for changing your favourite superstar's body. Each body is tailor-made, and that's where the 'personal' in personal trainer comes into play. Your workout has to be personal—customized for the individual. Most people I see are 'personal' breakers! The objective of most trainers is to get famous quickly. So they just go ahead and give a free-size programme to all their clients. It doesn't matter if the client is over 65 years of age or is complaining about shoulder pain.

I also don't want you to ever think that you can only train if you have a dedicated personal trainer watching your every move and guiding you. I started off with practicing Ashtanga Yoga in the very comforts of my home without a trainer by my side. And I think I managed just fine!

If you can't do without one, here's a checklist:

- Check the trainer's certification (ASCM, ACE).
- Ask the trainer his/her area of specialization—for example, injuries, special populations (older people), or bodybuilding. If it's in your budget to hire the best, get a trainer who is qualified in sports medicine. Like for me, my specialization is weight training and women's bodies.
- Choose a trainer according to your goal. For instance, if you want to train for a marathon, choose a trainer who is good with endurance training.
- Ask for a referral. Speak to other people who have trained under the instructor.

- ✓ Take a trial session. Remember you will be spending a lot of time with your trainer. Is the trainer soft or too aggressive? The trainer's personality has to agree with you.

Once you choose a trainer, make sure that you have certain ground rules. The trainer should talk to you about your goals, about your lifestyle, and only then make a programme. You should make sure that the time that he is training you, he needs to be focusing on you alone—not gossiping with a hot girl on the other machine.

This is how I go about with my clients. I want to have a fair idea about how this should ideally work. First up, I ask them to fill up a health consent form. They are asked details about any medication that they may be taking, if they suffer from any allergies, and their family history. I also ask them to list any cardiovascular problems, joint injuries, or musculoskeletal problems that they may have or have had in the past. These are just a few. I have a list of 4 pages of health appraisals for them to fill. All of this is important to know before you put any individual on an exercise programme.

A tip for the trainers as well—get your client to sign a health disclaimer. Some clients do crazy things outside the studio or gym and then blame the health problem on the trainer.

Personally for me, a doctor's go ahead is very important. I don't start my sessions unless I have the entire medical history. I give the go-ahead to my trainers only after I personally go through the medical history. In case the client has suffered an injury and wants to work out, we always work with the physiotherapist or doctor concerned and put down the correct protocol for post-rehab and pre-rehab treatment.

My trainers then do simple tests to observe the client's strength, flexibility, and stamina levels and tell me. The first few sessions are just evaluation and then the actual programme begins. Sometimes, we get stubborn clients who want to lose 5 kgs in 1 month—I always say the goal should be about being fit. The maximum weight that you can lose is 2.5 kgs to 3 kgs in a month, not more than that. If they don't agree, I tell them to go elsewhere. Then they go to other trainers, use unnatural methods, injure themselves or bloat, and soon they are back in my office.

I also believe in adding variety and fun to exercise programmes. For me, to add a playground element to training is very important. As adults, we forget to play. I believe you can train anywhere. I like teaching clients how to train by themselves, and not become overly dependent on their trainers. Many clients travel a lot—so they are taught to be self-reliant; so they can work out in the hotel gym or in their hotel room abroad using resistance bands or a TRX, or at their place of holiday, or they can take a swim. They are in touch with me and my team of trainers over email or messages.

As far as diet is concerned, even though I know a lot about food, I am not qualified to give a full-fledged diet to my clients. So I work with 2–3 nutritionists who believe in balanced meals, not fads. The meal plan is then mailed to the trainer and the client.

I also talk to my clients about sleep, hydration, and stress levels and many other magic mantras that need to be kept in mind. If they want to do a new exercise class like Pilates or something else which my trainers are not qualified to teach, I may tell them to go to the other classes. But they need to inform us so that the body is not overtrained. The entire process gets customized—many times they open up to me about smoking or alcohol problems—I always listen. That's why the term 'lifestyle coach'.

IT'S ALL IN YOUR MIND

Your thoughts and feelings have a significant impact on your physical and mental well-being which in turn has an important bearing on weight training. When you are upset, your heart is racing, your breath is shallow and rapid, and you may even sweat. That's an example of your mind–body connection.

When you train muscles, you tap into mind-body connection through your neuromuscular system. Before you can contract a muscle fibre, the nervous system must run a communication network from your brain through the spinal cord and out to the individual muscle fiber. In the early stages of training, before your start seeing visible external results your body is laying down the neural network. The more extensive your neural network, the more individual muscle fibre contract.

You need to disconnect your mind from all the distracting thoughts around you—be it the blasting music being played at the gym or the new gym enthusiasts trying to out-train each other. Take me for instance. While doing a single-leg lunge on a wobbly strap, I can easily shut my eyes and mind to all the distractions around me and yet not fall off or lose balance because years of practice have conditioned my body to get used to the routine. This is my mind–body connection at work and this is what I want all of you to strive to achieve.

So you have nothing to lose and possibly more effective training results to gain by focusing your mind on your target muscles as you do your exercise. When you are ready to train, clear your mind, see yourself going through your workout smoothly and successfully.

Visualize your strong and toned body, and believe in your ability to lift weights. It makes a difference.

INJURIES

Ouch…that hurts!

Have you suffered a shin splint while running? Or have you had a sudden catch in your lower back when you bent down to pick something from the floor or even just sneezed? Injuries have become a part and parcel of our daily lives. An injury is defined as anything that causes damage to the human body. Now that you have learnt about biomechanics you know that an injury happens when you ignore the most basic rule. You HAVE to strengthen all the muscles equally and in a balanced manner in order to have healthy joints. If you do a particular movement, the primary, secondary, and auxiliary muscles work in tandem. When you work on your muscles the right way, your recovery rate will be much faster.

It is disheartening to see that every time we get an injury, we feel like our life has come to a standstill. Through this section, I want to tell you that almost 90 percent of injuries can be avoided by taking proper preventive action. Of course, the 10 percent is left to fate and we can't do much about it. Be realistic about your fitness goals, don't overdo it, and you'll see that injuries can be prevented.

> I have never had an injury because of my training; it's because of the action that I do in my movies.
>
> —SHAHRUKH KHAN, ACTOR

Prevention is better than cure—so goes the cliché. I truly stand by it. I also believe in treating the pain when you just begin to feel it, instead of letting it progress to a full-blown injury. There is always a higher probability of getting injured when you are into active, intense sports. A lot of times when you are training for a marathon or trekking, you may suffer injuries. When you do something intense, you never know when the body can give up. But with proper care, you can prevent it from happening.

When you suffer from an injury, I don't want your life to come to a standstill. Of course rest it out, follow the doctor's instructions, do breathing and meditation. But ask your doctor when you can start moving. Movement is key—not vigorous exercises but a mild routine like walking or physiotherapy. If an injured person recovers without mild exercising, the muscles around the injured area will get stiff in a shortened position and will remain weak. This muscle then ends up being the weak link. So when you return to your activity, the chain reaction starts. Other muscles start overcompensating and you soon have a muscle imbalance in the body.

On the other hand, being adamant about getting back to an exercise routine without adequate rest is just plain silly. You have to listen to your body and allow it to heal.

EVERY JOINT HAS A 'CORE'

The only core that people know of is the abs and lower back, but you need to understand that every joint has a core. What does the term 'core' mean? For example, if you take the elbow joint, the muscles surrounding the area protect that particular joint. Those muscles are the core of the elbow joint and have to be strengthened equally to protect that elbow joint from impact and injuries. Sometimes people get obsessed about training their core muscles and work only on their abdominal muscles or the lower back. Understand that every joint has a core and every core has to equally be trained in order for that particular joint to take less impact and be injury-free. This is the only way to have optimum skeletal health. It is imperative that we work on those muscles to keep the joint flexible and healthy.

I spoke to Dr Aijaz Ashai, one of the country's most respected physiotherapists who trains sport stars such as

Sachin Tendulkar and Mahesh Bhupathi, on all the areas of the body that are prone to injuries and he shared his valuable insights on it:

Neck

The neck (cervical spine) is composed of 7 cervical vertebrae held together by ligaments which provide stability to the spine. The muscles in the neck allow motion and support for the weight of the head. However, because it is less protected than the rest of the spine, the neck can be vulnerable to injury and disorders that produce pain and restrict motion. For many people, neck pain is a temporary condition that disappears with time. Others need medical diagnosis and treatment to relieve the pain.

Core of the neck joint: the cervical and trapezius muscles. These are the muscles you need to strengthen to maintain flexibility of the neck region.

Common ailments, problems, and injuries

Osteoarthritis: can harm the joints in the neck and cause severe stiffness and pain. Osteoarthritis typically occurs in the upper neck area.

Cervical Disk Degeneration (Spondylosis): The cervical disk acts as a shock absorber between the bones in the neck. In cervical disk degeneration (which typically occurs in people ages 40 years and older), the normal gelatine-like centre of the disk degenerates and the space between the vertebrae narrows. The cervical disk may also protrude and put pressure on the spinal cord or nerve roots when the rim of the disk weakens. This is known as a herniated cervical disk.

Do not confuse this with spondylitis, which is inflammation of the vertebral joints caused either due to excessive strain or ageing.

People use the terms 'spondylosis' and 'spondylitis' interchangeably. While they are both painful conditions that affect the spine, they are in fact quite different. Such people make the mistake of doing the same exercises for both spondylosis and spondylitis when they shouldn't.

Since there is inflammation in spondylitis, you must never exercise those muscles till the pain subsides. A lot of women suffer from spondylitis. They cook and stir for long periods of time, and their muscles are not strong. Their neck muscles become stiff and hence, the spondylitis. On the other hand, spondylosis is the degeneration of the joint due to age or muscle weakness, so you must do exercises to strengthen the muscle.

Solutions

FOR SPONDYLOSIS:

Isometric neck exercises, isometric shoulder girdle exercises, and then stretching. Never do stretching when you start the exercises. Start with isometric strengthening because there is a lot of lactic acid accumulation in the muscles. When you do isometrics, you release the lactic acid and your muscle becomes stronger and the circulation is maximized. But when you try to stretch it, you might sprain or pull the muscle fibres; that causes more pain. So rather than starting with stretches, you first need to do isometric exercises and then the stretches.

FOR SPONDYLITIS:

No exercises are recommended till the pain and inflammation goes away. Once the pain subsides, start with simple stretches to increase flexibility, not with strengthening exercises.

Shoulder

The shoulder joint is the body's most mobile joint since it can turn in many directions. But this advantage also makes the shoulder an easy joint to dislocate. There are two joints at the shoulder—the glenohumeral joint which is the main ball-and-socket junction and the acromioclavicular joint located in the shoulder at the junction of the collar bone and the shoulder blade. Most shoulder motion occurs at the ball-and-socket glenohumeral joint, but for full motion of the shoulder, the acromioclavicular joint should also be functioning normally. The three bones of the shoulder are the arm bone (humerus), shoulder blade (scapula), and collarbone (clavicle).

Core of the shoulder: The triceps and serratus anterior—these are the muscles that you need to strengthen to prevent injuries to the shoulder joint.

Common ailments/injuries

Shoulder dislocation: A partial dislocation means the head of the upper arm bone (humerus) is partially out of the socket. A complete dislocation means it is all the way out of the socket. Both partial and complete dislocation can cause pain and unsteadiness in the shoulder. Symptoms include swelling, numbness, or bruising of the joint.

Sometimes dislocation may tear ligaments or tendons in the shoulder or damage nerves. A common type of shoulder dislocation is when the shoulder slips forward (anterior instability). This means the upper arm bone moved forward and down out of its joint. It may happen when the arm is put in a throwing position.

Solution: Visit a doctor immediately. He may suggest putting the shoulder in a sling. Plenty of rest is needed. The sore area can be iced 3 to 4 times a day. After the pain and swelling subsides, you can begin rehabilitation exercises under the supervision of the doctor or a physiotherapist. Begin with gentle muscle toning exercises. Later, weight training can be added. If shoulder dislocation becomes a chronic condition, a brace can sometimes help. However, if therapy and bracing fail, surgery may be needed to repair or tighten the torn or stretched ligaments that help hold the joint in place.

Frozen shoulder: It causes pain and stiffness in the shoulder. Over time, the shoulder becomes very hard to move. Though anybody can have a case of frozen shoulder, it most commonly affects people between the ages of 40 and 60, and occurs in women more often than men. Bad posture can also lead to frozen shoulder. The shoulder capsule thickens and becomes tight and, stiff bands of tissue, called adhesions, develop. Sometimes, there is less synovial fluid in the joint.

Solution: The doctor will check the range of motion of the shoulder joint. Most of the time, the condition improves with physical therapy which includes stretching or range of motion exercises for the shoulder. Sometimes heat is used to help loosen the shoulder up before the stretching exercises. Stretches, such as forward flexion of the shoulder and the crossover arm stretch, help to loosen the muscles of the shoulder. Yoga asanas like Gomukhasana (cow's face pose), Garudasana (eagle pose), and Dhanurasana (bow pose) prevent further discomfort and lower the risk of disability. Make sure that your posture is right and incorporate strengthening exercises in your routine.

Rotator cuff injuries: As I mentioned in the biomechanics chapter, the rotator cuff is a group of muscles and tendons attached to the bones of the shoulder joint, providing stability and facilitating shoulder movement. The muscles and tendons in the rotator cuff group may be damaged in a variety of ways. Damage can occur from an acute injury (say, a fall or accident), chronic overuse (like throwing a ball or lifting), or

Before You Start Exercising

from gradual degeneration of the muscle and tendon that can occur with ageing. In weightlifting, these muscles are often injured during bench presses and shoulder presses. You may have torn your rotator cuff if you feel a persistent ache or a sharp pain within your shoulder at a specific point during the exercise. You are unable to raise your arm in front of you and over your head. An irritation or swelling in the tendons could lead to a condition known as rotator cuff tendinitis. Both these injuries lead to pain, swelling and stiffness on moving your shoulder. Muscle strengthening and stretching exercises are crucial to make the joints stronger and flexible.

Solution: If you lift any weight over 5 pounds, your rotator cuff magically shuts off and your big muscles like deltoids take over. So ideally start with light weights or a resistance band. If you have injured your rotator cuff muscle, stop performing any exercises that cause you pain or soreness in that area. Skip all overhead pressing movements for as long as your healthcare provider tell you to. You shouldn't exercise while you have any pain. Lighten up your load on the bench press to a weight where you don't feel any pain. Limit the distance when you move the bar—so elbows should be parallel to the shoulder at a 90 degrees angle and don't try and bring the bar close to your chest because you are taking the muscle beyond the range of motion. Or skip the exercise altogether. You can strengthen your shoulder by isometric shoulder exercises, wall push-ups, internal and external rotation exercises (with band), and shoulder blade retraction (with or without band).

Elbow

The elbow joint is made up of three bones—the humerus (bone in the upper arm) the ulna, and the radius (two bones in the lower arm). The bony protrusions at the bottom of the humerus are called epicondyles. These bones are connected by muscles, ligaments, and tendons to form the elbow joint. Together, these structures allow us to use our elbows like a hinge to bend our arms.

The elbow is not as susceptible to injuries as weight bearing joints like the knee and the hips, but it still has its fair share of injuries. The elbow can be affected by typical injuries, such as broken bones and stress fractures, as well as inflammation, such as tendonitis, arthritis, and bursitis.

Core of the elbow joint: pronator of the forearms and the biceps. You have to strengthen the biceps and the forearm muscles.

Common injuries

Golfer's Elbow: In making a golf swing, the medial tendon gets stressed, especially if a non-overlapping (baseball style) grip is used. Many people, however, who develop the condition, have never handled a golf club.

Tennis elbow: It is a condition where the outer or lateral part of the elbow becomes sore and tender. Avoid an ultrasound when you suffer from tennis elbow. Due to the ultrasound light, the covering of the bone gets burnt, further leading to periostitis, an inflammation of the bone.

Solution: Tennis elbow and golfer's elbow have nothing to do with the elbow and everything to do with the wrist. Basically it is a scar tissue which you need to release and then strengthen. Chronic overuse stresses the extensor muscles, causing tiny tears in the tendons that result in inflammation, tenderness, and pain. The body responds by forming scar tissue that helps shore up the area. Repetitive injury prevents the scar tissue from healing properly, so it remains weak and painful. The scar tissue fibres get adherent and almost connected to each other. So whenever you try to do any activity, it becomes very painful. Try to release soft tissue with friction therapy

Before You Start Exercising

and then put ice on that. You need to begin with stretching slowly the muscles and then strengthening.

What most people do is that they try to strengthen it initially and it becomes tighter. The scar tissue doesn't stay forever if you mobilize it. This is called friction treatment.

You should ideally do isometrics to strengthen the forearm and wrist muscles, so the injury doesn't reoccur. Once you increase the elasticity of the fibre, you strengthen it. Don't ever massage any muscle which is inflamed. Tennis elbow occurs when repetitive stress causes small tears in the tendon that connects the extensor muscles—which run between the wrist and elbow—to the lateral epicondyle. So you should first and foremost rest it. Let the inflammation subside and then strengthen it.*

Wrist: It is the part of the hand that is nearest the forearm and consists of the carpal bones and the associated soft tissues. The eight carpal bones are arranged in two rows. One row of carpal bones joins the long bones of the forearm (the radius, and, indirectly, the ulna). Another row of carpal bones meets the hand at the five metacarpal bones that make up the palm.

Core of the wrist: Wrist flexors, extensors, and the palmar group of muscles form the core of the wrist joint.

Common injuries

Wrist Pain: It occurs when the ulna gets strained, and the strain comes on the muscle. You may have overloaded the muscle. Some people injure their wrists by bending them too much while lifting weights. The wrists should be aligned with your forearms. A lot of yogasanas put a lot of pressure on the wrists because most yoga practitioners have this tendency to dig their wrists into the mat, thus causing pain.

---

* If you want to read more, I recommend this link: http://www.hughston.com/hha/a.seven.htm

Solution: To prevent wrist injuries, do regular wrist curls and reverse wrist curls. Those with mild wrist pain as a result of asanas should focus on how they place their hands on the mat during a weight-bearing asana. The attempt should be to bring pressure to each of your fingers, down to the tip. Once the weight comes on the palm of the hand, the pressure will come off the wrist. Engaging leg muscles in the exercise is also a good trick to help take off some of the load from the wrists.

> STRAIN VS. SPRAIN
>
> Strain is different from sprain. Strain comes from the word 'stress', which means you overloaded the muscle which is why there was a strain. When you pull or overstrain the ligament, it becomes a 'sprain'. So you use ice on the ligament when you sprain it. Again when you want to get back to an exercise programme after a sprain, you first need to strengthen the muscle and then start lifting heavy weights.

Spine

The back provides support for the head and the trunk of the human body. It's one of the strongest areas of the body and allows for a great deal of flexibility and movement. A key area of the back is the spinal canal, which provides nerves to the rest of the body. This is the reason why you may feel radiating pain in other parts of the body when a spinal nerve gets pinched.

For example, if you suffer from radiating pain which goes all the way from your buttock to the back of your leg, you may be suffering from sciatica. The pain is produced by an irritation of the nerve roots that lead to the sciatic nerve. The sciatic nerve is formed by nerve roots that run from the spinal cord into the lower back, it goes down through the buttock, and then its branches extend down the back of the leg to the ankle and foot.

Before You Start Exercising

The spine consists of many vertebrae, which are bony structures that make up its skeletal formation. Vertebrae are separated by disks which cushion and support each vertebra. The human spinal column is made up of 33 bones—7 vertebrae in the cervical region (C1 to C7), 12 in the thoracic region (T1 to T12), 5 in the lumbar region (L1 to L5), 5 in the sacral region (S1–S5), and 4 in the coccygeal region which are fused together(Co). At the very bottom of the spine is the sacroiliac (SI) joint.

If you have a history of back problems, you can just as easily throw out your back reaching for an apple as you can while lifting weights in the wrong way. But because the weight constantly challenges your ability to stabilize your spine and maintain good form, it increases the risk of triggering an old injury or developing a new one. Always take precautions for your lower back when you lift weights. The trick is to pull your abdominals inward. By tightening your abs, you create a natural girdle to support and protect your lower back.

Most common abnormalities of the spine: You need to check if you have an abnormal curvature of the spine. A healthy spine has a gentle curve, which helps absorb stress from body's movement and gravity. The spine should ideally run down straight in the middle of the back. When abnormalities occur, the natural curvature of the spine is misaligned as in the case of:

Lordosis: Spine curves significantly inward at the lower back. The cervical spine (neck) and lumbar spine (lower back) have an inward curvature that is medically referred to as lordosis or 'lordotic' curvature where the spine is bent backward.

Kyphosis: Abnormally rounded upper back. The most common symptoms for patients with an abnormal kyphosis are the appearance of poor posture with a hump appearance of the back or 'hunchback,' back pain, muscle fatigue, and stiffness in the back.

Scoliosis: Sideways curve to the spine. The curve is often S-shaped or C-shaped. Scoliosis can occur from design at birth or from rotation or an abnormal twisting of the vertebrae from pain.

The normal curves of the spine allow the head to be balanced directly over the pelvis. If one or more of these curves is either too great or too small, the head may not be properly balanced over the pelvis. This can lead to back pain, stiffness, and an altered gait or walking pattern.

Solution: The doctor will perform a physical examination and recommend getting an X-ray done. Physical therapy is the treatment given—usually strengthening exercises for the back. In some cases, surgery is also recommended.

Core of the spine: It is the hip, lower back, and abdominals. This is the core that is most known and talked about. These are the muscles you need to train if you want to protect your spine and prevent pain.

Common ailments, problems, and injuries

LOWER BACK PAIN:

Almost 90 percent people develop compression of the vertebrae in the lower back, specifically in L4 and L5 (lumbar region), because that's where the load comes when you lift the weights. If you lift one kg, after bending the knees in the correct biomechanical manner, the pressure on the spinal disc is one kg only. But if you lift one kg, bending directly from the spine, it gets multiplied to 100 kg.

That's why when you see women picking up a baby which may be just 3–4 kg, they say they have got a catch. The weight of the baby itself is minimal. But it's the way you lift it; if you lift the baby incorrectly the weight can amount to 400 kg on the spinal disc. That's why you feel the compression most on L4 and L5.

Solution: The most common complaint by people who have lower back pain is that they have been advised to sit straight. But this makes the back pain worse. The basic cause of this is that if you look at the biomechanics of the spine, it is curved. So if you sit rod-straight, you will not just hurt your lower back but even your upper back muscles will get stiff. So the more you keep it relaxed, the better is the spine. The more you try to keep it erect, the more you are causing an overload on the spine. (Refer to page 345 for ways to strengthen your lower back.)

What you need to do is to strengthen the erector spinae—the back muscles—as well as your abdominal muscles and muscles of the hips. When you enter a gym or a workout area, do you often see people working on their abs and neglecting strengthening their lower back? This often leads to an injury, some kind of pain or a catch. You need to do your training in the reverse order—strengthen the back first and then the abdominals. Lower back muscles work in tandem with the abdominal muscles, located directly in front of them, when you bend your spine backwards or when you move your torso. Strengthening your lower back muscles will help prevent muscle imbalance in your core. Strong lower back muscles ensure that your spine is protected when you do any sort of abdominal muscle exercise.

Now you know that doing umpteen amounts of abdominal exercises will not help you lose belly fat. It's an overall diet, cardio and weight training programme that will give you results. The best thing is to work on the spine first. This way you can strengthen the spinal muscles and then you can do everything else.

The bridge pose is a good exercise that will strengthen an unstable back. Many times, you see people who are fit and regular gym-goers, but they have pain on the side of the back. It's not in the middle of the back but on the side—the pain of the sacroiliac joint pain. These two joints are the base of the back. If they go up and down, your whole spine moves, it gets deviated and your muscle balance gets imbalanced. So what we need to do is strengthen the glutes so that your sacroiliac joint stays in position.

Bridge Pose: Lie down on your back, bend both knees to 90 degrees, push the back up and hold the position. Once you hold it for 10 counts, squeeze your glutes. Tighten them. This will help your sacroiliac joint to stay in position. For the advanced bridge pose, you lift one leg straight at the same level as the other knee. Keep it there. You will see maximum people dropping to one side. If they are able to hold it, that's when the stability starts. If that is stable, the pressure on the spine is minimum. This is the best and foremost exercise for back strengthening. If you start with this, you can move on to other back exercises like Superman, one leg raises, and dead lifts.

What you need to do is start with the hip and back strengthening exercises first and then work on the abdominals to strengthen your core. When you do any back or hip exercise, you need to hold your lower abs in. That's how you automatically work on the core. Even when you are sitting, if you tuck your lower abs in, your back becomes straight. If you leave it, your back is relaxed. If you want to straighten your back, you need to just push your abs in, not pull your back up. When you do any exercise, tuck your lower abs in to support your back so that there is no strain in your lower back. This starts working on your core.

Twisting moves like axe chop with a medicine ball/resistance band will help strengthen your lower back.

Alexander technique is another method that helps cure back pain. This technique teaches you the appropriate amount of effort required for a particular activity, It does not involve exercises or treatments, but an active exploration of the mind and body that helps you discover new balance in the body by releasing unnecessary tension.

Slip disc (also called herniated disc): The discs in the spine are protective shock-absorbing pads between the vertebrae, also called as inter-vertebral disks. Although they do not actually 'slip,' a disk may move, split, or rupture. This causes the inner gel portion of the disk to escape into the surrounding tissue. This leaking, jelly-like substance can place pressure on the spinal cord or on an adjacent nerve. This is what causes severe pain, numbness, or weakness either around the damaged disk or anywhere along the area supplied by that nerve. This condition is also known as a herniated disk, ruptured disk, or prolapsed disk. The most frequently affected area is in the low back, but any disk can rupture, including those in the neck.

You can suffer a slip disc due to several reasons. It could be as a result of ageing, where the discs lose elasticity. It could also be an injury from improper lifting, especially if accompanied by twisting or turning; and excessive strain forces associated with physical activities.

The pain often starts slowly. It may get worse when you sneeze, cough, or laugh. Sometimes, it gets worse when you stand for long and for some people, the pain increases at night time.

Solution: You should consult your doctor for any neck or back pain significant enough to limit activity or if it lasts more than a few days.*

Hip

The hip joint is a ball and socket joint located where the thigh bone meets the pelvis. The top of the thigh bone (femur) is a

---

* Go to this link for more information on slipped disc injury: http://www.nhs.uk/Conditions/Slipped-disc/Pages/Treatment .aspx

ball that fits into the socket formed by a cavity in the pelvic bone. Ligaments form a capsule around the joint that holds the ball in the socket. The capsule contains synovial fluid that lubricates the joint. The bony joint surfaces are coated with cartilage, important for friction-free movement. In sports, we usually talk about the hip flexors; the skeletal muscles which help flex the femur to pull the knee upward.

It is very important to strengthen and stretch your hip flexors. One of the muscles involved in flexing the hip is the rectus femoris, which is situated in the middle of the front of the thigh. When you are sitting and if you want to clear the ground by lifting your feet, you need to use your rectus femoris or your hip flexors.

Core of the hip: is the gluteus medius and maximus

Common injuries

Groin injuries: When people don't exercise to strengthen the hip flexors, they suffer from maximum injuries in the groin because the rectus femoris stays weak. You then start applying pressure on your knee and even the knee is not able to take the load. The pressure then comes on to the groin, which leads to an injury. All those who run on the roads, get either shin pain or groin pain, due to tight hip flexors.

The groin is a drainage system in our body. We have four drainage systems in our body— four channels—two on the axilla and two near the groin. If our waste products don't move from these areas, you feel stiffness, pain, and often, swelling occurs.

THE BODY'S DRAINAGE SYSTEM

The lymphatic system is a one-way drainage system which transports a colourless fluid called lymph, which consists of fluid, plasma proteins, fats, cells, and debris in the form of dead blood cells and bacteria, from the tissues to the blood vascular system.

Before You Start Exercising

> It is also part of the body's immune system, filtering the lymph as it passes through the lymph nodes, killing bacteria by the action of blood cells called phagocytes, and producing another form of blood cell called lymphocytes. Nodes are usually situated in groups, such as are found in the axilla (armpit) or inguinal area (groin).*

Solutions: You have to stretch the groin and strengthen the hip. For the groin, I would mainly recommend the adductor stretch—which is crossing the leg (the butterfly stretch). Breathe and relax into the stretch, don't flap your legs too hard. Be careful with the knee. People tend to push it down.

No form of training is wrong—neither yoga nor Pilates or gym training—it's the way you do it. If you are going to do it wrong, it will lead to an injury. For the hips, you need to work on the gluteus medius. For the back and the groin, you need to work on the adductor muscles, which are the gluteus maximus and the hip flexors.

An effective exercise to stretch the hip flexor muscle is the Pigeon Pose Stretch.

1. From Downward Facing Dog: Step both feet together and bring your right knee forward between your hands so that your outer right leg is resting on the mat.
2. If your hips are more open, inch your right foot away from you. Make sure your left hip is always pointing down towards the mat.
3. Stay here with your hands resting on your right leg or walk your hands out in front of you, allowing your torso to rest over your right knee.
4. Hold here, breathing into any areas of tightness and tension for at least five breaths.

---

* http://www.lymphoedema.com.au/LymphaticSystem.html

5. Then place your hands on the mat in front of you, tuck your left toes, and step your right foot back. Step your left foot forward, and repeat the Pigeon Pose Stretch on the left side.

Hip replacement surgery: The gluteus medius is the muscle you need to concentrate on. Do not do any exercises which will move the hip in the pre-op rehab of hip replacement surgery. You need to do isometric contraction exercises—contract the gluteus muscle, hold it for ten counts, and relax it. Increase the count to make it stronger. Once the surgery is done, even if you lose 40 percent of the strength of the muscle, you have already built up 100 percent strength and your 60 percent strength is still there. But if you don't strengthen in pre-op and you go for a surgery, you lose 40 percent plus you lose other strength too and you have to start from zero and the recovery period is longer.

The best thing is the isometric contraction of the surrounding muscles. Now for the hip, you can't do anything else except the isometric exercises. For the knee, you can work on the hip. For the hip, there is no other specific joint that you can work on. You can exercise the muscles around the hips, work on the glutes, and do the bridge pose. This keeps muscles stronger. Once you get the surgery done, it is already strong enough to take the load. So the recovery in walking is much easier.

It is important to work on the gluteus medius muscle. You see many people limp after a hip surgery. That's not because of the shortening of the bone or because of the surgery. It's because the gluteus medius stays weak, it stays like that forever. They are not able to strengthen it later on and they keep on limping. So strengthening of the gluteus medius muscle, pre-op, is a must.

For more on hip injuries, I highly recommend this link: http://www.coreperformance.com/knowledge/injury-pain/hip-injuries.html

Knee

Remember the plane of movement of the knee that I talked about in the chapter on biomechanics? The knee has two articulations—flexion which involves bending the joint resulting in a decrease of angle and extension which is straightening the joint leading to an increase of angle. It's the largest joint in the body. It acts like a hinge joint connecting the thigh bone (femur) in the upper leg to the shin bone (tibia) in the lower leg. In front of these bones lies another bone—the kneecap (patella). The knee joint is enclosed in a fibrous capsule containing synovial fluid which provides lubrication to the joint. This capsule is called bursa, and they are found in several major joints in the body.

There are four main ligaments in your knee—two outside the joint (medial and lateral collateral ligaments), and two inside the joint (anterior and posterior cruciate ligaments). This complex set of ligaments helps stabilize the knee, which bears a substantial part of body weight when you run and walk. Additionally, the knee has menisci which are horseshoe-shaped pads of cartilage that act as a shock absorber between the bones. Individually, they are known as lateral and medial meniscus.

Core of the knee joint: The lower ends of the quadriceps and hamstrings, and the upper end of the calf muscles. You need to strengthen these muscles to keep the knee joint strong.

Ligaments in the knee: Ligaments stabilize the joints. The muscle is supposed to take the entire body weight, the ligament holds joints in position, and the joints are supposed to take the least pressure of the body weight. If your muscle is weak, then pressure comes on the ligament. That's how you sprain the ligament. For instance, if you do a rotational movement of the knee, you will twist the knee and injure the ligament. When you twist it, you sprain or tear the ligament. Ligaments are not supposed to take the weight; they are supposed to stabilize the joint in a biomechanical way. If you change the biomechanics, the ligament is going to tear. That's why you need to strengthen the muscles which are the core of the joints. Only then will the muscles take the entire body weight and there will be less impact on the ligaments and joints.

Haven't you seen that it's mostly footballers who face knee problems? This is because they have all kinds of movements on the field. It's not just straight running, they run laterally too which lead to osteoarthritis injuries. Any kind of sportsperson can suffer from these injuries because they do multi-dimensional movements while they are playing, which can cause a sprain to the ligament. Now you cannot tell them not to do this kind of movement. Their only way out is that their fitness levels and muscle strength has to be higher than an average person.

Also, IT band syndrome is the leading cause of lateral knee pain in runners.

You cannot strengthen ligaments. You can strengthen the muscle that covers the ligament. Remember it is the muscle that takes the load, not the ligament. Once the muscle is strong, your joint can take the load even if you are turning and twisting. Everything is balanced by the muscle. Starting from the hip, your gluteus medius has to be strong to support you when you twist, turn, squat, or jump. If that muscle is weak, the pressure comes on the other muscles which are not supposed to take that load in the first place. They overcompensate for the weak gluteus medius and they come under pressure. This leads to muscle tears and joint pain and this causes injury.

To prevent injury to the knee, you need to strengthen mainly the quadriceps muscles (the thigh muscle). You have to increase the power of the quadriceps muscle because it is the loading muscle. When you sit, stand, run, you climb—you

Before You Start Exercising

use your quadriceps muscle. But at the same time, you need to have flexibility of the hamstring muscle. You don't need power in your hamstrings, you need strength and flexibility.

When you climb a step, you put load on one leg but the other leg pushes you. That's when the hamstring comes into action. If your right leg is on the step, and your left leg is down, it's the left leg that needs to push you up, otherwise you will cause too much of load in the right leg. If your hamstrings are strong and flexible, the chances of injury in your quadriceps is less.

When you want to sprint, the load comes on the gluteus maximus. So if you want to run faster, you want to strengthen the gluteus maximus.

If your knee is injured, you don't have a full range of motion. If you try to work on that, you will tend to damage it more.

So if you need to do something with the knee, you need to work on the hip and calf muscles. People always ask me why I make them work on the other muscles when it's their knee that's hurt. My answer to them is that load gets shifted from the hip joint to the knee joint. And if one's calf muscles are not strong, this is a double whammy to the knee. If the calf muscles and one's hip is strong, minimal is the load on the knee.

Arthritis is the most common disease that affects bones in your knees. The cartilage in the knee gradually wears away, causing pain and swelling. Injuries to ligaments and tendons also causes knee problems.

The best strengthening exercise for the knee is to walk on the beach. When you walk on the sand, especially in water, there is a natural resistance offered to your muscles from the sand and water. This helps to strengthen your muscles. Everyone likes running on concrete roads, no one runs on the beach. They land up having shin and knee pain. The solution is running on the beach for 2–3 weeks and then begin running on the roads. You will see a difference. Try to run on softer terrain. You will build up endurance, stamina, and strength.

Common Knee Injuries: The most common injury is the medial menisci injury—the inner side of the knee. It can happen with squats and lunges. This happens due to strain or misalignment during exercise. The other cause can be twisting of the knee or weak muscles in the thigh. Overloading of the joint and pain may be caused due to too much of running on a hard surface. If you do too many lunges and squats while your muscle is weak, it can injure your knee, regardless of age, though the risk is higher in those above 40. Solution: you need to strengthen the muscles. Non-weight bearing exercises where you hold and contract. You can also use the maximum weight and less reps method to strengthen that muscle. If you have to go for a surgery, you need to work on the knee and hip muscle. Strengthen the quads and hamstrings so there is minimum pressure on the medial aspect of the knee joint. By now you know that the gluteus medius is the main muscle which takes the weight and the load off the body.

ACL injury—anterior cruciate ligament injury: (it is behind the knee and holds the knee joint in position). Injuries occur when there is a lot of knee twisting in any heavy kind of sport or in turning movements. If you are running and turning, say while playing soccer, rugby, squash, and tennis—that can cause an ACL tear. Then the knee starts buckling.

In India, we don't do much of hamstring strengthening. ACL injury is maximum as most of the time the strain comes on that. To avoid it, we have to do hamstring strengthening exercises.

Solution: Once a ligament injury happens, you have to go for surgery if it is completely torn. If only a few ligament fibres are torn, then you can go for strengthening. You start with hamstrings, calves, and then move on to the gluteus maximus and finally, the quadriceps muscles. In other ligament injury cases, we start the quad strengthening first. In an ACL injury, we start with the hamstrings first.

Before You Start Exercising

If it is completely torn, you can't do anything except go for surgery. If it is only a partial tear and functionally they are fine, then you can just strengthen muscle.

Dr Ashai says, 'A famous cricketer had an ACL tear but is still playing cricket—Yuvraj Singh. In 2004, I checked his knee. We decided we won't go for surgery; we will do rehabilitation. From that day he has never had a problem. Many people say if you don't go for surgery, you will suffer from osteoarthritis of the knee. Remember it is only for people who don't strengthen the knee.'

If people strengthen the muscle groups around the knee, there will be no degeneration of the knee. If you don't strengthen it, the other part of the cartilage also starts decaying. If you strengthen the muscle, minimum erosion happens and so you can save the knee joint.

It used to take six months for people to recover from this surgery, and now it has come down to four months. Sportspeople need to take a break for four months. They do upper body exercises, gym training with sitting exercises, hydrotherapy, core strengthening—there are a lot of options to continue their exercises. Breathing and meditation exercises (done either on a chair or while lying down) is also highly recommended.

What if you are 'knock-kneed'?

'Genu Valgum' (knock-kneed)—where your knees are moving inwards—is a condition often seen in women with big hips and thin legs so that when they walk, the knees rubs against each other, creating a lot of pressure. The chance of osteoarthritis is a lot more in these cases. What we tell them is that they need to work on their hips so that the pressure is felt most on the hips and minimum on the knees. At the same time we do the VMO Training (Vastus Medialis Training) for the quads. We tell them to do the training for the Vastus Lateralis for then. They have to strengthen the outer side of the knee. We usually work on the inner side of the thigh but in this case, we work more on the outer side of the thigh. That is biomechanically correct. So once the biomechanics is corrected, they walk straight.

Sore knees: Pinpointing the source of the problem can be difficult with knee injuries because the injury can come in many varieties, and have many different causes. Runners walkers ward off many common knee injuries by performing quadriceps exercises. If any leg exercise causes you pain, skip or modify it. Some people try to protect their knees from injury by wrapping them in yards of bandages.

Solution: To help protect your knees, make sure that you strengthen both your front and rear thigh muscles. Stretching is also helpful in keeping all the muscles that surround the knee loose.

For more on knee injuries, visit this site: http://www.knee-pain-explained.com/common-knee-injuries.html

Ankle

The ankle joint is a hinge type joint that participates in movement and is involved in lower limb stability. It's formed where your leg meets with your foot. The ankle consists of three bones: the tibia (one of the lower leg bones), the fibula (the other lower leg bone), and the talus. There are four major ligaments in the ankle—the deltoid ligament, anterior talofibular ligament, the posterior talofibular ligament, and the calcaneofibular ligament. Your ankles and feet are an important part of everyday movement because they support the weight of your entire body. They are prone to overuse, injuries and ankle foot pain from incorrect posture.

Core of the ankle: is the calf, tibialis anterior, and the peronei.

Common injuries

Ankle sprain: Most people have twisted an ankle at some point in their life. But if your ankle gets swollen and painful after you twist it, you have most likely sprained it. Ankle sprain occurs when one or more ligaments of the ankle is torn or partially torn. The ligaments of the ankle hold the ankle bones and joints in position. They protect the ankle joint from abnormal movements—especially twisting, turning, and rolling of the foot. Ligaments usually stretch within their limits and then go back to their normal position. When a ligament is forced to stretch beyond its normal range, a sprain occurs. A severe sprain causes actual tearing of the elastic fibres. Years ago, when people had a sprained ankle they put a cast. It's not like that anymore. Now, patients insist on physiotherapy.

Solution: See your doctor to diagnose a sprained ankle. He or she may check your X-ray report to make sure you don't have a broken bone in the ankle or foot. A broken bone can have similar symptoms of pain and swelling. For a mild sprain, RICE method is good enough (Refer to page 266). The doctor may suggest physiotherapy. Resistance bands can be used for mild rotations when the injured ankle can bear weight mildly, so that we get the ankle to stabilize slowly. People with flexible hips and knee joints recover faster from ankle sprain. So develop flexibility in joints to avoid getting an ankle injury.

Wobble boards and BOSU ball are much more advanced forms of strengthening the muscles around the ankle. They should only be used once you have fully recovered and your doctor and trainer give you the go-ahead. For more details on ankle injury, this is a great site to visit: http://www.nlm.nih.gov/medlineplus/ankleinjuriesanddisorders.html

Achilles Tendonitis: It occurs when the tendon has been overstressed or overworked. Two most common causes are lack of flexibility and overpronation. This is usually caused by sports, especially if an athlete suddenly changes the intensity or amount of exercise. Tight calf muscles and lack of flexibility can also cause stress to the tendon. As we get older, our tendons become less flexible, which is why middle-age athletes tend to be more susceptible to Achilles tendonitis. Poor athletic equipment or a sudden change in footwear can also cause Achilles tendonitis.

Solution: X-rays and occasionally, an MRI, are needed to evaluate a patient for tears within the tendon. If there is a thought of surgical treatment, an MRI may be helpful for preoperative evaluation and planning. Treatment of Achilles tendonitis begins with resting the tendon to allow the inflammation to settle down. In more serious situations, adequate rest may require crutches or immobilization of the ankle. There are different treatments for Achilles tendonitis, including ice, manual therapies, medications, injections, and surgery.

DIFFERENT REHABILITATION METHODS

Hydrotherapy: It's exercising in water with the healing force of the water jets—the resistance makes your muscles and joints stronger. Nowadays, they have underwater treadmills and spinning bikes where you are submerged in water, waist-deep.

Combo unit: This is the latest medical technology. If you want to do rehab as soon as possible without putting any pressure on the joints, the combo-machine can be used. You can start strength training using this unit on the first day after your surgery. This is known as contraction strength training. The machine helps to contract the muscle—we call it combo machine. There are different modes—there is a strengthening mode, an isometric mode, and a kinetic mode.

Hydrocortizone Injections: You have to do pre-op rehab before going for these treatments. You have to do 140 percent strength training in the gym because post these injections you lose 40 percent strength of the ligaments. That's why we recommend to not give these injections to anyone who is above 45–50 years of age. They will be able to strength train as much. But in South Africa and Australia, cricketers strengthen the muscles first and then they take it.

Dr Ashai says, 'I met Javagal Srinath and he said "They put me on hydrocortisone but they never put me on strengthening exercises after that. Since I did not experience pain, I continued to play cricket. I never expected my joint to get damaged".'

Injecting Gel in the Cartilage: It has never been successful. Once the ligament is torn, it never heals. It is only the menisci—the inner side which is the cartilage—where the circulation takes place. There is no blood circulation in the ligaments—once it is torn, it is torn. You have to suture it and strengthen the muscle in order to save it. Around 20 percent of the inner circle where the circulation is can get healed. The outer surface does not heal. If menisci is chipped and it does not get healed, then they do arthroscopy on the knee; this is only when the knee gets locked. If it is not getting locked, you don't need to operate it. Only muscle strengthening is required.

Inflammation: This is where most Bollywood stars go wrong, because they do not rest first and strengthen the muscles. You need to take rest and use ice to heal it. You need to strengthen the muscle and only then get back to the treadmill. Dr Ashai says, 'Suniel Shetty's daughter would get inflamed knees every now and then when she was shooting for her movie. She was training with a well-known trainer. I told her to get off the training programme and strengthen the muscle first before she goes on to her dancing moves. She never had pain after that.' If you strengthen the hips, you avoid the vicious cycle of pain. For Bollywood stars, it's the pressure of performing day after day—they do not give their joints and muscles time to rest and recover. Hence this leads into serious knee issues which reoccur and eventually they need a surgery.

After the inflammation subsides, start strengthening exercises. In this phase, use cables. Put the cable strap around your ankle and perform hip exercises. Resistance bands can be used. Tie the bands around your ankles and walk sideways. This will help strengthen your gluteus medius muscles.

IT bands (iliotibial band) exercises are a must. The iliotibial (IT) band is a tough group of fibres that run along the outside region of the thigh. The following IT band exercises help to strengthen the knee:

Side stretch: Stand with your left foot crossed in front of your right, and lean your upper body to the left with your hands overhead. Lean as far as you can without bending your knees.

Leg Lift: Lie on your side with your elbow on the floor. Lift your upper leg up about a foot and return to the starting position. Do 20–30 on each side.

Backward T Stretch: Stand, feet together, facing a wall about 6 to 12 inches away. Hold your arms to your sides like you're forming a T. Without bending your knees, reach down and back as far as you can with your right hand.

RICE: For mild injuries, RICE is the best way to help speed up the recovery process. It stands for Rest, Ice, Compression, and Elevation. To fully understand how this works, let's look at each one individually:

Rest: Your body's first reaction is to begin the repair process by stopping the bleeding by forming a clot around the injured tissues inside your body. You need to rest the injured area to allow the clot to be formed.

Ice: When applied to an injured area, it has a numbing effect that reduces pain and offers temporary relief.

Compression: Applying some type of compressive wrap to an injured area can greatly reduce the amount of initial swelling.

Elevation: Refers to keeping the injured body part in a position higher than the level of the heart. For example, if you have sprained your ankle, you should prop your foot on a small pillow while lying down. When your leg is raised, gravity works to reduce the swelling and relieve pressure from the injury.

After you have completed the RICE process, you ask yourself, 'Now what?' You will always understand how your body feels. Is the pain good or bad? Does it hurt a lot or has the swelling subsided? After a minor injury, swelling should be reduced within the first couple of days and a gradual return to activity is recommended. If you are still in pain and have significant swelling for more than a day or two, you need medical assistance.

If the swelling has subsided, work on gaining full range of motion by lightly moving the injured body part and stretching to a comfortable range. Next, begin to strengthen the area with normal daily activities and then progress to sport activities.

When you are injured, it's not the end of the world. Always look for activities that will not tax your injured area to move around. You can gauge your recovery by pain—eventually the pain will subside.

Ice Baths: Sportspeople like hockey players or cricketers who play intensely for many hours can suffer from muscle soreness. They usually soak themselves in ice cubes in a bath tub. They know that soreness is good because muscles are being developed. So a quick relief is required. These ice baths cause blood vessels from forming waste products in that specific area. So the area starts warming up again and this helps the healing process happen better. But this is only for athletic players.

Heat: If you suffer from arthritis pain, you can use a heating pad or hot water bags. But for sports injuries, you need to use ice. Heat can be used when pain persists for a couple of months. Ice is used for swellings while heat is used for aches and pains. For chronic injuries you need to apply ice. Later, when scarred tissue is formed, heat can be applied so that the range of motion gets better.

Sometimes you realize that when you get a pull, you get temporary relief when you put a hot water towel or bag. That's because the hurt maybe in a muscle deep inside. Just a bottle won't help because the heat is limited to an outer area. Deeper scar tissues need ultrasound machines.

Heat is also good if you have had an injury and have recovered. Suppose somebody is going back to the sports field after they have recovered from an injury, then it's okay to use a hot towel or a hot water bottle to help prevent the muscle from further exertion. Muscles are supple. So you need this kind of superficial warm up. This has to be done before exercise, not after. Do not use heat on a fresh injury.

Massages: They will definitely make you feel better post-workout. They don't help in speeding up recovery but will give you temporary relief. They just make you relaxed but don't take away your injury. If need be, if you are a sportsperson, it is better to go to a sports massage therapist or a chiropractor. Many elite athletes consider sports massage as an essential part of their training and recovery routine. These athletes report that a sports massage helps them train more effectively, improve performance, prevent injury, and recover quickly. Do not do a deep tissue massage—it may just cause more damage.

Tapes: Taping and strapping techniques are commonly used by physiotherapists, athletic trainers, and sports therapists in the treatment, support, and prevention of sports injuries. Tapes are used to give extra support and reassurance to injured joints and soft tissues. Various taping and strapping materials can be used depending on the type of tape job required. Different taping methods are used for problems with different anatomical locations.

Sports injuries are on the rise these days. Simply put, a sports injury is one that occurs as a result of playing sports, exercising, or accidents. Such injuries are mainly caused by trauma, direct impact, or overuse of a particular body part. Sports trainers or coaches are hired these days to assist in the recovery.*

By now you know that with proper knowledge, you can prevent the chances of getting an injury. But if you do get one, there is no reason why you should stop living. With specific strengthening and flexibility exercises, it is possible for the injury site to come to its original functional state in no time. So use this chapter to heal from an unwanted injury and move on!

---

* If you want to read more on sports injuries, visit this link: http://www.pponline.co.uk/encyc/0181.hm

3

Programming

Dance walking, body barre, antigravity yoga, hot pilates, gravity surfing, core fusion, urban rebounding, boot camp, flywheel indoor cycling, arial silk, warrior fitness, masala bhangra, burlesque dancing, kama sensual yoga, yoga with your dog, yamuna ball body rolling, kiwisweat, cheerfit dance cardio, booty bounce, boxercise, fencing, rock-climbing, fit wall, body pump, body balance—the kinds of exercise classes are endless.

There are so many different exercise training methods out there. No wonder people are confused about how to work out and what to do. Most people join a new aerobic class without evaluating their own fitness levels and medical history, body type and shape, their fitness goals or their age, just because their neighbour or a friend—or better still, a celebrity or a famous actor—lost weight after doing it.

There is too much of an information overload in the fitness world. Many a times, people sign up for classes and then never show up, or they jump from one class to another. Then they wonder why they injure themselves and never get the body they want in the first place.

Do you know why people don't have a healthy and fit body, even after doing endless workouts? It's because they focus mainly on cardiovascular activity, which is any aerobic activity such as running or cycling that will help improve the consumption of oxygen in the body.

Think about it. You want to lose weight. One fine day, you decide enough is enough and enroll in a gym. You start your exercise programme by hitting the treadmill. You lose a kilo in a month, but you are not happy. Your trainer tells you to run harder and faster. You then not only do endless hours of cardiovascular activity, you also starve yourself. At the end of three months, you have a body which is still not toned, you have severe pain in your knees, and you look haggard. Depressed with how things are going, you then give up your exercise programme and start binge eating. Now you are not just back to square one, you are worse off! All you have to show for months of sweat and toil is an acute joint pain, sallow skin, and a few more kilos than what you started off with.

Do you want to know why? Because doing excessive cardio is a dummy's solution to losing weight! How long do you want to continue being a dummy?

To make sure that you will never harm your body like this again, I want to lay down some hard facts.

First, let's get the premise right. When you say you want to lose weight, what you're really saying is that you want to lose that unattractive 'fat'. It's important to get this fact right. You want less flab, you want more definition, you want to be fit, and you definitely don't want injuries.

THE SECRET TO BURNING FAT

Any cardiovascular activity, if done with certain intensity, does burn fat but the effect stops the minute you jump off that treadmill, elliptical trainer, or the recumbent bike. Instead, if you build muscle through weight training, you burn fat all day long.

This is a very important point to understand. For example, if you do 1 hour of cardio and 1 hour of weight training, you may burn more calories during your cardio session and less during your weight training routine. However, overall the total number of calories burnt in weight training will exceed that of cardiovascular exercise because the body continues to burn calories throughout the day, even after you have stopped lifting the weights.

This is because muscle is an active tissue that burns calories 24/7, even as you sleep, eat, or perform simple activities like combing your hair or brushing your teeth. Imagine muscle mass to be a slow fire in your body that is burning calories all day long. The more muscle you have, the more you stoke the fire, and the more calories you burn.

So wouldn't it make sense to build muscle to boost your fire-burning capacity or metabolism when it is the single largest calorie expenditure process in your body?

DO THE MATH, LOSE THE FAT

Sure, any cardiovascular exercise will help you lose weight, but it will not help you lose fat fast. Not as fast as weight training does. Here's an interesting fact—one pound of muscle burns 6.5 calories per hour while one pound of fat burns 1.2 calories per hour. You need to burn 3500 calories to lose a little less than half a kilo of fat. On an average, you will burn about 150–200 calories if you run for half an hour on the treadmill. This, of course, varies with body weight and intensity. But what I am trying to say is that it is a very small amount of calories burnt. Cardiovascular activity does help burn calories but when fat loss is your goal, cardiovascular exercise alone does not work.

That's the biggest weapon I am giving you to lose the fat—
BUILD MUSCLE.

> I have weight-trained ever since I was 18-years-old. Everybody seems to think that cardio is going to get you to lose a lot of weight. But weight-training really converts fat into muscle and it is proven that it shows faster results and actual weight loss and toning. I think for women also, as they get older, weight training is amazing to keep your muscle toned. Your muscles also start responding much slower than what they are used to earlier. The more frequently you are going to keep that memory in that muscle, the better you are going to look for a longer time in life.
>
> LARA DUTTA, ACTOR

HOW MUCH SHOULD YOU EXERCISE?

The most common misconception people have is that they feel if they don't exercise every day, they will gain weight. So they beat themselves up for missing their run or drive themselves crazy if they slept through their weight training session at the gym. Here's what I want you to understand: The opposite is true. You don't have to train that much to get optimum health benefits as well as the body shape and size you want.

Research backs this up. A study published in the journal *Medicine & Science* in *Sports & Exercise* in the US shows that a more relaxed approach to working out is more beneficial than working out almost daily.

Group A: Lifts weights once a week + performs cardio like jogging or cycling on another day (Total of 2 workouts per week).

Group B: Lifts weights twice a week + performs cardio like jogging or cycling twice a week (Total of 4 workouts per week).

Group C: Three weightlifting and three endurance sessions (Total of 6 workouts per week).

The researchers tracked the women's blood levels of cytokines, a substance related to stress that is thought to be one of the signals the nervous system uses to determine if someone is overdoing things physically. They also measured the women's changing aerobic capacities, muscle strength, body fat, moods, and energy expenditure over the course of each week.

By the end of the four-month experiment, all of the women had gained endurance, strength, and lost body fat. The scientists had not asked the women to change their eating habits. There were, remarkably, almost no differences in fitness gains among the groups. The women working out twice a week had become as powerful and aerobically fit as those who had worked out six times a week.

However, the women exercising four times per week were now expending far more energy, over all, than the women in either of the other two groups. They were burning about 225 additional calories each day, beyond what they expended while exercising. The twice-a-week exercisers also were using more energy each day than they had been at first, burning almost 100 calories more daily, in addition to the calories used during workouts.

But the women who had been assigned to exercise six times per week were now expending considerably less daily energy than they had been at the experiment's beginning, the equivalent of almost 200 fewer calories each day. These women complained about how it took too much time. They were physically tired all the time.

The most important finding of this study for me is that less may be more. Quality is better than quantity. Sometimes when you stress yourself out by too much exercising, it has an adverse effect on the body. Your stress hormones hit the roof, your endocrine system goes out of whack, your body goes into self-preservation mode and holds on to fat, and your immune system shuts down. You start getting allergies, colds

Programming

and coughs often, and you generally look gaunt and fatigued. You also run a much higher risk of getting injured. For most, just two intense sessions may not be good enough to meet your fitness goals—ideally four effective, smart workouts will produce the best results.

Exercise is a way of reducing and dealing with stress. Don't do something that gives you stress. Build your exercise routine based on how much you enjoy working out, not because you have to.

TIME OR DISTANCE?

So what category do you fall in—one who works out with a time goal in mind or one who has a distance goal and won't mind however long it takes to accomplish it?

If your're one of those who has a packed schedule in a day, time-based workouts are better because then you'll set a goal of getting the most productive workout in the shortest time period. This form of workout is also best if your objective is to gain speed, or to burn more calories. If you have a specific distance goal to reach in the long-term, you're better off not leaving it up to chance.

I believe you'll see better results, achieve progress, and avoid a plateau if you're able to combine both. If you're working out by distance, try to cover the same mileage in less time each week, so you know you're pushing the pace. And if you're working within a time frame, with each session you should aim to log more miles, lift more weight, or gain more flexibility.

4PF: WHAT'S THAT?

So, let's get down straight to it. How do you go about building an effective exercise programme? If you want to achieve a fit, muscular, lean, athletic, and injury-free body, you have to make sure that you have incorporated the **4PFs** in your exercise programme. Take a body barre class for example. It is considered a full body workout since it combines a number of disciplines like yoga, Pilates, weight training, and ballet barre to tone your whole body while developing balance, strength, and flexibility. The 60-minute ballet-inspired exercise programme is designed to burn fat and calories by combining the various components mentioned. And what's the end result? A beautiful lean body with sculpted, tightened, and elongated muscles. Since body barre improves posture, people even start feeling taller after practising it! I feel body barre is the most complete workout since it combines all the 4PFs. This is not to say you can't dabble in other forms of workout. So if you like doing rebounding, do it twice a week and couple it with body pump twice or thrice a week because that will ensure your full-body workout is taken care of. You need to be smart about your training choices. You can't be living in a humid climate like Mumbai and do a hot Pilates or a hot yoga class just because everybody else is doing it. Be wise and choose a training method keeping your fitness goal, fitness levels, age, body type, and body shape in mind, not because a third person is doing it. The four of fitness, or 4PFs, that have to be in your workout programme are **strength, endurance, flexibility,** and **balance**.

Strength Training: It is the process of exercising with progressively heavier resistance for the purpose of strengthening the musculoskeletal system. It is also referred to as weightlifting, weight training, body sculpting, toning, bodybuilding, and resistance training.

Endurance Training: It is any kind of aerobic activity which builds stamina and endurance levels. It improves the cardiovascular and lung capacity of any individual.

Flexibility Training: It refers to the ability of your joints to move through a full range of motion. Having flexibility in your muscles allows more movement around the joints and helps in better posture, reduc risk of injury, and reduces relaxes the mind and body.

Balance Training: It comprises exercises that are designed to improve ability to withstand challenges from postural sway. Equipments like stability balls, BOSU trainer, wobble boards, and so on—all create that unstable surface which causes more muscles to activate than if you were just standing on a stable surface.

When you incorporate the 4PFs in your exercise routine, make sure that the biomechanics of your body is maintained. Whether it is endurance or strength factor, or your flexibility or balance, make sure that you keep in mind the biomechanics and alignment of the movements (Refer to the chapter titled 'The Way We Move', pg 3). The main message that I am trying to drive home through this book is that your body is a magnificent machine which was built to move only in a certain way—the most optimal way. To chisel the body into perfection, you have work on it the way it's supposed to move—through certain moves. Your body's anatomy including muscles, bones, ligaments, tendons, was designed to move only in a certain way. It's designed to pull, push, twist, squat, lunge, walk, run, and jump. These moves, which come naturally to the body, are called functional moves.

MAKE STRENGTH TRAINING THE BASE

Build a programme which makes strength training the base. In a week, whatever training you do, make sure you do strength or resistance training at least three times a week. Add a cardiovascular routine you enjoy—it could be running, dancing, playing soccer, or other field sports. Make sure you add flexibility training through your stretches and balance. You can add classes like yoga, body balance, body barre, qi gong, or Tai Chi to name a few that will help you increase your flexibility, balance as well as strength. Incorporate balance exercises that are done on the floor—for both beginners as well as advanced fitness enthusiasts. Even martial arts are an excellent way to add all 4PFs. You cannot escape strength training, be it strength, resistance, or body weight training. Without strength training, your muscles will not get conditioned, strong, or ever have good definition nor will your body get compact, fit, and injury-free.

You could lift weights and yoga to get an ideal mix. Or you could do TRX suspension training and combine it with a dance class. You could also do weight training with a body balance or a stretch class. This is what I call fusion fitness. It is fusing workouts together keeping in mind that all the aspects of the 4PFs are incorporated. When you're training, keep in mind the strict disciplines like strength training, yoga, or martial arts which have been around for ages.

The idea is to get all the 4PFs with an emphasis on strength training, keeping in mind the importance of incorporating flexibility and balance. Endurance training is important, but make sure you customize it to your goals and age. For instance, if you are above 40, have never run before in your life, and decide to run a marathon, make sure you condition your muscles first, start a good walking programme, and then advance slowly to running. Otherwise, you are sure to suffer from joint pains and injuries.

While cardiovascular exercise is a great way of burning fat, adding strength training to your workouts will earn you extra calories every day. You'll even be burning extra calories while you're sleeping or sitting on the couch, watching the latest sitcom.

Muscle weighs more per square inch than fat. So your kilos may not change but your clothes will feel baggier and you will soon see a healthier, slimmer, and better-toned reflection in the mirror.

Programming

Building muscle reduces the risk of injury. Strong muscles, tendons, and ligaments are much more capable of withstanding stress, and the improved flexibility gained by strength training also reduces the likelihood of pulled muscles and back pain. It has a positive effect on insulin resistance, resting metabolism, blood pressure, body fat, and colon health which are all linked to illnesses such as diabetes, heart disease, and cancer.

I'm not telling you to start lifting 100 kilos or do crazy amount of chest presses. Start slowly and work your way up. Never force yourself to do any exercise class that you are not comfortable with. Remember that now you are educated about stress hormones—cortisol—and how excess secretion can lead to an increase in body fat and the chances of an injury. So do what you love, balance it out with strength training. Start with baby steps. I promise you that once you start seeing results, you will want to educate yourself further and do more.

WHY STRENGTH TRAINING?

First of all, let's define strength training. It is any exercise that uses resistance to strengthen and condition the musculoskeletal system, improving muscle tone and endurance. 'Strength training' is also called 'weight training' and 'resistance training'.

It's simple logic as to why weight training works more effectively than any other programme.

When you lift weights or use resistance, your muscles contract and they use energy. The more intense the muscle contraction, the more energy the muscles use to perform the movements. Over time, the contractions can become so intense that your muscles will use more oxygen than your body can provide. Your body then works overtime to replenish the oxygen levels as well as nutrients and build good quality muscle. This is the reason why weight training, which involves intense muscle contractions, helps build muscle mass.

Even when we are sleeping, our muscles use more than 25 percent of our energy. When you consistently work on strength training, you will achieve an increase in lean muscle mass throughout your body and increase your Basal Metabolic Rate. In other words, you can actually condition your metabolism to work better and more efficiently even when you are at rest.

The formula is simple: the higher your muscle mass, the greater your metabolic rate wiil be. Imagine a burner inside your body. When you weight train and build muscle, you stoke the wood and start burning a slow fire. As you build muscle, the fire becomes stronger and keeps melting fat round the clock even when you are not exercising. So it's essential to build your lean muscle mass if you want to keep your metabolism at its highest levels.

Adding just half a kilo of muscle will help you keep off an extra 35 to 50 calories a day. This is the reason why men and women who have a muscular, toned body because of a solid strength training routine don't need to really worry if they eat a little more than their calorific needs on a vacation. This is the reason why I don't get worked up if I skip two or three exercise sessions because I have to tend to my son if he is ill. The body forgives you those extra calories or missed exercise sessions because you have built lean muscle mass. And this helps keep the metabolism ticking and prevents fat and kilos sticking to the body easily.

A tip: don't just focus on the weighing scale when you are strength training. It's quite possible that the scale won't budge at all. However, you will notice big changes in your appearance. Your clothes will seem loose or you may feel that your arms are looking more defined.

Muscles are a lot denser than fat. So it's easy to figure out that if you lose body fat, even if you build some muscles, you will end up with a smaller body. But now your body will be firm, toned and tight, not saggy.

The best way to monitor your progress is by a combination of the scale, measurements, and your body fat percentage. Knowing your body fat percentage will tell you how much muscle you are building and how much fat you are losing. If you went by the weighing scale alone, you would not get a right reading and you won't be able to track your progress. If you are losing muscle—a situation we have to avoid at all cost when body fat reduction is the goal—buy a skinfold calliper (See 'Before You Start Exercising' pg 188) and keep a note of the changes in your body fat percentage rather than just focusing on your weight.

THE REASONS YOU NEED TO MAKE MUSCLES YOUR BEST FRIEND

Muscles rev up your body's system: When you increase your power and strength by building muscles, you will immediately experience a boost in your energy levels. Your digestion and elimination processes will improve. You will be in a happy state of mind as your body will release happy hormones or 'endorphins' which make you feel good. Your brain will get a rest from the constant thoughts of work and daily life as you focus on physical exercise. Your stress levels will automatically dip. You will sleep better and you will wake up refreshed.

Muscles keep you healthy: Your cardiovascular circulation and lung capacity increase when you strength train. Researchers think that weight-bearing exercises may induce biochemical changes that improve the body's ability to form bone tissue. Studies have shown that consistent strength training can increase bone density and prevent osteoporosis. In people at high risk of diabetes, strength training can decrease blood sugar levels. It also reduces arthritis pain because strong muscles help support and protect joints. Building muscle also promotes weight loss, which reduces pressure on your joints.

Muscles burn fat: Your body fat percentage will automatically reduce once you start weight training. You already know that lean muscle mass gives your metabolic rate a big jump. It's like putting a big bonfire in your body. The more muscle you build, the more fire you stoke. You want to keep this fire burning brightly so that you can melt away your body fat even when the body is at rest. Your blood pressure lowers with just as little as 4 kilos of weight loss.

Muscles give your body the best shape: Muscle is much denser than fat. This is the reason why when you build muscles, your body gets tight and firm and your clothes look good on you. Unless you pump your body with steroids, you will not develop unnaturally large muscles. This is true especially for women who are scared to pick up weights.

Muscles keep you young: Building muscle can literally turn back your genetic clock. By making your body work harder through weight training, you force it to stay younger. Muscle and connective tissue are our body's supporting structure. As we age they deteriorate unless given regular stimulus. Studies have proven that regular and progressive weight training activates our body to repair and regenerate.

Muscles make you confident: When you build muscle and develop the discipline of weight training regularly, you will gain a giant boost in confidence and self-esteem. You will walk taller, you can wear clothes you want with ease, and you will be able to use your body more efficiently in daily movements. Gone will be the person who is insecure and troubled by routine aches and pains. You will notice that you will do all other daily activities with ease.

Programming

> The one difference I have felt when I started training is that I feel much more compact. I feel tighter, I feel fitter, I like the way my body looks, even though it was always thin. But now it looks more athletic which I like. I also feel more energetic even though I may have slept for only 4–5 hours. I was a lot more lethargic earlier. These are the changes that have happened to me, which is why I think I like the fitness aspect of it.
>
> PRIYANKA CHOPRA, ACTOR

MEN-O-PAUSE: MUSCLES KEEPS ANDROPAUSE AT BAY IN OLDER MEN

Andropause is the male counterpart of female menopause. Usually this affects men who are more than 40 years of age. During andropause, the testosterone levels in a man's body begin to dip. Men then begin to experience symptoms of andropause such as low sex drive, decreased energy, problems in sleeping, nervousness, a reduction in motivation, or a loss of interest in some activities they once enjoyed.

During andropause, the most common change in older men is sarcopenia—the loss of muscle mass that occurs with ageing. The consequences of sarcopenia are decreased muscle strength and power and neuromuscular impairments that affect balance. This can lead to an increased risk of falling and developing fractures. For older men who wish to improve or maintain muscle mass, experts say that resistance training is more effective than simply taking hormone therapy to boost testosterone levels.

THE TRUTH ABOUT TONING

I often hear people say that they want to look toned. What does the term 'toning' really mean?

It means having a lean, fit, and lithe look where the body is compact and tight, and there is no flab in sight. It means that the muscles are not bulky and beefy like a bodybuilder's, but more defined and sharpened.

Toning can be achieved by a combination of weight training and high-intensity conditioning. When several major muscle groups are trained over a period of time in an effective manner, the body burns off fat and builds lean muscle mass. This is what gives the body the sexy, toned, sharp physique.

I have had so many clients and friends who come up to me and say they have lost oodles of weight and got to almost where their goal is. But they are not happy with their body shape. Their body still looks flabby, feels soft and spongy, there is cellulite on their thighs, their arms still jiggle, and their tummy doesn't look toned. It is definitely not the kind of body they were hoping for.

For a body that you can be proud of even when you are naked, you have to strength train. You won't be palpitating about the muffin-tops or the flab on your arms. You don't burn body fat by doing cardiovascular exercises alone. Look around you—you will see that people who do hours of dancing, spinning, running or any kind of endless aerobic classes will have no definition to their body. Yes, your cardiovascular strength improves; your lung capacity gets a boost, and your VO2 Max levels rise. (Refer to 'Endurance Training', pg 229) But you need to add strength training to get muscle definition, slash your body fat percentage, and build strong bones. Now that you know all the benefits of strength training, you know that it has to be a part of your exercise routine.

If you do an excessive amount of cardio—be it dancing or running—and neglect strength training, you are going to suffer from injuries. Strength training protects the joints and the ligaments and strengthens the core. All of this combined prevents injuries in the long run. You will notice that most of the dancers who don't incorporate weight training will have some kind of knee or back pain. Group aerobic classes are the worst offenders. I believe everyone's body is made differently and exercises need to be customized to the kind of body you have. You can suffer from injuries if you strain your body to work out just because others in class are able to do it.

Overtraining with cardiovascular activities is the biggest mistake people do. Killing yourself doesn't mean you will get results faster. Basically, cardio and aerobics are not the solution to fighting body fat. People have this myth that cardio is the solution to losing fat. Even though you will lose inches, you will realize that the fat is still stubbornly where it was. So you need to aim at cutting body fat. Strength training is my biggest weapon to staying healthy and young. It's what makes a person strong inside and out.

SOME MYTHS BUSTED ABOUT TONING!

If I lift heavy, I will become bulky.

Many people are afraid of lifting heavy weights, especially women. What few women realize is that you need to have muscles on your frame in order to get a sexy, toned body. You can't shape bone or fat. Like I said, muscle is your friend; don't make it out to be a monster. Heavier weights, in fact, builds the strength of the muscles and helps boost your metabolism and burn fat. It's really not about lifting heavy or light; it's about working your muscles to fatigue. This is the most effective way of helping you reach your goal of toning your muscles than any other process. The time it takes to reach fatigue with light weights is much longer than the time it takes to reach fatigue with heavier weights. It's as simple as that. If you're like most people who are hard-pressed for time, it makes more sense to lift heavy and then rush back home!

I will achieve the toned, flab-free look if I do loads of cardio.

If you have consistently been hitting the treadmill or pounding the pavement doing miles of cardio, kudos to you, but you are only fatiguing yourself and setting yourself up for injuries. Yes, cardio will help you burn fat but it will not be able to help you build the lean muscle mass you are looking for. This is the reason why people who do endless cardio never have the toned physique that weight trainers have. When you lift weights, you create micro-tears in your muscle fibres. Your body then repairs these tears to build stronger muscles. Note here, I didn't say bulkier muscles. Yes, your muscle size will increase a bit, but unless you are genetically disposed to building muscle or you are pumping steroids, your body will not have Popeye kind of muscles. That requires intense training and lifting very heavy, and a disciplined diet. Bodybuilders put in hours to build their physique, so you need not worry! What you will achieve is boosting your muscle mass, which will help give you the toned physique you are looking for. You have to make weight training a part of your programme if you want to get the toned look.

I will get the toned, lithe muscles if I practice yoga or Pilates.

I am a big fan of yoga; I have been practicing for many years now. Yoga, Pilates, and martial art forms help improve flexibility and balance, and the range of motion of the joints increase. Also in Yoga and Pilates, you challenge yourself when you lift your own body weight. But as your body weight decreases, the challenge becomes minimal. Your body needs to be constantly challenged if it has to build muscle mass. These exercise forms do build a lot of muscle mass, but you need to do it with the right combination of strength

Programming

training and other exercise programmes that challenge your body in different ways.

No exercise form 'lengthens' the muscles. Muscles are of a certain length because they attach to your bones; they cannot get any longer. A wide variety of movements and exercises can help you strengthen your muscles without necessarily making them bigger. In fact, you can develop a lot of muscular strength without your muscles ever increasing in size.

WHY LIFTING HEAVY HELPS YOU GET A TONED BODY?

Understand this. There are two types of muscle tones—myogenic muscle tone and neurogenic muscle tone. You need both for a sexy, toned look and a hard, defined body.

Myogenic tone is the residual tension in a resting muscle, i.e. how hard your muscles are when you are at rest. Myogenic tone is affected by the density of your muscles and is improved by using heavy weights and low rep training workouts.

Neurogenic tone is the level of tension in a muscle in a working or flexed state. That is how hard a muscle is when you are training it or just flexing it. Neurogenic tone is improved due to the effect of lower rep training—less than 7 repetitions.

Lower rep training with heavier weights is by far the best way to get a lean, defined, and tight body. It helps to increase the neurogenic tone of muscles.

Training with heavy weights improves both myogenic and neurogenic tone. When you melt away the fat in the body, you need to build lean muscle mass to get a toned, sexy body. Incorporate training with heavy weights and low reps to get an amazing body.

Genetics determine the actual shape of your muscles. But always remember that you are in control of how big you want to get. You can always modify your routine and stop building strength in the areas you don't want to get bigger. If you approach your training this way and are mindful to the changes in your body, you can sculpt your body the way you want it and get fantastic fitness results.

STRENGTH TRAINING: DIFFERENT METHODS

There are several ways you can strength train at home or at the gym.

- **Body weight:** You can do many exercises with little or no equipment. Functional moves like squats, push-ups, pull-ups, abdominal twists can all be done without any equipment. Yoga and Pilates are other ways to use body weight to strength train
- **Free weights:** Barbells and dumbbells are classic strength-training equipments
- **Weight machines:** Gyms offer various resistance machines. If you have limited space at home, try and invest in a multipurpose gym that allows you to do all workouts in the comfort of your home
- **Accessories like resistance tubes/bands:** It is inexpensive, lightweight tubing that provides resistance when stretched. You can choose from many types of resistance tubes in any sporting goods store
- **TRX Suspension training:** It is a form of resistance training that requires the use of the TRX Suspension Trainer, a portable performance training tool, that leverages gravity and the user's body weight to do several exercises

FUNCTIONAL FITNESS AS A PART OF STRENGTH TRAINING

I want to drive home the message that our bodies are designed to work in a certain way. I want to emphasize that the muscles are designed in such a way that they are all connected to ligaments, cartilages, and to the bones, so you can move, work, and function well in your daily lives. It's not just your big muscles which work; it's also your stabilizing muscles that work in tandem for movement. That is why I am giving you these timeless exercise moves that work on your core muscles and help you function at your optimal best.

When you work all your muscles in the way that your body meant for you to function, you know you are on the right path—and this means doing functional moves like squats, lunges, twists, dead lifts, pushing and pulling moves, walking, and running.

These are a few timeless moves because they mimic everyday activities and help you keep your body functionally fit. I have given you some of the moves below. They focus on building a body capable of doing real-life activities in real-life situations, not just lifting heavy weights in a gym. For instance, squats help you sit cross-legged even as you age, and helps to keep your knees and legs strong and build balance.

Functional moves work on more than one major muscle group. They are not isolation moves but compound moves which integrate your bigger and smaller muscles and make them work in tandem. They help you increase core strength, flexibility and balance, and your overall stamina levels.

It's important that you incorporate these functional moves in your strength training programme. You can begin without weights, advance to weights, and finally do variations with balance equipment.

HOW TO DO A SQUAT

Perfect form is vital if you want to get the most out of this fabulous move. It's easy to hurt your lower back and knee if you don't get it right. Squat exercises make a good conditioning workout, toning your legs while helping you build strength in your quadriceps and gluteal muscles.

MUSCLES WORKED:

- ❖ Quadriceps
- ❖ Hamstrings
- ❖ Glutes

Equipment used:

Squat rack

1. Begin with arms extended in front of you at shoulder level.
2. Make sure your feet are shoulder–width apart.
3. Tighten your abdominal muscles. Lower your body until your thighs are parallel to the ground.
4. Do not lift your heels from the ground. Your position should mimic that of sitting in a chair.
5. Keep your knees in line with your toes without pointing your toes out.
6. Tighten your buttocks and quadriceps muscles. As you lower, breathe in.
7. When you straighten up, exhale.

Dial it down: Take the support of a ledge on a wall and then squat

Pump it up!: Squat with Bar Weight

1. Set the bar in a rack at mid-chest level. Grip the bar with as narrow a grip as possible.
2. Your feet should be under the bar, hip–width apart.
3. Squat under the bar and put it on your upper back. Do not rest it on your neck.
4. Take a deep breath and squat up to un-rack the bar.
5. Take one step back with each leg. Never step forward with the bar.
6. Make a mental check that your head is in line with your torso, chest up and shoulder blades are squeezed together.
7. Initiate the squat by pushing your hips back. Never bend your knees first.
8. Bend your knees while pushing your hips back and down.

Programming

9. Push your knees out to the sides as you squat down. Never allow your knees to buckle in.
10. Squat down so your hips hit at least parallel while keeping everything tight.
11. Reverse the squat by driving your heels through the floor.
12. As you rise, keep your knees out and drive your hips forward.
13. Squeeze your glutes hard at the top.

HOW TO DO A LUNGE

Muscles worked:

- Quadriceps
- Gluteus Maximus
- Hamstrings

Equipment used:

Dumbbells

- **Lunge with dumbbells**

1. Hold a pair of dumbbells and stand up straight. Don't lock your knees.
2. Hold the dumbbells down at your sides. You are now in the starting position.
3. Step forward with your left leg while maintaining your balance and squat down through your hips.
4. Keep your torso straight and head up. Don't allow your knee to track out over your toes.
5. Push yourself back to the starting position by using your heel to drive you.
6. Repeat this movement with your right leg.

Dial it down: Do the same movements without weights

Pump it up!: Do it with Lunge variations.

Reverse Lunge

1. Stand straight with legs about shoulder–width apart.
2. Take one step behind you, so you move into the traditional lunge position.
3. Once you're in the full lunge position, rise back up and step the opposite leg behind the body.
4. You are moving backward doing the reverse lunges.

Lateral Lunge

1. Here you lift one leg off the ground and take a large step sideways.
2. Bend at both knees until your lower body is close to the ground.
3. Rise up once again while you bring the stationary leg to meet the other.

HOW TO DO AN OVERHEAD PRESS

Muscles worked:

- Posterior deltoids
- Triceps
- Trapezius

Equipments used:

- Squat rack
- Dumbbell

1. Position your feet shoulder–width apart. Keep your chest high and elbows in front of the bar.
2. Put the bar on the front of your shoulders with a tight grip just outside your shoulders.
3. Un-rack the bar.
4. Press the elbows forward so that they are in front of the barbell and keep your chest up.

5. Take a deep breath and squeeze your glutes hard to protect your lower back.
6. Start pressing the bar. Tilt your head back so that the bar can pass in a straight line.
8. Press your head through and torso forward once the bar has passed your head.
9. Tense your whole body at the top.
10. Lower the bar to the top of your chest, close to your clavicle bone.

Pump it up!: Seated Dumbbell Military Press

1. Raise a dumbbell to your shoulders. Sit at the end of a bench, with your feet at about shoulder width, flat on the floor.
2. Keep your chest high and your back straight.
3. Press bar to arm's length overhead. Use a slow, steady motion, without swinging.
4. Lower slowly to starting position. It can also be done while standing.

HOW TO DO A DEAD LIFT

Muscles worked:

- Gluteus maximus
- Hamstrings
- Quadriceps

Equipment used:

- Bar or barbell

I strongly believe that both men and women should dead lift. Don't pay attention to anyone who tells you that dead lifts are dangerous. All exercises are dangerous if you do them wrong. Dead lifts, if done with the correct technique, is the best exercise to build your lower body muscles and to get your back strong and to prevent lower back pains.

1. Always start with the bar on the floor. Stand with your feet hip–width apart, bar above the centre of your feet.
2. Grab the bar with an overhand grip just outside your shins.
3. Bend your knees until your shins hit the bar.
4. Arch your lower back, lift your chest, shoulders, back and down, head in line with your spine.
5. Take a deep breath. Initiate the pull by driving your heels into the floor.
6. As the bar comes past the knees, drive the hip forwards.
7. Squeeze your glutes at the top. Do not lean back past vertical.
8. Initiate the lowering portion by pushing your hips back.
9. Keep your lower back tight.
10. Bend your knees once the bar reaches knee level.
11. Keep the bar close to your body at all times.

HOW TO DO A CHIN-UP/PULL-UP

Muscles used:

- Latissimus dorsi
- Brachialis
- Teres major
- Rhomboids
- Trapezius
- Abdominal muscles

Equipment used:

- Pull-up bar
- CrossFit resistance band

The pull-up is the best way to work the biggest muscle group in your upper body—your latissimus dorsi.

Programming

1. Grip the bar hard. Don't take too wide a grip.
2. For pull-ups, a grip just wider than shoulder-width apart works best. For chin-ups, use a shoulder–width reverse grip.
3. Take a deep breath, bend your legs, cross your feet behind you, squeeze your glutes, keep your chest up, look up, and start pulling yourself towards the bar.
4. Once your chin is over the bar, reverse the motion and return under control to the starting position.

Dial it down: Pull-up with a resistance band:

This is not a regular resistance band which physiotherapists use; this is a band is part of the CrossFit exercise equipment called CrossFit Resistance Bands.

1. Take the pull-up bar off of the stand. Slide the handles of the resistance band onto the pole so that it forms one continuous loop. The centre of the band should be on the floor.
2. Insert the bar back into the pull-up stand. Slide the resistance bands to the centre of the bar.
3. Grip the bar with your hands. Extend your hands past your shoulders at a distance of 10 to 12 inches for good form.
4. Place your right foot into the resistance band so that the band is in the middle of your shoe. Holding onto the bar, pull yourself up and put your other foot in the same position, so that you are basically standing on the resistance band.
5. Pull yourself up, and when you release back down, do so slowly, feeling the resistance band push against you as you lower down.
6. As you raise yourself back up, let the resistance band do some of the work as it essentially bounces you back to the top.

7. Step down carefully when you finish your workout. Release yourself down from the bar, still holding your hands as far to the ground as you can get. Step one foot out carefully, and then the other.

Pump it up!: Isometric Pull-ups

Try adding a 30–45 second hold at the end of your regular pull-up workout. Once you are comfortable with the 45 seconds hold, add weights.

HOW TO DO A PUSH-UP

Muscles worked:

- Abdominals
- Deltoids
- Pectoralis major
- Tricpes brachi

Equipment used:

- Mat

1. Assume a prone position on the floor or a mat. Keep your feet together.
2. Position hands palms-down on the floor, approximately shoulder–width apart.
3. Curl your toes upward (towards your head) so that the balls of your feet touch the ground.
4. Raise yourself using your arms. At this point, your weight should be supported by your hands and the balls of your feet.
5. Make a straight line from your head to your heels. This position is called a 'plank,' which is used for various exercises. This is the beginning and the end position of a single push-up.
6. Lower your torso to the ground until your elbows form a 90 degree angle. Keep your elbows close to your body for more resistance.

7. Keep your head facing forward. Your nose should be pointed directly ahead. Draw a breath as you lower yourself.
8. Raise yourself by attempting to push the ground away from your body.
9. Breathe out as you push. The power for that push will inevitably come from your shoulders and chest.
10. Continue the push until your arms are almost in a straight line (but not locked).

Dial it down: You can also begin with your knees down on the floor to make the exercise slightly easier.

Pump it up!:

- **Diamond Push-up:** Bring your hands together in the shape of a diamond. Now do the push-up with your hands in this form. This mainly works the triceps.
- **Superman Push-up:** Do a standard push-up or a basic variation of push-up. When you finish lowering yourself, bend your knee to the side so that it comes to your shoulder. Do individual sets for each leg, or alternate between legs. If done properly, this should engage the core in addition to the upper body.

HOW TO DO THE PLANK

Muscles worked:

- Erector spinae
- Rectus abdominis
- Transverse abdominus

Equipments used:

- Mat
- Swiss ball or balance ball
- Cable machine or resistance band
- Weight plates

Whether you're a beginner or an advanced fitness enthusiast, the plank is a good exercise to add to your workout routine. It helps strengthen the abdominal abdominals along with providing numerous other benefits.

1. On a mat, get down so that you're balancing on the forearms and toes, with the body in a flat tabletop-like position.
2. Keep your neck and spine in the neutral position.
3. Don't let the back and hips drop or rise upwards.
4. Raise or lower your hips to the optimal position where you feel maximum tension in the core and feel no pressure on your lower back.
5. Hold that position.

Pump it up!:

- **Add weight plates to your back:** If you have a training partner, you can ask to add plates to your back for any of the static planks. Generally, a weighted vest works better—the weight won't shift, and it's distributed around your body.
- **Plank on a Balance Ball (for advanced fitness enthusiasts; and to be done under supervision):**

1. Start by getting into the plank position with your forearms on the balance ball and your toes on the floor.
2. Keep your abs contracted and your back straight—you should form a straight line from your head to your toes.
3. Hold this position for as long as you can, without sagging or arching your hips.
4. To increase the difficulty, keep feet close together or lift one foot off the floor.
5. To decrease the difficulty level, spread your feet wide apart for a larger base of support.

PLANK VARIATIONS

Plank with Twist:

1. Get into the plank position with your forearms on the floor, abs engaged, back straight, and toes tucked under.
2. Twist your entire lower body (from the torso down) to the right, keeping your arms, shoulders, and head still, legs and feet together.
3. Hold for 5 seconds, then return to centre.
4. Repeat, twisting towards the left.

Side Plank Row:

1. Position yourself next to a low cable machine (or attach a resistance band, with or without a handle, to a secure low object) and get into the side plank position facing the cable.
2. Grab the handle with your free hand, palm facing the floor.
3. Brace your core and, without allowing your torso to lean forward or backward, pull the cable until it's at or near the side of your rib-cage.
4. Slowly return to the starting position, again keeping your core still and moving only your arm. That's one rep. Do 10 to 12 reps, then repeat on the other side.

Side Plank with Rotation

1. Lie on the right side with your elbow on the floor under your shoulder, and hips stacked.
2. Push hips up, forming a straight line from head to heels; and extend left arm above shoulder.
3. Bring your left arm under your body, rotating the upper body towards the right.
4. Hold for 1 count; return to start.
5. Switch sides and repeat.

HOW TO DO TWISTERS: THE IDEAL MOVES FOR ABS

I do not believe in simple crunches. Using twisting moves engages the obliques, the rectus abdominis, and the other smaller stabilizing muscles. This improves core strength and activates and strengthens all the muscles that help support the spine.

Muscles Worked

- Internal Obliques
- External Obliques
- Rectus abdominis

Equipments used:

- Dumbbells
- Weight plates
- Medicine ball
- Resistance band/plate

Wood-Chop with a Resistance Band/Plate

1. Stand with your feet shoulder–width apart and knees slightly bent.
2. Attach one end of the band to a stationary object and wrap the other end around both hands.
3. Start with your arms up above the shoulder closest to the attachment.
4. Keeping the elbows straight, and pull your hands down, across your body to the opposite hip.
5. Concentrate on using your abdominals to twist from one side to the other. Contract your abdominals at all times.
6. Slowly return to the starting position.

Russian Twist with Dumbbells/Weight Plate/Medicine Ball

1. Sit on a mat, holding a dumbbell with both hands.
2. Hold the dumbbell out in front at the height of your waist.
3. Twist the torso to take the dumbbell all the way to the right, and then to the left.

Pump it up!: Lift your feet off the mat and balance yourself on the buttocks, while performing the Russian twist. Make sure you keep your core tight to avoid straining your lower back.

I must add here that there are many other twisting moves, but I will be covering only these two in the book.

FOR MEN WHO WANT TO BUILD SIZE

When attempting to maximize growth, many people make the common mistake of increasing training volume and intensity. Instead, you should perform fewer repetitions and total sets and rest longer between sets. Follow this broad guideline for your training programme to build bigger, better muscles.

- **Do Heavy Compound Movements:** Dead lifts, bench presses, shoulder presses, squats, and pull-ups are the most efficient for stimulating more muscle growth. Build your workouts around them.
- **Use Isolation Moves For a Specific Purpose:** Isolation movements are for definition, not building muscle mass. Drop the majority of them from your routine except, of course, when training arms.
- **Train to Fatigue with Low-rep Range:** Do heavy weights in the 6–8 rep range to stimulate muscle growth. Avoid high-rep sets, except for warm-ups.
- **Free Weights are the Way to Go:** Cable and machine

moves are not good mass-builders. Use free weights if you want to build size.
- ❖ **Avoid Extreme Cardio:** Don't perform more than three 30-minute sessions of cardio per week. You will achieve two objectives: your cardiovascular performance will improve and you won't burn too many calories which can lead to the loss of muscle mass.
- ❖ **Don't Overtrain:** Keep training sessions to no more than four per week to avoid injuries or fatigue. Muscles grow in the time when you rest. Train four times weekly and try to complete all workouts in 60 minutes or less.

HOW TO EASE MUSCLE SORENESS

When you begin weight training or pump up your routine a few notches by making it more intense, it is normal to experience muscle soreness the next day. You might have a tough time moving your limbs or even climbing down the stairs, let alone heading back to the gym for another workout session. This usually means that you are suffering from DOMS.

Delayed onset muscle soreness (DOMS) is muscle pain, muscle soreness, or muscle stiffness that occurs in the day or two after exercise. This muscle soreness is most frequently felt when you begin a new exercise programme, change your exercise routine, or dramatically increase the duration or intensity of your exercise routine.

Here are some simple and effective ways to reduce DOMS:

1. **Light Exercise:** When you feel like it's a struggle to move and you are tempted to stay in bed, it's better to go for a walk or do light stretches. A little movement helps the body become less stiff because the excess toxins in the muscles get eased out. Breathing exercises can help too as it will allow more oxygen into the muscles, helping them to heal.

2. **Taking an Ice Bath:** This option is not for the fainthearted. Many sports athletes do this—after a hard, vigorous game, take a bath with ice-cold water (about 55°F or 13°C). You will feel your muscles first tense up and then gradually relax as the cold water washes over your body. As a precautionary measure, always take advice of your doctor before exposing your body to sudden temperatures.
3. **Massage:** This may be an easier option for many. A massage will increase the blood flow in the body and help you relax if the muscles are tense. There is a lot of controversy around taking a deep tissue massage to soothe away the soreness as some experts say it may damage muscle fibres. It is recommended that you take a longer massage from a sports massage therapist.
4. **Using Foam Rollers and Tension/Stress Balls:** A foam roller is a long, cylindrical piece of foam, and it is one of the most versatile pieces of gym equipment that can help you work out knots in your tensed muscles. Lie on your back and place the foam roller under the muscle which is most stressed. Roll directly into it and hold it for 30–60 seconds. Start with light, quick motions and progress to deeper rolls. This activates your muscle's proprioceptors and prompts the muscle to reflexively relax. You should never feel sharp pain or any sort of tingling sensation. For a more concentrated effect, especially in your neck and back region, consider rolling on a tension or stress ball (it is shaped like a tennis ball).
5. **Keep Yourself Hydrated:** Tank up on the H2O. Have lots of water to flush out the toxins from your body. Studies show that a cup and a half of tart cherries or one cup of tart cherry juice, without added sugar, can significantly reduce muscle inflammation. The anti-inflammatory and antioxidant properties in tart cherries—and other

fruit juices like grape, pomegranate, acai, blueberry, and cranberry—act as natural NSAIDs (non-steroidal anti-inflammatory drugs, such as ibuprofen and aspirin), reducing muscle soreness.

Ultimately the key is consistent strength training along with the right amount of cardiovascular activity. By now, you know that strength training has to become the base of any training routine you do and that it provides benefits like no other. When you begin seeing your body mould into a beautiful, toned, sexy physique, the exhilaration and the high you will feel will be like no other.

BOOST YOUR ENDURANCE LEVELS

Endurance is the ability of the human body to be resilient under any kind of physical stress. If you can run behind a thief who has stolen your wallet without getting breathless, or if you are able to hike a mountain comfortably, you know your body has high endurance levels.

Endurance training is a great way to get fit because it is challenging, improves the condition of your heart and lungs, and helps in muscle growth. It keeps your cardiovascular system in order and increases your stamina levels.

Endurance training is any kind of athletic training which helps improve stamina, endurance, and overall athletic performance. Sportspeople undergo vigorous endurance training when they prepare for sports events like marathon-running, sprints, field sports, boxing, and wrestling.

This kind of strenuous training helps you raise your lactate threshold. During intense exercise, muscles produce waste products like excessive lactic acid that can contribute to muscle soreness. Too much accumulated waste products can make exercise painful and exhausting. With endurance training, the buildup of waste products in your muscles will eventually reduce. The result will be more stamina and less body fatigue. This also means that you have effectively increased your lactate threshold and decreased your chances of injury.

There are several kinds of endurance training and can be broadly divided into

Aerobic Training: This involves exercises which are done at a pace where the person is pumping enough oxygen and fuel into the body at a sustainable rate.

Why is it important for an athlete?

Aerobic training increases the oxygen transport and utilization in the body while also increasing the strength of the heart and lungs. Any kind of aerobic training must provide a sufficient cardiovascular overload to stimulate increase in the athlete's heart stroke volume and cardiac output.

Why should I do it?

The benefits are endless and include strengthening the hardest working muscle in your body—your heart; raising HDL (good) cholesterol, lowering LDL (bad) cholesterol; and strengthening the respiratory system. Continuous aerobic endurance routines help to improve your oxygen uptake.

Start Slow: Walking, jogging at a slow pace, leisure swim, stationary cycling.

Pump it Up!: Marathon, triathlon, swimming, basketball, football, boxing, track and field events under one mile, soccer, volleyball, and cross-country skiing.

Anaerobic Training: This training focuses on improving how long the body can perform while there is less oxygen being pumped into the muscles. Most types of anaerobic exercises are associated with weightlifting and are described as movements that are carried out 'without oxygen'. This means that at a molecular level, the body cannot provide enough oxygen to accomplish the move. Anaerobic endurance training workouts will push the body near the limit of failure through repetitious, high intensity or short recovery workouts.

Why is it important for an athlete?

A sprint runner or a footballer who has to make a sudden dash across the field uses the body's anaerobic system and has to train to increase the anaerobic threshold levels to avoid fatigue. It helps to increase the lactate threshold, the size of the fast twitch muscle fibres, and the resting levels of ATP and glycogen in the muscles.

Why do I need to do it?

Different types of anaerobic exercises are used to build muscle mass. Muscles that are trained under anaerobic conditions develop in a different way than muscles that are trained for activities that are of a long duration. Muscles bulk up quickly, becoming very strong. This is due to the contraction of muscle fibre.

Start Slow: Any kind of weightlifting activities and functional moves like squats, push-ups, pull-ups, and twisting moves.

Pump it Up!: Advanced weightlifting routines, any kind of sprints like running or cycling, TRX suspension training, jumping rope at a fast pace, or any sport which is a rapid burst of exercise—for example, quick runs between wickets and cricket fielding.

INTERVAL TRAINING

It involves practicing different types of anaerobic exercises such as weightlifting in tandem with aerobic exercises such as cycling, jogging, and jumping rope. It is an efficient way to lose weight and build muscle. Interval training helps improve the heart's ability to pump blood. If you're doing high-intensity interval training and still not seeing results, it's because you're not hitting the right heart rate intensity. To calculate your maximum heart rate, use 220 minus your age.

As a general rule, aim to work between 85 and 90 percent of your maximum heart rate on intense bursts. Then recover for as long as it takes you to get back to 60–70 percent of your maximum rate. Invest in a heart-rate monitor if you can, so that there's less scope of error.

You need to go easy on the recovery to allow your body to expend a close to maximal effort on the next burst.

Why is it important for an athlete?

Interval training leads to an increase in cardiovascular efficiency, as well as increased tolerance to the build-up of lactic acid. These changes result in improved performance, greater speed, and endurance.

Why do I need to do it?

The combination of both exercises is an effective way to lose weight and keep it off for good. More than anything else, it helps you jazz up your exercise routine. Turning up your intensity in short intervals can add variety to your exercise routine.

Start Slow: If walking, add short jogging intervals. Add short sprints if you have been jogging for a while.

Pump it Up!: High Intensity Training (HIT); High Intensity Interval Training (HIIT); Fartlek Training.

HIT A WEIGHT LOSS PLATEAU?
WORK THE DIFFERENT ENERGY PATHWAYS

Endurance training also helps increase the efficiency of the three main energy systems of the body—the ATP–CP system, the glycolysis/lactic acid system, and the oxidative system. When you hit a weight-loss plateau or are unable to increase the speed when you run, the best way to make a change is change the demands you make on the three energy systems of your body.

You can work on your body aerobically or anaerobically. An activity is termed aerobic when the majority of energy needed is derived aerobically. These activities are usually greater than ninety seconds in duration and involve low to moderate power workout intensity. Examples of aerobic activity include running on the treadmill or swimming for twenty minutes, and watching TV. You mainly work on the oxidative system in aerobic exercises.

Your body can also release energy anaerobically, i.e. in the absence of oxygen. Activities are considered anaerobic when the majority of the energy needed is derived anaerobically. These activities are of less than two minutes in duration and involve moderate to high power output or intensity. Examples of anaerobic activity include running a 100-metre sprint, squatting, and doing pull-ups. You work the ATP–CP system and the glycolysis/lactic acid system in anaerobic exercise.

Activities which include aerobic and anaerobic training are CrossFit Training and Tabata training.

CrossFit is a fitness training method which incorporates cardio, weights, plyometrics, and other full body movements into its routine. If you've ever been to a boot camp, you've probably done a light version of CrossFit.

Tabata training is basically another form of high intensity interval training (HIIT). The difference is that while HIIT usually involves strictly cardio exercises such as running, biking, or skipping, Tabata training uses some form of resistance or weights. But the principle is the same in both methods—work hard for x minutes then rest for x/2 (half the time) minutes or variations of it.

Speed Strength Training: It helps develop muscle coordination as well as speed and agility. Speed strength comes from the neuromuscular system's ability to create a large impulse in the shortest amount of time. The stronger you are, the more speed you will be able to generate. This kind of training is usually done by above-average fitness enthusiasts and sportspeople.

Why is it important for an athlete?

This is a quality necessary in many sports—it helps build speed, power, and explosiveness. Speed training can help your body prevent injury, especially during strenuous activity.

Start Slow: Adding sprints while running.

Pump it Up! Plyometrics exercises like leaps over obstacles, squat jumps, vertical jumps with power, sideways one-legged leaps, power skipping; uphill sprints; agility drills. (For more details on CrossFit, Fartlek, and different kinds of training, refer to 'Before You Start Exercising', pg 231.)

ALWAYS PROCEED WITH CAUTION

You should consult a personal trainer or coach to develop an endurance training programme if you are looking for a plan which is suited to a particular athlete and sport. The programme will vary in intensity at various points to keep you in condition without causing damage or injury.

People who have been injured should not plunge back into an endurance training programme soon after recovery. Always consult your doctor or physiotherapist before resuming activity after an injury. The experts may recommend adjustments to the training plan to accommodate healing.

Endurance training can be taxing on the body and you should never just jump into it. Always build your levels slow and steady, and make sure that you listen to your body. If you are attempting a CrossFit class and are uncomfortable with the height of the box jump, it's best to avoid it till you build strength. I was very uncomfortable doing short sprints during the first CrossFit class that I took because I know my body. I realized that weight training, TRX, and yoga would work for me. What works for you may be a different combination. I do feel that a high-intensity aerobics class is best suited to people below the age of 35. After that age, you should ideally do weight training and light cardio, weight training and cardio with a combination of yoga and pilates, and activities that do not stress your joints.

Remember endurance training is fun; it helps boost the 'play' element when you work out and you will feel stronger and leaner. But always exercise caution—slow and steady is the way to go!

RUN YOUR WAY TO FITNESS

Many people who enjoy running enroll themselves for marathons across the country. Marathon running is a great way to improve not just your fitness levels, but your endurance levels as well. Marathons across India, including the Mumbai Marathon, have inspired many to take up running and fitness for life and while this is heartening to see, I feel people need to really educate themselves about the ABCs of running. I still see people practicing on concrete roads without proper warm-up, bad posture, and wrong shoes. Many make a strange thumping noise as they run—a sure-shot sign that they are going to hurt themselves. I see many men running with braces on their knees. Any sort of endurance activity needs to be enjoyed and done with proper technique and education.

Running is a pretty democratic sport—you don't need a fancy gym or expensive equipment. You just need to put on your shoes and run. However, make sure you have weighed the pros and cons of running. If you are a rookie, begin by walking first, building your muscles strength, and then run. Running can impact the joints and cause an injury for life, if not done with the right technique.

Even though my years of training allows me to run like a pro, I prefer to walk–run instead of simply running because when you club the two together and not focus on running alone, it gives your joints a break. If you are not built to run, don't force yourself to run a marathon because it's the cool thing to do since everyone you know has signed up for it. There are several other ways to build stamina in the body—running a marathon is not the only way.

ABSOLUTE BEGINNER'S PLAN FOR A RUNNER

Once you have decided that you want to start a running programme, start by making a proper training plan. Track your progress in a diary or excel sheet on your computer. Always warm-up and stretch before you begin a workout. A good warm-up for runners should start off with a brisk walk or jogging in one place to raise your heart one rate. Loosen and activate your muscles with 5 to 10 minutes of dynamic stretches and form drills such as lunges, skipping, and high-knees running.

First begin by walking 4–5 times a week for 25–30 minutes. Once you can do this easily without being breathless, add jogging intervals of 30–45 seconds in your walking programme at a pace that feels comfortable to you. As time goes on, make the running intervals longer till you are able to run for 30 minutes at a stretch. It is important that you increase the distance that you run and the pace at a slow and steady rate to avoid injuries. After you finish your run, always walk briskly and then decrease the pace till the heart-rate comes down to normal.

Follow a proper cool-down programme where you stretch your lower body muscles and shoulder muscles. Be consistent with your running programme. It's better to run twice a week, every week, than to run half a dozen times one week and then do no running for the next couple of weeks. Also remember to consult your doctor before beginning any sort of training programme. Always wear a heart rate monitor.

MASTER THE RIGHT RUNNING TECHNIQUE

It's essential to master the right alignment of the body when you run. This will keep you injury free and prevent any sort of muscular imbalance.

YOU KNOW YOU ARE RUNNING RIGHT WHEN YOU...

Keep Your Head Straight: Fix your gaze in front of you. Avoid looking at your feet or the ground because this will create tension in your shoulders and neck.

Don't Hunch: Keep your shoulders relaxed while you run. Hunching tenses muscles of the shoulders and chest and allows less oxygen to get to the muscles while running, thus causing fatigue.

Keep Your Hands Relaxed: Don't clench your fists. You should not let them loose either. Keep your arms at a 90-degree angle and swing them to increase or decrease pace as you run. The arm movement should move you forward; don't swing them sideways.

Lean Forward While Running: This helps you land in the middle of your foot and helps you increase power in your stride as you are automatically propelled forward.

Keep Your Hips Stable: Don't rock your hips from side to side. Keep your core tight and your hips forward-facing. This will help prevent lower back and hip pain.

Don't Lift Your Knees Too High: Avoid unnatural movements and bouncy steps. Your knee should lift forward, rather than upward.

Land in the Middle of the Foot: Avoid striking the ground with your heel or toes first. You should aim for a mid-foot strike and your foot should land below your hips—not out in front of you.

Don't Make a Thumping Sound When You Land Your Foot: Your landing should be soft, with minimum impact on the knees. Aim for short steps.

Breathe Rhythmically: Avoid shallow breaths. You need to breathe rhythmically so that your inhalation and exhalation matches your cadence. (Refer to Breathing Technique mentioned below).

> Mastering the right running technique is important. The concept of a high-knee run is very different from running on a treadmill or just going for a run on the road or on the beach. It is really maximizing your stride. You are propelling yourself forward, and in that momentum, to lift your knee really high, and then stretch your leg as much as you can possibly forward before it comes down, just increases the length on each stride. When you watch Usain bolt-run, they did this amazing study where over that 100-metre dash, where people take about 43–44 strides, he ends up taking 40–41. So he just maximizes the reach on each stride that he takes. That is such a gift to have.
>
> FARHAN AKHTAR, ACTOR

HOW TO BREATHE WHILE RUNNING

Research shows that rhythmic breathing while running helps in keeping injuries at bay. Rhythmic breathing involves coordinating your foot strike with inhalation and exhalation in such a way that you land alternately on your right and left foot at the beginning of every exhalation. Most often, runners land on the same foot (either just right or left) when they begin to exhale. When you exhale, your diaphragm relaxes. This creates less stability in your core and so, landing on the same foot makes for a perfect setting for an injury. Rhythmic breathing helps reduce the impact of stress on the foot and the body, because it is shared equally by both sides of the body.*

It's important to concentrate on the way you breathe when you run. Many people don't pay any attention to that. When you concentrate on your inhalation and exhalation, you can achieve centredness by focussing your mind on the activity you are doing and increasing the efficiency of the muscles during movement. Rhythmic breathing is calming and allows you to remain as relaxed as possible, removing any stress which could inhibit your performance.

How to practice rhythmic breathing?

First learn to breathe from the belly (also called diaphragm breathing). Then:

- Lie down on your back on a mat
- Keep your upper chest and shoulders still
- Focus on raising your belly as you inhale
- Lower your belly as you exhale
- Inhale and exhale through both your nose and mouth

Incorporate rhythmic breathing in your running routine

Most runners tend to have a 2:2 pattern of breathing—they inhale for two foot strikes and exhale for two. Some breathe

---

* *(Source: http://m.runnersworld.com/running-tips/running-air-breathing-technique?cm_mmc=Twitter-_-RunnersWorld-_-Content-Training-_-RunningOnAir)*

Programming

in for three steps and exhale for three steps. Both have the same result—the exhalation is always on the same side.

The recommended rhythmic breathing pattern is 3:2, where you inhale for three counts and exhale for two. First practice it by:

- Lying on your back with your knees bent and feet flat on the floor.
- Breathing through your nose and your mouth. As you inhale, fill your belly with air.
- Inhaling to the count of 3 and exhaling to the count of 2.
- Once you become comfortable, add foot taps to mimic walking steps.

You will find it easy now to incorporate it when you run moderately. When you climb uphill or change to a fast pace, you can change the ratio to 2:1, where you inhale for two counts and exhale for 1. Your body requires more oxygen when you increase speed because your muscles are working harder.

Once you start breathing rhythmically, you will notice a difference in your running routines. You will find yourself more focussed, less susceptible to injuries, and will enjoy your running more.

> Breathing is crucial because the moment the breathing technique goes off, you start getting a terrible stitch in your side. That is the first thing that happens. Only when you focus on your breath, you can get rid of that terrible stitch. When you start concentrating on your breathing, then you stop worrying about distance. You stop worrying about how much time you have been running for, because there is a certain kind of meditative quality which applies in yoga or anything else that you do.
>
> FARHAN AKHTAR, ACTOR

POWER MOVES EVERY RUNNER SHOULD DO

It's extremely important that you train your body anaerobically when you take up an endurance training programme. Strength training strengthens all the connective tissues, helping to avoid strains, sprains, and tendonitis. It also reduces or completely eliminates kneecap pain, or 'runner's knee' and helps prevent a whole list of runner's injuries like iliotibial band syndrome, nagging hip and low back pain, shin splints, Achilles tendonitis, and heel pain.

Unlike aerobic exercise—which is of a longer duration and allows your muscles to continue to receive oxygen—anaerobic training involves short bursts that starve your muscles of oxygen. It uses the fast-twitch fibres of your muscles and helps you be faster and stronger. I recommend a combination of functional moves like push-ups, pulling movements, twists, and squats. Functional training helps strengthen weak muscle groups and provides balance to the whole body.

What does arm strength have to do with running? Everything! The faster your arms, the faster your legs are going to be. Lack of upper body strength, not lower, is often responsible for the slowdown towards the end of a run. Running requires that your right arm works in tandem with your left leg, and vice versa in a counterbalancing fashion to propel you forward. When your arms and shoulders tire while you run, your legs automatically slow down and affect your running performance. You need to build upper body stabilization and strengthen your core and increase your muscle mass to boost your athletic strength. Your core is the command centre during running because it controls rotational movements between the upper body and the lower extremities.

I have listed a few sample moves which will help work the hips, the core, the upper body and improve balance and have also incorporated accessories like a BOSU ball and a stability ball because these large vinyl balls add a new dimension to exercise: instability. To counteract this instability, your body, while balancing on the ball, causes groups of core muscles and smaller stabilizing muscles to work in unison. Exercises done on an unstable surface help stabilize your spine to prevent injury to the lower back and hips. These exercises improve foot balance and stabilization and help prevent 'power leaks' while running. When your foot hits the ground, some energy can be wasted if not stable.

Before attempting any kind of training programme, always get a go-ahead from your doctor or orthopaedic. You need to slowly and steadily build up strength and stamina in your body to keep injuries at bay.

The super moves:

1. *Overhead Press on Swiss Ball:* Sit on a Swiss Ball. Start with dumbbells at your shoulders, palms facing in. Press the dumbbells straight overhead, until your arms are straight. Maintain an erect torso. Return to the starting position, and repeat.
2. *Dumbbell Push-up with Back Row:* Place a pair of hex dumbbells at the spot where you position your hands. Grasp the dumbbell handles and set yourself in a push-up position. Lower your body to the floor, pause, then push yourself back up. Once you're back in the starting position, row the dumbbell in your right hand to the side of your chest, by pulling it upward and bending your arm. Pause, then lower the dumbbell back down, and repeat the same movement with your left arm. That's one repetition.
3. *Advanced Bridge with Stability Ball:* Lie face up on the floor. Place your heels on top of the ball, hip–width apart. Place your arms out to your sides to stabilize

your body as you squeeze your glutes, lifting your hips into line between your shoulders and heels. Hold for a slow count of five. Slowly lower back to the starting position.

4. *Medicine Ball Rotation on Swiss Ball:* Hold a 3-8 pound medicine ball and lie with your back on a stability ball, feet flat on the floor, hip–width apart. Raise the ball straight over your chest. Rotating from your hips, twist your upper body as far to the right as possible, keeping the ball in line with your chest. Then immediately rotate to the left. That's one repetition.

5. *Plank:* Start on the floor, resting on your forearms and knees. Step your feet out one at a time, coming into a plank position. Contract your abs to prevent your booty from sticking up or sinking. Your spine should be parallel to the floor, with your abs pulling toward the ceiling. Hold for 30 seconds, and work your way up to one minute as you get stronger. You can add variations like side plank, rocking plank, and up–down plank.

6. *Forward Lunge on a BOSU Ball:* Lunges on a BOSU ball may be stationary or dynamic. In stationary lunges, keep your legs in a lunge position, bending your joints to move your body up and down. Dynamic lunges are more difficult because you are balancing on one foot in the middle of the exercise as you step forward, backward, or diagonally. To perform a forward lunge, position the BOSU in front of you at a comfortable distance for a lunge such that when you lower your body to the floor, your hips and knees form nearly 90-degree angles. Suck your navel towards your back to enhance stability. Your arms should be in front of you to help you balance. Step your right leg forward, planting it securely and fully on the BOSU. Contract your leg muscles and push through your heels to stand up with your feet together. Step forward again with the

same leg or your other leg. Always do the exercise near an immovable bar or machine so you can hold the bar when needed.
7. *Stability Ball Wall Squat:* Position the stability ball between the wall and your lower back. Stand with your feet wider than shoulder–width and about 12" out in front of you. Lean back against the ball and continuously push your body back against the ball as you perform the exercise. Inhale as you slowly lower your body by bending at your knees and hips. Go down until your upper legs are parallel to the floor. Roll the ball between your lower back and the wall for the duration of the entire movement. Pause, then exhale as you slowly return to the starting position to finish one repetition.

Squatting has various benefits for runners, from helping you prevent knee injuries and making you run faster to helping you climb hills with ease and increasing endurance levels.

Knee Exercises for Runners

These knee exercises strengthen all the muscles supporting the knee, including the vastus medialis, and iliotibial band (ITB). You can do this as part of your warm-up or cool-down, or even as a part of your flexibility training programme.

1. *Knee Bends:* Stand a foot away from a wall with your knees hip–width apart and your feet pointing slightly outwards. Slide your back down the wall by slowly bending your knees. Let the knees point in the same direction as your toes. As you come up, focus on tensing the thigh muscles and your buttocks.
2. *Thigh Contractions:* Sit up straight on a chair. Slowly straighten and raise your right leg until straight with your foot pointing slightly outwards. Squeeze your right

thigh muscles and hold this position for 10 seconds. Repeat with the other leg.

3. *Hamstring Stretch:* Sit on the edge of a chair. Keep your left leg bent and straighten your right leg. Place the right heel on the ground with your foot pointing slightly outwards. Bend towards your right leg to stretch your hamstrings. Make sure you keep your back straight and bend from the hip.
4. *IT Band Stretch:* To stretch your right ITB, cross your right leg behind your left leg. Keeping your feet on the ground, lean towards your left side and push you right hip outwards. Don't bend forwards or stick your buttocks out. You should feel the stretch along your outer right thigh and hip.

You can add squats, crossover squats, and lunges if you want to increase the length of the flexibility session as a part of your running programme.

HOW TO STRETCH AFTER A RUN

A proper stretching routine after a run will help you to enjoy your endurance training for life by preventing injuries. Breathe deeply while doing these exercises.

1. *Thigh Stretch:* Grab the top of your left foot behind you and gently pull your heel towards your left buttock to stretch the front of the thigh, keeping the knees touching. Avoid leaning forwards or to the side. Repeat with the other leg.
2. *Hamstring Stretch:* Stand with your right leg just in front of the other and your hands on your hips. Keeping your right leg straight and toes pointing up, bend your left leg. Bend towards your right leg, keeping your back straight.
3. *Calf Stretch:* Step your right leg forward and bend it slightly, while keeping your back leg straight. Both

feet should point forward. Push your left heel into the ground, keeping your left leg straight. You should feel the stretch at the back of your left leg, below the knee. Repeat with the opposite leg.

5. *Butterfly Stretch for Hip Flexors:* Sit with your knees bent so that your feet are flat on the ground. Lower your knees until the soles of your feet are flat against one another. Gently grip the arches of your feet with your hands, one hand on each foot, and rest your elbows on your knees. Slowly press down on your knees with your elbows until you feel a stretch in your hips and inner thighs. You should avoid bouncing your knees up and down, as this detracts from the effectiveness of the stretch. Hold this pose for 10 to 15 breaths and then release.

6. *Lower Back Stretch:* Lie on your back with both feet flat on the floor. Pull your right knee to your chest until you feel a stretch in your lower back. Hold for upto 15 seconds and repeat with the left leg. Then pull both knees to your chest and hold for upto 15 seconds.

7. *Buttock Stretch:* Lie on your back with your knees bent and both feet flat on the floor. Cross your right leg over your left thigh. Grasp the back of your left thigh with both hands and pull the left leg towards your chest. Repeat with the opposite leg.

SECRETS TO RUN A FASTER MARATHON

If you are serious about shaving off those seconds and stepping it up at the next marathon, here are a few tips to beat your personal record.

While Training:

- Add sprints to your training programme: Begin small. Start with shorter sprints and then build up the speed.

- Practice Running Uphill: It increases the flexibility and strength in your muscles and tendons and reduces the risk of injury. Again, start by practicing with smaller inclines on the treadmill and increase it slowly and steadily.
- Incorporate Strength-training Moves: Make sure you mix it up with variations of functional moves like squats, lunges, step-ups, and pushing and pulling movements.
- Practice on the Actual Marathon-route: Familiarizing yourself with the course before the main event will give you an added advantage over other runners and help you run faster.

On Marathon Day:

- Sleep Right: Make sure you have an early night. The better rested you are, the better will be your performance on the day of the marathon. Don't practice running too close to bedtime, a day before; it will keep you awake.
- Eat and Hydrate Yourself: Eat a low-fibre (200–50) calorie meal with a balance of proteins and carbohydrates one or two hours before you run. You could have a tablespoon of peanut butter on a slice of whole wheat bread or almonds and a glass of milk. Find out what works for you. Drink 2–3 glasses of water two hours before you run to make sure you are adequately hydrated.
- Warm-up: Light jogging or brisk walking is recommended half an hour before the race. Dynamic stretches to open up the body will help raise the body temperature and you will be ready to go once the marathon kicks off.
- Start Off Strong and Finish Strong: Research shows that starting the first part of the race at a slightly faster

speed than your normal pace can result in a shorter overall time. For the last few kilometres, increase your pace. Sprint to the finish line, aim for the gold!

FINDING THE RIGHT SHOES

Don't go for the first shoe you spot in a shop just because it is on discount or in your favourite colour. Wearing right shoes is probably the single most important aspect of any kind of endurance training programme. A good pair of shoes can make or break your workout. Nowadays, you get all kind of shoes—for running, walking, and cross-training. So how do you know which one's right for you?

Consider Your Footprint

The trick is to know your footprint first. Here's a simple way—lightly wet the bottom of one foot and step on a sheet of paper. Check the shape of your footprint. If you have a flat foot, you will leave a complete footprint. If your footprint is a very slim version and is cut in more than half vertically, then you have a high arch. A normal foot will show about half the footprint because of the arch of the foot. Once you know what kind of foot you have, you can then buy a shoe with the right fit to address your problems.

Know Your Pronation

Most runners hit the ground on the outside of their heel. The rest of the foot comes down and rolls slightly inward as it meets the surface. This down and inward roll rotation is called pronation. This movement helps your body absorb shock and is important for maintaining the right alignment when running.

However, when the foot rolls in too much, it is called excessive pronation or overpronation and can cause an injury. Overpronation is most common among runners with flat feet and bowed legs. These kinds of runners need shoes with good motion-control properties.

Runners with a high arch tend to suffer from under-pronation. They tend to hit the ground with a thumping sound because their feet are not able to make the inward rolling motion. The recommended shoes are the kinds which have plenty of cushioning to absorb the shock.

Understanding your personal pronation type is crucial to choosing the proper running shoes. When you have a problem with pronation of the foot, visit your physiotherapist. The physiotherapist will assist you with orthotic inserts or arch support insoles which can be put in your shoes to help with excessive pronation. Foot-balance custom insoles support your feet properly in the neutral position to aid in stability and facilitate healthy foot function.

Getting the Right Fit

If you are buying shoes for endurance training, it's very important that you try it out yourself. Telling your relatives to pick out the latest model from abroad without actually trying it yourself is a big NO. You need to know three things—the length and width of your foot and the arch length. All three of those numbers together determine what size you should wear. Each shoe can be made a little differently. A 10 and a half isn't a universal 10 and a half in all shoes.

Most shoe stores now allow you to test-run around in a pair of shoes. The best time to shop is in the afternoon because your feet tend to swell during the day. Your feet tend to change over time so measure both feet, particularly the width, whenever you buy new shoes. And always try the shoes on with the kind of socks you normally wear. Your toes should be able to wiggle when you try on the shoes. They should not feel like they are being pushed against each other. The shoe should hug your heel; you shouldn't feel like the foot will slip out.

Customize the Shoe for your Activity

A shoe made for running is very different from a shoe made for sports like football or basketball. Make sure that you pick up the right kind of shoe for the kind of endurance workout you are doing. Running shoes usually don't provide lateral stability because you move forward when you run. They are made to give you support and stability as you land your foot forward in the running gait cycle. On the other hand, shoes made for field sports are built to stabilize your foot laterally because you move your foot diagonally, forward as well as backward.

Similarly, running shoes are different than walking shoes because when you walk briskly, you tend to have a heavier heel strike. During running, your foot lands heel first. Running shoes need to have more cushioning on the forefoot, while walking shoes should have stiffer rubber to support the heel.

If you do a variety of activities like hiking, running, and walking, cross–trainers are a good choice. But if you are a serious runner, cross trainers are best avoided because they weigh more than the standard running shoes and are not as flexible and well-cushioned. When you start feeling strange aches and feel that the shoes are not supporting your feet, it's time to get a new pair.

Qualities of a Good Running Shoe

- **Fit:** A good shoe must hug your feet like a sock. However, it should not be tight
- **Cushioning:** Shoes should provide enough cushioning to absorb impact to protect joints
- **Light weight:** It should not feel heavy when you run.
- **Flexibility:** You should be able to flex or bend the front of the shoe. This will ease the movement when you push off with the ball of the foot

- **Stability:** A stable shoe controls the inward rolling motion of the foot when you run
- **Breathability:** Shoes that absorb sweat quickly reduce the risk of bacterial or fungal infection

STRETCH YOURSELF TO AN INJURY-FREE AND FIT BODY

An effective fitness programme is more than just aerobic training or strength building. To really reap the benefits of exercise, you need to add flexibility and balance training to the mix. Flexibility is not about doing crazy yoga postures or twisting and turning your body in several directions like a gymnast. A gentle stretch relaxes the muscles, letting them release and grow supple. It helps the ligaments of the body too. As I had mentioned before, you cannot strengthen ligaments, only the muscle that covers the ligament. Remember it is the muscle that takes the load, not the ligament. Once the muscle is strong, your joint can take the load even if you are turning and twisting. Everything is balanced by the muscle.

Flexibility is about taking care of not just your major muscle groups, but also the smaller stabilizing muscles and ligaments which are important to maintain the proper biomechanics of the body.

WHY FLEXIBILITY IS IMPERATIVE

I love observing people in the gym when they are working out. I get upset with the way many people workout day after day, without realizing that they are giving themselves a lifetime of injuries and muscle tears. Almost 90 percent of the people do not do a proper warm-up before and after they begin their workout. I have seen them jump on to treadmills without warming up their bodies. Many a time, I have seen young children play an intense soccer game and their coaches do not train them to condition their muscles—no wonder that the kids suffer from lower back pain, knee joint injuries, shin splints, and ankle twists. Add to that, once they finish their vigorous aerobic activity, they happily go back home without a cool-down. They don't stretch and let their heart-rate come down smoothly and steadily

Warm-ups, stretching, and cool-downs are imperative to maintain the suppleness of the muscles, keep joints strong, and prevent injuries. It is not a waste of time—it helps boost athletic performance and can keep you going longer in your workouts. Even if you have never worked out, you need to incorporate a stretching routine in your life unless you want to end up with a bad posture, joint pains, and shrinking muscles as you age. Yoga and Tai Chi are excellent ways of maintaining flexibility even as you age.

It is important to keep the body flexible, as we were meant to be. Flexibility is about stretching muscles and opening up the body joints to its entire range of motion. We should be able to sit cross-legged, touch our toes, and kick a ball without hurting our knees. But as we age, we lose muscle, strength, and size. This can affect the range of motion of the joints of the body, leading to stiffness if we don't stretch our muscles enough. Other factors also enter the picture—if you spend hours at a desk job, your hip flexors become tight. If you run for hours and do not stretch enough, your leg muscles can become short and stiff.

Stretching is too often neglected by exercisers who are too pressed to fit workouts into their busy schedules. This common mistake can reduce the effectiveness of exercise because better flexibility results in better fitness. By increasing your flexibility, you can improve your ability to move around. You will have less muscle tension and your posture will most likely improve. More importantly, stretching after each workout reduces your risk of injury.

MYTH VS FACT

Most people are fed into believing that stretching can make them longer and leaner. Now I'm not denying that muscle is lengthened when you stretch, but the fact is that the opposing muscle gets shortened in the process. The moment you release the stretch, the muscles come back to their normal position. It's just a temporary effect and it's physically impossible to make your muscles grow longer! Please also keep in mind that stretching burns very few calories. It is more beneficial for increasing your flexibility and range of motion.

> **THE FLEXIBILITY FIVE-STAR: WHY YOU NEED TO DO IT**
>
> ✓ **Improved performance in strength and endurance training:** Flexible joints allow for a greater range of motion and you are able to do your exercises more effectively.
> ✓ **Better posture:** Flexibility improves muscular balance and posture by realigning tissue. This reduces the effort it takes to maintain good posture throughout the day.
> ✓ **Reduces muscle soreness by easing lactic acid build-up in muscles:** After you workout a particular muscle, there will be a substance called lactic acid leftover from the workout. Lactic acid is what causes that tightness and soreness the next day. Stretching actually helps remove excess lactic acid from the muscle.
> ✓ **Prevents joint pain:** Stretching helps prevent joint pain by keeping muscles strong and supple. The muscles protect the joint and prevent it from taking the entire impact of any activity.
> ✓ **Increases blood circulation and nutrients to tissue:** Stretching increases tissue temperature, which in turn increases circulation and nutrient transport. This allows greater elasticity of surrounding tissues and increases performance.

Programming

> ### ALL YOU NEED KNOW ABOUT WARM-UPS
>
> I remember when Melvin, my running coach, and I first started training together on the first few days. I got very excited, did warm-ups and stretches and then running sessions. After a few days, the warm-ups and stretching session became very boring. He told me that most injuries happen because people start taking this part of five to ten minutes warm-up sessions very lightly. They start feeling like one day if I don't do it, nothing will happen. He said that it is THE most crucial thing—to avoid injury, make sure your body is warmed-up and then you have stretched it enough before taking it into a zone where you want to max your potential in any front. He drilled that into my head. So from warming-up to stretches that happened before every single shot, he always made me warm up. He made me stretch again. Then, he made me cool down again. This was before every shot. So there was a tent that was set up on every field that we shot, on every location that we shot. So we could do a five-minute warm-up run before we shot, then he would meet me at the end of the shot and then we would do a cool-down run and go into the tent and do a cool-down stretch routine. In my head, this became a part of my take. So like you prepare yourself for everything—before every take, this is what I HAD to do. This is why there has been no injury whatsoever. Most things that are important are boring!
>
> FARHAN AKHTAR, ACTOR

Why do I need to do a warm-up before a workout?

If you don't want to injure yourself, you have to do a warm-up. It's as simple as that. Warm-up is one of the most important parts of your workout or sports activity. It is any type of low impact activity which is done prior to stretching or any kind of strenuous exercise. The warm-up routine prepares all the systems of the human body by gradually increasing demand on these systems. The goal is to raise total body temperature, elevate the heart rate, and condition the muscles before beginning vigorous activity.

Warm-ups reduce the potential for muscle pulls and joint pains. They also help reduce muscle soreness because higher temperatures and increased blood flow due to warm-up help in the smooth flow of oxygen to the muscles. This prevents the build-up of toxins and waste products in the muscles which can lead to soreness.

How intense should the warm-ups be?

It's not 'One size fits all'. A proper warm-up should raise your body temperature by 1 or 2^0C. There are different kinds of warm-up routines and the intensity needs to be tailored according to the activity you are going to perform.

Passive Warm-up: You increase body temperature without physical activity but by external means such as wearing warm clothes like a sweatshirt or massaging a specific muscle. The advantage of a passive warm-up is that no energy is spent during the warm-up period. However, it is best to use passive stretching in combination with an active warm-up.

Active Warm-up: It can be divided into general and sports-specific warm-ups. The general warm-up uses low intensity movements like walking or slow jogging in one place. It helps increase muscle temperature. Specific warm-up exercises are generally used by weight lifters and sports athletes—the actions mimic the sport or activity they are about to do. For example, a bowler will warm-up using arm swings, which is rotating the arms clockwise and then anti-clockwise to warm-up his arm muscles. This way, he increases the temperature of the specific body part that will be used the most. The simplest way to warm-up is by doing an aerobic activity at an easy pace. If cycling is what you plan to do, start out slowly in a low gear.

How much time should I spend on warm-ups?

This again depends on the activity you are about to take up. A warm-up routine of 5–8 minutes is generally enough to warm-up the body for more strenuous exercise. There are several factors you need to take into account. For instance, if your muscles are sore from the previous day's workout, take time to stretch and ease away the pain. Always make sure to take into account the environmental temperature and the kind of clothing you have worn. Your muscles will warm-up sooner if it is a hot day or if you are wearing warm clothes. Don't spend too much time on warm-ups—say more than 15 minutes. You will end up tiring your muscles before even having begun your exercise routine.

Is warm-up the same as stretching?

No, warm-up is not stretching! You have to warm-up before you begin stretching your muscles. If you stretch your muscles before warming-up and raising your body temperature, your muscles will be cold and more prone to injuries, pulls, and tears. A good warm-up routine helps open up joints to their full range of motion. First, do a warm-up like a brisk walk or jog in one place, raise your body temperature, elevate your heart-rate slowly and steadily and then, begin the stretches.

STRETCHHHHHH!

Now that your body is warmed up, you need to stretch to increase the efficiency and suppleness of the muscles. There are different kinds of stretching:

#*Passive Stretching (Relaxed Stretching):* It is when you stretch a muscle and hold it with an external force, like another part of your body, or with the assistance of a partner or an accessory like a resistance band or a towel. It's slow and relaxed, and is useful to relieve spasms in muscles that are healing post-injury. You can use a resistance band or a towel in case you are not able to touch your toes, or your trainer or a partner could help. You should always check with your doctor first to see if it is okay to attempt to stretch injured muscles. Bringing your leg up high and then holding it there with your hand is an instance of passive stretching.

#*Static Stretching:* Is any kind of stretch that does not use motion. However, it is not the same as passive stretching. In static stretching, you stretch to the farthest point and then hold the stretch for 15–30 seconds. On the other hand, in passive stretching, you are relaxed and make no contribution to the range of motion. Instead, an external force like a partner or an accessory is used to hold the passive stretch so that the effort is less and you are relaxed. When you sit with your legs in front of you and hold your toes with your hand to stretch your leg muscles, you are performing a static stretch.

#*Active Stretching:* Is where you assume a position and then hold it there with no assistance other than using the strength of your agonist muscles (See pg 29 for more information on Agonist/Antagonist muscles). For example, lift your leg up high and then hold it there, without using any other force other than your leg muscles to keep the leg in that extended position. The tension of the agonists in an active stretch that helps to relax the antagonist muscles being stretched. Active stretching increases active flexibility and strengthens the agonistic muscles. Such stretches are usually quite difficult to hold and maintain for more than 10 seconds and rarely need to be held any longer than 15 seconds. Many yoga asanas are active stretches.

#*Dynamic Stretching:* It consists of controlled leg and arm swings that take you to the limits of your range of motion. In dynamic stretches, there are no bounces or 'jerky' movements. An example of dynamic stretching would be slow, controlled leg swings, arm swings, or torso twists. Dynamic stretching is quite useful as a part of your warm-up for an active or aerobic workout (such as a dance or a martial-arts class). Dynamic stretching exercises should be performed in sets of 8–12 repetitions. Do only those number of repetitions that can be done without decreasing your range of motion. An example of a dynamic stretch is a 'knee touch'. To perform knee touches, stand with your feet together. Bring your arms up in front of you at shoulder level. Lift the knee up so that it is parallel to the floor and touches your stretched-out hand. Lower the leg back to the floor. Perform 10 repetitions, alternating the right and left leg.

> **WHY I PREFER AND RECOMMEND DYNAMIC STRETCHES**
>
> I prefer doing dynamic stretches. They are an excellent full body warm-up before any type of intense activity—whether you're about to play sports, or lift weights. Just about every athlete—from runners to cricketers—is required to perform dynamic stretching before exercising as part of their warm-up routine. If you are going to do an advanced-level activity like CrossFit or suspension training programmes like TRX, kickboxing, or rock-climbing, you have to make dynamic stretches a part of your routine too.
>
> ✓ **Condition the entire body for strenuous activity:** Dynamic stretches warms up your body even faster than static stretches. This helps prevent injuries. For example, mimicking a jump rope action or jumping jacks helps elevate heart-rate and pumps oxygen to major muscle groups in the body faster.
> ✓ **Improve kinesthetic awareness:** Kinesthetic awareness is the understanding of where your body is in space and time. For example, if you try to touch the tips of your fingers together on both hands, that's a simple example of kinesthetic awareness. If you jog in one place, it doesn't really prepare you for the different movement patterns you may do on, say, a football field. This is where dynamic stretches help.
> ✓ **Improve flexibility:** Dynamic stretching can help improve the range of motion around the joints in your body to help you perform better in any kind of strenuous activity. This in turn helps in preventing any kind of injury.

#Isometric Stretching: It is one of the more advanced techniques. It involves the resistance of muscle groups through tensing of the stretched muscles. Isometric stretching is quite demanding on the muscle tendons and joints, and therefore, it should not be performed more than once per day for a given group of muscles.

The proper way to perform an isometric stretch is:

- Assume the position of a passive stretch for the desired muscle.
- Next, tense the stretched muscle for 7–15 seconds (resisting against some force that will not move, like the floor or a partner).
- Finally, relax the muscle for at least 20 seconds.

The most common way to put resistance for an isometric stretch is either by applying resistance manually to your own limbs, you can ask a partner to apply the resistance, or use a wall or the floor to provide resistance. An example of using a partner to provide resistance would be to have him hold your leg up high (and keep it there), while you attempt to force your leg back down to the ground. An example of using the wall to provide resistance would be the well-known 'push-the-wall' calf-stretch where you are actively pushing against the wall.

#PNF Stretching: It stands for Proprioceptive Neuromuscular Facilitation stretching. Sounds complicated? It's really not. It's a type of stretching done with a partner which combines passive stretching with isometric stretching. PNF was initially developed as a method of rehabilitating stroke victims. The stretched muscle should be rested and relaxed for at least 20 seconds before performing another PNF technique.

The most common PNF stretching techniques are:

- **Hold-relax (also called the contract-relax):** After assuming an initial passive stretch, the muscle being stretched is isometrically contracted for 7–15 seconds, then briefly relaxed for 2–3 seconds, and then immediately subjected to a passive stretch which stretches the muscle even further. This final passive stretch is held for 10-15 seconds. The muscle is then relaxed for 20 seconds before performing another PNF technique.
- **Hold–relax–contract:** This involves performing two isometric contractions: first of the agonists and then of the antagonists. The first part is similar to the hold-relax where, after assuming an initial passive stretch, the stretched muscle is isometrically contracted for 7–15 seconds. Then the muscle is relaxed while its antagonist immediately performs an isometric contraction that is held for 7–15 seconds. The muscles are then relaxed for 20 seconds before performing another PNF technique.

Example of a hamstring PNF stretch:

- Lie on your back with one leg straight and the other extended and raised off the floor
- Your partner's should slightly push against your raised leg
- Contract your hamstrings
- Stop contracting as your partner attempts to stretch your leg further

PNF stretching is also not recommended for children and people whose bones are still growing. Also like isometric stretching, PNF stretching helps strengthen the muscles that are contracted and therefore, it is good for increasing active flexibility as well as passive flexibility. Furthermore, as with isometric stretching, PNF stretching is very strenuous and should be performed for a given muscle group, not more than once per day.

#Ballistic Stretching: It uses the momentum of a moving body or a limb in an attempt to force it beyond its normal range of motion. This is stretching by bouncing into or out of a stretched position, using the stretched muscles as a spring. An example is bouncing down repeatedly to touch your toes. I don't consider this kind of stretching useful since it can lead to injuries. Ballistic stretching does not allow your muscles to adjust to, and relax in, the stretched position.

HOW TO BREATHE WHILE STRETCHING

It's important to take slow, relaxed breaths when you stretch, trying to exhale as the muscle is stretching. Proper breathing helps to relax the muscles and increases blood flow throughout the body.

The proper way to breathe is to inhale slowly through the nose, expanding the abdomen and not the chest. Hold the breath a moment, then exhale slowly through the mouth. Inhaling through the nose has several purposes including cleaning the air and insuring proper temperature of the oxygen intake.

As you breathe in, the diaphragm presses downward on the internal organs and squeezes the blood out of them. As you exhale, the abdomen, its organs and muscles, and their blood vessels flood with new blood. This rhythmic contraction and expansion of the abdominal blood vessels is partially responsible for the circulation of blood in the body. This pumping action is referred to as the respiratory pump which is important during stretching because of increased blood flow to the stretched muscles improves their elasticity and increases the rate at which lactic acid is purged from them.

DON'T SKIP YOUR COOL-DOWN ROUTINE!

Take time to stretch your muscles after you finish a vigorous workout. Ideally, you should start your cool-down within 5 minutes of a sport-specific activity—at a little more intense level to get your heart-rate down steadily. If you are jogging, begin to cool down by first jogging at a slower pace. The sport-specific activity should immediately be followed by stretching. First perform some light dynamic stretches until your heart-rate slows down to its normal rate; then perform some static stretches. Sport-specific activity, followed by stretching, can reduce cramping, tightening, and soreness in fatigued muscles and will make you feel better.

At the end of your cool-down routine, practice lying down on a mat and relaxing with your eyes closed and body still and loose. This Shavasana (Corpse Pose) will quiet the mind and relax the body. It helps ease the body back to its normal temperature and the oxygen levels also stabilize. (Refer to my first book *I'm Not Stressed* for more techniques on relaxation).

Get the most out of your flexibility training by following these simple guidelines:
- ✓ Always warm up before your stretch. Stretching cold muscles can cause injury.
- ✓ Stretch slowly and gently. Breathe into your stretch to avoid muscle tension. Relax and hold each stretch for 10 to 30 seconds.
- ✓ Do not bounce your stretches. Ballistic (bouncy) stretching can cause injury.
- ✓ Stretching should not hurt. You need to hold on to a point of tension. If you feel pain, take the stretch easier, breathe deeply, and relax.
- ✓ Never skip your cool-down routine unless you want to end up with sore muscles!

- ✓ Some people have stiff bodies, so they need to ease into stretches slowly. Static stretches are recommended for them. On the other hand, some people are too flexible. They tend to hyperflex, i.e. move the joint beyond its normal range of motion. This can cause injuries.
- ✓ When you perform any vigorous activity (like interval training), it is advisable to wear a heart-rate monitor to keep a check on your heart-rate so that it goes down steadily back to its normal rate.

IMPROVE YOUR BALANCE

I have been training for many years now and the one part of training I feel people really neglect is balance, even though it is the most important. Balance is simply the ability to maintain a line of gravity within a base of support with minimal postural sway or collapse. Do you know why most people run with that silly gait, when their hip collapses to the side each time their foot painfully hits the ground? Yes, it's because of lack of balance. Along with good eyes (visual balance) and ears (vestibular balance), you also need to have healthy joints (somatosensory balance) to maintain proper balance. Balance training has a range of benefits and leads to increased inner and core strength, flexibility, limited injuries, and even the right posture!

Good balance enhances performance in all kinds of sports. Have you suffered from a sprained ankle as a runner? You could have avoided the injury if you would have concentrated on balance training because it improves the neuromuscular system. In basketball, improved balance increases the player's movement, speed, and effectiveness on the court. It even helps you jump higher. The next time you want to slam dunk on the field, give balance training a try. As a footballer, the basic trick used is to fake spin in one direction and go in the other in order to fool the opponent. Balance training comes in handy here as well because it helps you improve agility, allowing you to change your centre of gravity without falling to the ground. If you like to do Mixed Martial Arts (MMA), balance training will help you to execute your kicks better.

Stand near a wall. Try standing on one leg without taking any support. Were you able to stand for more than a minute? That's great! But if you started swaying the moment you stood on one leg, you know you are in trouble. Developing good balance is essential when you're training, and it positively impacts your everyday life as well. However, it's an area often overlooked and ignored by fitness enthusiasts and sometimes even trainers.

Just like everybody needs to incorporate a flexibility programme—no matter what their activity level and age— the same goes with balance exercises. Whether you were born with excellent balance or you feel your coordination skills are dipping, practicing balance moves will help strengthen your muscles, better your posture, and improve your neuromuscular coordination.

If you add balance exercises to your exercise routine, everything—from running after your kids to climbing the stairs to even lifting heavy weights—will seem easier. Working with machines at your gym, running on a treadmill, or using the elliptical—all these activities isolate muscles. They force you to stay in a specific position to work only one muscle in one direction at a time, in a linear pattern on a one-dimensional plane. But the ways in which you have to move your body in everyday life are far from one-dimensional. Think of running up the stairs, cooking, twisting to see behind the car when reversing, or even playing a football match at your local grounds!

When you train with balance equipment, you start working not just your major muscle groups but the small stabilizing muscles, simply called stabilizers. Just like how a foundation stabilizes a house, your stabilizer muscles help to keep you balanced and upright when moving. Your stabilizer muscles are not directly involved in daily activities, but they help keep your body steady through isometric muscle contractions. This is the reason why balance exercises are most necessary.

Keeping your stabilizing muscles strong with balance exercises goes a long way in keeping your core strong and in preventing injuries. For example, weak knee stabilizer muscles can lead to injuries such as a torn ACL or meniscus, and weak ankle stabilizers are a primary cause of rolled and twisted ankles.

As we age, our balance skills dip and it is important to keep practicing it. Older people are more likely to trip, fall, and stumble while doing daily activities as the neuromuscular coordination wanes and the muscles become weak. These falls can lead to some scary injuries to the brain, hips, legs, feet, and even damage internal organs.

One of the best ways to improve balance is by practicing simple yoga asanas. Ballet and Tai Chi help too. Here are some of the ways to build a good balance programme.

#Tadasana (Mountain Pose): This is the most basic posture you can begin with.

- Stand tall. Align your feet parallel to each other by placing your heels slightly apart, with the second and middle toes pointing forward.
- Keep your thigh muscles tight without locking the knees.
- Keep your chin parallel to the floor maintaining the length through the neck.
- Let your arms hang loosely. Relax your eyes, tongue and facial muscles.
- Breathe slowly as you hold the pose for 30 seconds.

Note: If you have difficulty balancing, widen your feet a few inches keeping your second and middle toes pointing forward.

#Vrikshasana (Tree Pose):

- Stand tall. Align your feet parallel to each other by placing your heels slightly apart, with the second and middle toes pointing forward.
- Focus on a point in front of you. Lift the right leg to rest the sole of your right foot on the inside of the left thigh. Make sure the left leg is strong, pressing the foot flat into the floor.
- Try to keep the right knee bent at 90 degrees towards the right side. Keep your shoulders relaxed and rolled back and press the chest forward.
- If you feel very balanced here, try the next stage by inhaling and extending the arms over the head. Join the palms together with the thumbs crossed, stretch the elbows straight, and pull the arms upward.
- Hold the pose for 15–30 seconds , if comfortable.
- To come out of the pose, slowly exhale while bringing the arms down and then release the legs back into a standing position.
- Repeat on the other side.

There are several other poses you can perform to improve balance—Ekpadasana (One-Legged Pose), Natrajasana (Dancer's Pose), Utkatasana (Chair Pose), Virbhadrasana (Warrior Pose), and Trikonasana (Triangle Pose) are just a few.

USING BALANCE ACCESSORIES

Balance accessories usually provide an unstable surface that activates the proprioceptive system—the system that tells the body where its limbs are within space. This forces the stabilizers to work harder and helps in strengthening neuromuscular coordination. They are also used by physiotherapists to increase the strength of muscles in the advanced stages of healing. To add instability and get more muscles in the mix, try using the workout tools designed to challenge your balance:

Balance Balls (Exercise Ball, Fitness Ball, Workout Ball or Swiss Ball): It is a large inflatable ball, approximately knee high, typically placed on the floor. It is used to support the body in exercises done in a sitting position on the ball, lying across the ball, or gripping the ball between the hands, legs, or feet. It is the preferred tool to lift weights with, as the instability of the surface helps the core become stronger. The simple act of sitting on the ball forces the core to engage itself in order to prevent the ball from rolling away. The more inflated the ball is, the greater the element of instability.

Always check to make sure that the ball is properly inflated. Choose a ball of the correct size. Size can be determined by sitting on the ball. Ideally, the thighs should be parallel to the floor on the right size ball. Choose the ball according to your height:

4'11" to 5'4" height: 55 cm ball
5'4" to 5'11" height: 65 cm ball
5'11" to 6' 7" height: 75 cm ball

Always make sure you buy the anti-burst model from a good company; you are likely to hurt yourself if you skimp on the quality.

Balance Beam: It is a steel rod which usually runs along the wall or near the mirror in gyms, fitness clubs, or yoga studios. It can be used to practice several balance exercises.

Balance Discs (Dyna Discs, Balance Pads): It helps increase balance in standing exercises. Choose a disc based on the level of difficulty desired but appropriate to your skill level.

Standing on the discs immediately challenges balance due to the unstable surface. Advanced balance work can incorporate balancing on one leg atop the balance disc. They come in different shapes and colours (depending on the softness of the surface). The softer the surface, the more unstable it is—and the tougher it is to exercise with.

BOSU Ball: It is like a stability ball with a flat bottom, creating a half-moon shape. Short for 'Both Sides Up', the rounded, inflated side of the BOSU ball also functions similarly to a balance ball. Standing exercises can be performed with the flat side down standing on the inflated half. Alternatively, you can flip the ball over to increase the challenge by creating a highly unstable surface, balancing with the rounded side against the floor. Make sure to stand near a wall, because it can be extremely challenging. You can injure yourself if you are not careful. This is a useful balance accessory for runners because it helps increase ankle stability—you can use it to perform advance step exercises. But only above-average fit people should train with BOSU balls or you could end up injuring yourself.

Half-foam Rollers: Foam rollers are more typically used for active release of tight muscles, but the half-foam roller functions similar to a balance beam for balance exercises. Standing along the foam roller like a balance beam or standing with the feet perpendicular to the foam roller, both create an unstable surface that challenges the core and lower body muscles immediately.

Wobble Boards: These are similar to balance discs but are made of a rigid material such as wood or plastic. They may be designed to tilt forward or backward, side to side, or provide a full plane of instability with a rounded base. Wobble boards demand a high degree of balance and stability because they are rigid, and often used for therapy of the ankle and knees. Wobble boards are most effective for activating proprioceptive awareness for the coordination between brain signals and movement of body parts.

Remember, you don't need to use fancy equipments to improve balance. Simple things like standing or walking on sand strengthens the muscles and the core because of the instability it provides. You can even practice standing on one leg or performing simple squats to increase your balance levels.

SAY BYE-BYE TO LOWER BACK PAIN!

Most weightlifters and runners suffer from lower back pain and end up bringing their training to a halt. A lack of training in the lower body region (lower back, glutes, hamstrings, hip flexors, and the IT band) is one of the major reasons for poor spinal health. Instead, people focus most commonly on the abdominal muscles. This causes a muscle imbalance in the body and increases the risk of injury. Too often, the lower body region as well as the lower back is neglected because this muscle group is not seen as often in the mirror or as glorified like the other parts of the body like the arms, the chest, or the six-pack.

The lower back muscles are our biggest strength when attempting to produce power and precision through any range of motion. Whether you are working at home, training at the gym, running on a track, or swimming in the pool, the lower back is the key to any sort of sport or activity. The lower back muscle group protects your spine and holds your body in alignment, so a strong lower back protects you against injury and gives you a strong foundation for all-round muscle growth.

To appreciate why training the lower back is so important, imagine a chain running from your head to the toe. Each link helps hold the chain in place. When any link is weak, the entire chain collapses! Once you start paying attention to developing the vital link, that is the lower back, you will immediately feel the difference.

The major muscles of the lower back include the erector spinae muscle group, which run vertically on each side of the spine, and the deep spinal muscles (For more information, refer to 'The Way We Move', pg 19). These muscles in your lower back are the key to the stability of the rest of your body. Your weightlifting will become more powerful and efficient, your sprint will become faster on the track, and you will be able to do all your daily chores with ease, without worrying about a muscle catch or a pull.

Proper athletic positions require an extremely strong lower back. Remember that weightlifting and any kind of strenuous cardiovascular activity places a lot of strain and demand on the lower back. This is why it is most important that you train your lower back muscles to the range of motion as efficient and safe as possible.

BUILD A STRONG FOUNDATION: STRENGHTEN LOWER BACK MUSCLES

You can use a combination of stretches, lower back strengthening moves, and strength-training power moves to train your lower back muscles. I recommend dynamic stretches to strengthen your lower back because they mimic the movements you do in your daily activities such as twisting, bending, or leaning to one side. If you have suffered from an injury or lower back pain, you can begin with static stretches to open up your lower back muscles.

Back Flexibility Exercises

1. *Simple Spinal Stretch*: Sitting on the floor with your feet wider than your hips, bend your head forward, hinging at the hips. Breathe normally. As you go down, draw your chin towards your neck. Your hands should not

reach past your toes—you're not aiming to lie on the floor—and you shouldn't feel as if your back and spinal ligaments are being pulled. Once you feel the stretch through your back, slowly return to the starting position.

2. *Cat–Cow Stretch*: Get on to your hands and knees. Slowly alternate between arching and rounding your back. Do this slowly and gently, and don't force yourself. One cycle will take 3 to 4 seconds. Repeat the stretch 5 or 6 times. This helps activate all the three parts of your spine—upper, lower, and the middle of the back.

3. *Supine Spinal Rotation*: Lie on your back with knees bent and feet on the floor. Stretch your arms out to your sides, palms facing down. Rotate from the hips to bring your knees down to the right side. Lift your left hip up but keep your shoulders touching the floor. Try to keep your knees together and tip them over as far as you can, while keeping your hands on the floor. Hold for a minimum of 30 seconds. Return to starting position and repeat, dropping knees to the left this time.

4. *Supine Spinal Twist*: Lie on your back with knees bent and feet on the floor. Stretch your arms out to your sides, palms face down. Cross your right knee over your left knee, as if you're sitting in a chair, with your right foot off the floor. Drop your knees to the left; it doesn't have to go all the way to the floor. Breathe throughout the stretch; inhale and exhale for about 4 seconds each. Repeat on the other side.

5. *Seated Rotation Stretch*: Sitting on a chair with your feet flat on the floor, twist your upper body so your shoulders rotate to one side. You can use the chair for support. Go only as far as you can comfortably. Hold for 20 seconds, and return to the starting position. Repeat on the other side.

6. *Seated Spinal Twist*: Sit tall, extending both legs in front of you. Bend your right knee and cross it over the left thigh. Now bend the left knee (you can keep your left leg straight if necessary). Take the left elbow and place it on the outside of the right knee, then place your right hand on the floor behind you, looking over your right shoulder. Hold and breathe deeply for 15 to 30 seconds, and then release. Switch sides and repeat.

Exercises to Strengthen Lower Back Muscles

1. *Cobra Pose (Bhujanasana or Upward Dog)*: Lie down on your stomach and place your hands down on the ground close to your body. Relax your lower body and push your upper torso upward like a cobra lifting its head off the ground.
2. *Bridge Pose*: Lie on your back. Fold your knees and keep your feet hip-distance apart on the floor. Your knees and ankles should be in a straight line. Keep your arms beside your body, palms facing down. Inhaling, slowly lift your lower back, middle back, and upper back off the floor. Try to touch the chest to the chin without bringing the chin down, supporting your weight with your shoulders, arms, and feet. Feel your bottom firm up in this pose. If you wish, you could interlace the fingers and push the hands on the floor to lift the torso a little more upwards, or you could support your back with your palms. Hold for 10 seconds and relax your back on the floor.
3. *Superman*: Lay flat on your stomach with your arms straight out in front of you and legs straight out behind you. Keep your arms and legs shoulder–width apart for the duration of the exercise. For the beginner's version, begin by lifting your arms at the same time while keeping your legs on the floor. Then move on

to lifting your legs, this time keep your arms on the floor. Once you get comfortable, you can move onto lifting alternate legs and hands at the same time. Begin by lifting your right arm and left leg, and then your left arm and right leg. The most advanced stretch involves lifting both the arms and the legs at the same time. Keep your breathing controlled while exercising. Take slow deep breaths as you lift into this position. Breathe out slowly while lowering to your starting position.

4. *Kneeling Alternate Arm and Leg Lift*: Get on your hands and knees. Place your hands directly under your shoulders and knees directly under your hips. Your chin should be slightly tucked in and nose pointing down to avoid hurting your neck. Lift the right arm and left leg simultaneously (try to lift to the same height). The lifted arm and leg as well as the hip and shoulder should be in one line. Hold. Repeat with opposite limbs (left arm and right leg).

A resistance band is an excellent accessory that helps strengthen lower back muscles and keeps back pain away. There are several easy-to-perform resistance band exercises that you can do in the comfort of your own home.

5. *Side Bend*: In order to perform this exercise, you will need to place one foot on the resistance band and then hold both the ends of the band right above that foot. Keep the band short so that you can increase the tension as you pull it till your waist. Laterally bend towards the side of the foot that is above the band, and then revert to your original position. Repeat this exercise with the other foot as well.

6. *Lower Back Extension*: Sit on a chair and then place both your feet on the band, shoulder–width apart. Grab the ends of the band and leave your hands near your ankle on both sides, and bend down so that your

chest touches your knees. Now you must slowly sit back upright while allowing the band to get stretched further, and then go back to the crouched position for the next repetition.

Dynamic Stretches to Strengthen and Warm-up Lower Back Muscles

1. *Alternate Toe Touches*: The exercise stretches the muscles through spinal flexion and extension ranges of motion. Stand upright with your feet spread wider than your shoulders, toes directed forward, and knees flexed slightly. Extend your arms sideways, away from your body, at shoulder height. Without bending your knees, bend forward and rotate towards the left, moving your right hand to your left foot. Stand back up and repeat in the opposite direction, touching your right foot with your left hand. Continue alternating sides for 10 to 20 seconds.
2. *High Knee Touches*: Stand in one place with your feet hip–width apart. Drive your right knee towards your chest and quickly place it back on the ground. Follow immediately by driving your left knee towards your chest. Continue to alternate knees as quickly as you can. You can begin with slower, controlled movements and then increase the pace. Do this for a minute.

Power Moves for a Strong Lower Back

(Note: Avoid these power exercises if you have arthritis, knee problems, or lower back pain).

Dead Lift

1. Always start with the bar on the floor. Stand with your feet hip–width apart—bar above the centre of your feet.
2. Hold the bar with an overhand grip just outside your shins.

3. Bend your knees until your shins hit the bar.
4. Arch your lower back and lift your chest, shoulders back and down, head in line with your spine.
5. Take a deep breath and start pulling the weight by driving your heels into the floor.
6. As the bar comes past the knees, push the hip forward.
7. Squeeze your glutes at the top.
8. Now push your hips back as you get the weight down.
9. Bend your knees once the bar reaches knee level and slowly release the grip on the weight.

A dead lift, when done correctly, is the best exercise to strengthen the lower back. Make sure you don't round your back at any time. Practice the dead lift technique without any weights for a few repetitions. When you add the weight, remember to keep the bar close to your body at all times.

Squat

1. Set the bar in a rack at mid-chest level. Grip the bar with as narrow a grip as possible.
2. Position your feet under the bar, hip–width apart.
3. Squat under the bar and put it on your upper back—not on your neck.
4. Take a deep breath and squat up to un-rack the bar.
5. Take one step back with each leg.
6. Set your heels shoulder-width apart with your feet pointing slightly outwards.
7. Head should be in line with your torso, chest up, and shoulder blades squeezed together.
8. Always start the squat by pushing your hips back. Don't bend your knees first.
9. Push your knees out to the sides as you squat down.
10. Squat down so your hips are parallel while keeping everything tight.
11. Rise by driving your heels through the floor.

12. As you rise, keep your knees out, and drive your hips forward. Squeeze your glutes hard at the top.

When you un-rack the bar, always take a step back and not forward. And never, ever do a half-squat. Here's why—your knee joint is at its most stable position when fully flexed or extended. So you will injure yourself when you do it only half-way; there is a lot of pressure on the knee joint.

Lunge

1. Start with your feet next to each other, with six inches between them. Keep your arms by your side, pelvis in a neutral position, with abdominals gently pulled in.
2. Step forward approximately two feet with the right leg, and bend both knees until the back knee is six inches from the floor. Keep your weight distributed evenly on both legs. The back heel should be lifted up.
3. Push-up with the right leg, and lift back to the starting position.
4. Repeat on the other side.

First, practice a lunge in front of a mirror to make sure you get the form right. There are two common mistakes—one is that that front knee should not go beyond your toe when you lunge and secondly, avoid leaning back or forward and make sure your back is in a straight line when you lunge forward.

Using the Hyperextension Bench

You can also advance to a hyperextension bench in the gym—it's great for core strengthening and building the lower back muscles.

1. Adjust the hyperextension bench so that your waist is in line with the top of the pad. Lie face down and position your feet firmly on the platform, tucking your ankles securely under footpads.

2. Cross your arms in front of you or hands behind your neck.
3. Bend at the waist and slowly lower your body towards the ground until you reach about 65–75 degrees.
4. Pause briefly at the bottom and then raise yourself back up to the starting position where your back is in a straight line with your lower body.
5. Repeat.

Hyperextension Variation 1 on a Swiss Ball:

1. Position yourself on top of a stability ball. Lie on your stomach and chest. Your legs should be fully extended behind you and toes planted on the floor.
2. Place your hands behind your head. Tighten your core and contract your glutes.
3. Slowly raise your torso upward. Hold for a second at the top. Make sure your glutes remain tight.
4. Lower yourself all the way back down until your chest touches the ball.
5. To make this exercise less difficult, you can place your arms across your chest.

Hyperextension Variation 2 on a Swiss Ball:

1. Lie face down with your torso and hips resting on the ball, and place your hands on the floor in front of you for balance.
2. Raise your legs so that they are even with your body.
3. Keeping your toes turned out, squeeze your glutes and lower back to extend your straight legs up to the ceiling.
4. Lower to the straight position, and repeat.
5. Squeeze your glutes and hold for a few seconds at the top of the move for an added burn.

These power moves are important because they help to not just strengthen and build the lower back muscles (erector spinae), but also the major muscles of the lower body. They help in stabilizing the torso and in preventing lower back injuries. Concentrate on every link in the body's main chain—including the glutes, hamstrings, and core—and build each one to maintain the proper muscular balance of the body. Be patient and make each repetition count. You need to be very careful and aware of your lower back muscles at all times. Be sure to train the abdominal muscles as well. Consistency and efficiency is important because together they will help develop a faster, stronger, healthier, and more functional body.

Ten Rules for a Strong Back

1. **Move Your Body:** The more you move and stay active, the healthier you will be. Keep your body well-conditioned, maintain a healthy weight, and exercise regularly. If you are a couch potato, start small with a walk 4–5 times a week. Make it your goal to start moving.
2. **Keep Your Core Strong:** Your abdominal muscles, hip, and lower back have to be strong and work in harmony to avoid any sort of misalignment of the spine. You don't need to be a world-class athlete or a model or a fitness fanatic to benefit from a toned core. Strong core muscles make simple, daily activities more manageable. Core muscles provide the postural support necessary to stay balanced when the body is in motion.
3. **Be Posture-perfect!:** Most times, we think that practicing a perfect posture involves keeping your spine ramrod straight. Good posture is actually quite simple. A normal spine is shaped like an 'S' curve. To maintain good posture, your goal is to keep this natural curve in balance while standing, sitting, or lying down. If the natural curve is displaced, your spine becomes unstable. Your muscles, ligaments, and joints have to work much

harder to support your head, which inevitably leads to muscle fatigue and back pain.

4. **Take Breaks if You Sit for Long Periods of Time:** If you have a desk job, take a break and move around every hour. It could be a simple stretch or even a simple walk to a co-worker's cubicle. This helps relieve pressure on the spine. Make sure your computer screens is set at eye level and that your seat is positioned to where your legs are at a 90-degree angle, with your feet tilted slightly upward. You can also substitute your office chair for a Swiss ball built-in chair. By sitting upright on the ball, you can simultaneously strengthen your core, abs, and back while also relieving pressure from any sort of built-up compression on the spine.

5. **Sleep Right:** Don't just sit right, sleep right too! Research shows that sleeping on your side on a firm, yet comfortable mattress helps take most of the stress off the spine. You can even tuck a pillow between your legs to take the pressure off the hips. On the other hand, sleeping on your stomach is considered the worst because it exaggerates the spinal arch of the body and may cause strain.

6. **Don't Ignore the Symptoms of Lower Back Pain:** You have to learn to listen to your body. If you feel a nagging pain in your lower back while weightlifting or running, don't ignore it. Don't assume it will go away. It's a sign that you are doing something wrong or that there is a lack of alignment when you are exercising. Stop what you are doing and rest your back till the pain subsides. If the pain persists, it's time to see your doctor.

7. **Heal Your Back:** If you experience back pain, rest it for a day. But never bring your activity to a complete stand-still. Something as simple as a walk or a leisure swim will keep the area stimulated.

8. **Avoid Certain Exercises till Your Back is Completely Healed:** While physical activity is an excellent way to strengthen the back and help the healing process, some moves should be avoided if your back hurts. Military presses and weight-assisted lunges are not recommended because they can axially load the spinal column (compress the spine from the head area—as when a person dives into shallow water and lands headfirst). Running can also be risky. Make sure to talk to your chiropractor or doctor before you begin a heavy exercise programme, after a back injury.
9. **Proper Biomechanics of the Body = Strong Back:** You need to make sure that your workouts exercise all the muscles of the body equally. Any sort of muscle imbalance can throw your spinal health out of alignment. If your major muscles aren't strong and balanced, they will tend to fatigue faster, taking energy away from other smaller muscles, and change your stride and alignment, increasing the risk of injury.
10. **Make Sure You Do Your Back Strengthening Exercises Before You Work on Your Abdominals:** This way you will not put too much strain on your lower back when you are performing abdominal exercises. Always support your lower back by tucking in your lower abdominal muscles and maintain a strong core.

Working Your Abdominals

I write for *Femina's* 'Fitness Q&A' column, and every month, the maximum queries are on belly fat. By now, you know that your abdominal muscles are not just the six-pack or the lower and upper abdomen. There are four abdominal muscles—the rectus abdominis, internal and external obliques, and the transversus abdominis. (To understand more about the importance of these muscles, refer to 'The Way We Move', pg 24)). It's important to understand that you cannot reduce fat from the mid-section by doing crunches—it's just not an effective way!

There is a lot of misinformation floating around the subject of training the abdominal muscles. Hundreds of gadgets and machines on TV and magazines promise to sculpt your abs or melt away the fat from the belly region. But really there is nothing unique in the way you train your abdominal muscles—it is like any other muscle in the body. The principle that applies to training your chest or biceps and triceps is the same that needs to be applied to training your abdominals.

Here's what you need to keep in mind when you begin with Ab-solute training:

- Progressively increase the intensity of your ab workouts
- Space your workouts properly to avoid overtraining or undertraining your ab muscles

On each successive workout, aim for a 5 to 15 percent increase in the weights you use. If you can't get a 5 percent increase if your abs are sore, it's time to add more days off between your workouts because you need to let your ab muscles recover from the training. To force new development, you need to increase the intensity.

IT'S NOT JUST THE ABS, IT'S ALSO THE SPINE

Another reason why it's important for you to train your abdominal muscles is because it keeps your spine strong, helps you to do daily activities with ease, and prevents injuries when you twist and turn. Strong abs help you sit straight and enables you to do all kinds of activities—from pushing a grocery market trolley cart to carrying your kids to climbing stairs without getting a backache. All your abdominal muscles work together to support and move the spine.

Most people get a backache or a sudden painful 'catch' when they twist with a jerk or jump over some object. Strong abdominal muscles and proper biomechanical movements help in preventing these injuries.

I do understand the need for washboard abs or a six-pack because your favourite model is flaunting it or it's a goal that you would like to achieve to feel good about yourself. However, you have to understand that if it's in your genes to store fat... above your rectus abdominis muscle, the six-pack won't show, no matter how much you train or how less you eat. Take heart from the fact that most celebrities get this look with excellent make-up techniques as well as helpful Photoshop tools. Very few of them are genetically gifted and most resort to unnatural supplements for a quick-fix.

So it's better to feel good about your abdominals being strong enough to support your back, instead of hemming and hawing that you don't have a six-pack.

Here's the absolute right way to train abs:

1. **Skip Sit-ups!:** People always think they will get a toned midsection with any sit-up type movement. It's not true. Sit-ups work mostly on your hip flexors and lower back muscles, more than your abdominal muscles. Design an effective abdominal programme and target the right muscles.
2. **Variation is Key:** It's important to target abdominal muscles from every angle. This will promote growth and definition. I don't believe in old-school crunches. Crunches performed on a Swiss ball are much more effective because the instability of the surface helps target the small stabilizing muscles, works your lower back as well as all the major muscles of the abdomen. It is important to know that any one exercise will not target one specific abdominal muscle at one time.
3. **Work Out with Balance Accessories:** Adding balance equipments like balance pads and Swiss balls (Refer to pg 341 for balance accessories) will make the exercises

more advanced. When you use balance accessories, the unstable surface makes your core work harder by recruiting more muscle fibres for any action performed.
4. **Intense Cardio Sessions are a Must:** Remember I said 'intense'. You can't just stroll on a treadmill and expect fat to went. Use interval training techniques like a walk-run-sprint, walk on an incline, or perform circuit training in the gym by using the exercise bike and then using a rower. The heart then needs to pump blood into several major muscle groups in the body and this gives a major push to the fat loss process. Try to stay away from the same workout routines—make it a little more intense each time. You can use accessories like battling ropes, thick ropes which are tied at one end. The objective is to create waves by slamming the ropes on the ground. They are a fun, quick, and alternative way to work out your arms, back, legs, and especially target the core—not to mention the ultimate stress buster! So mix up the equipment you use and inject a sense of play in your routines.
5. **Fitness Enthusiasts Should Perform HIIT:** If you have high fitness level, perform High Intensity Interval Training. This will lower your body fat percentage and speed up the fat burning process by giving your metabolism a boost. Make sure you take your age into account before attempting intense exercises like CrossFit. If you are 30–35 years of age, it is better to mix an intense activity with yoga, pilates, Tai Chi.
6. **Shock Your Body Each Time:** Always keep your body guessing. Give it something new. Your abdominals are like any other muscle. It responds to the way you train. Try to make your exercise session more intense every four weeks. Make it more challenging than the last session by using a heavier weight, increasing the rep range, or the tempo of lifting weights.

7. **Eat Right!:** We have heard the term that abs are made in the kitchen, The layer of fat is not going to get melt away if you are not eating right. Here the common notion is that if you cut down on oil or fat, the belly fat goes away...that's not true! If your diet is deficient in vitamins and minerals or if it is full of sugar, then it will not work. You also need to incorporate healthy sources of protein such as lean (not processed) meat like chicken or turkey, and plant-based protein (Refer to the chapter on 'Diet', pg 93).
8. **Watch Your Alcohol Intake:** If you are trying to lean down, alcohol will pose a problem. It is inevitable to have alcohol when you are socializing. Then add to it, alcohol always seems to go hand in hand with greasy food. If you want to get rid of the mid-section flab, you need to stop having alcohol.
9. **Make Your Abdominal Training the Last Thing You Do in Your Workout:** If you are only concentrating your abdominals, always work on your lower back muscles first and then move onto abdominals. This helps in two ways—one, it strengthens the lower back and prevents strain on that region. Second, when people start working their abs first, they fatigue the muscles and put excessive pressure on the lower back.

   On the days you are doing an intense lower body workout with squats and lunges, or are going to lift heavy weights, and if you wish to do an ab workout, always do it last. This is because while you are doing an intense lower body routine, you are using the muscles of the core. It's not a good idea to fatigue these muscles of the core first by doing abdominal exercises. You will start losing form and it will end in an injury. So hit your ab training after compound exercises or after lifting heavy weights. Even here do work on lower back muscles before working out your ab muscles.

10. **Do More Reps:** It's important that you train your abdominal muscles with more repetitions but ideally, start counting your repetitions after you feel a muscle burn. Perform 8–15 repetitions after the burn. For advance fitness enthusiasts, heavy weights to your ab routine. When you look at obliques or six-packs, they may look like separate muscles, but the truth is they are not. They just appear separate and distinct. It's really one long muscle. However, you may always feel one section is working more than the other. But in reality, the entire muscle group is being worked on. For example, if you are doing leg raises with proper form, you will get maximum activation from the sternum to the waist line. Lifting heavy weights will force abdominal muscles to work harder to stabilize the body. In order to get a strong mid-section, you need to work on balance.
11. **Do the Twist!:** Twisting moves are more effective for abdominal training. If you are doing a hanging knee raise, first do it slowly and in a controlled manner and then add a medicine ball between your knees—it works on your lower body and abs. Before you add weight, make sure you complete a set without weights. All abdominal exercises need to be slow and controlled and then you can add weights. When your reps start becoming too easy, you need to add weights with a medicine ball or standard weights.

EXERCISES FOR ABDOMINAL TRAINING:

1. Band Resisted Jackknife

This is one of the best exercises for abdominal training because it forces you to move your hips and thighs against resistance while keeping your core stable. This exercise helps you build core strength needed for stability during lower body exercises like squats and dead lifts.

How To Do It: Secure a looped (CrossFit) resistance band to a pull up bar and suspend your ankles in the end as you assume a push-up position. Without rounding your back, bend your knees, and pull them towards your torso. Pause, and return to the starting position. Do 3 sets of 8 reps.

2. Kettlebell Pullover Crunch

Lie on your back and place the kettlebell on the floor just over your head. Lay it down on its side so that the handle is facing your head. Reach over your head and grab the handle of the kettlebell with both hands. Lift your legs. Raise your legs off the floor and bring them to a point where your feet are parallel to the ceiling. Your hips will be bent at 90-degrees. Now pull your arms above your head and do a crunch—all in one, smooth motion. Lift the kettlebell up in the air as you do this. Now slowly lower it back down and repeat the whole process.

Training your abdominal muscles in the most effective manner will ensure that you have a strong back for life. I also recommend a Swiss ball chair for people who work for hours on a desk. It would be a good idea to replace your ordinary office chair with a chair which has a built-in Swiss ball. Research shows it helps people focus better and improve that balance and core strength. They come in different sizes and colours. I would also recommend it for school students and kids at home. I feel it should be introduced in schools because it helps one focus and improve posture. These kids spend the better part of their day in school; it is better to teach them how to sit right. The Swiss ball chair is a magical piece of equipment which increases blood flow leading to more alertness, keeps your back from getting stiff, and prevents posture problems.

PLAY WITH FITNESS ACCESSORIES

There are several fitness accessories in the market and every day, I hear of a new one which hits the shelves or gyms. I have included the timeless fitness equipments as well as some of the new ones that I believe in.

Resistance Bands and Tubes: It's a great alternative to hand weights for resistance and strength training, especially if you travel a lot. Resistance bands look like large rubber bands and usually come in different colours according to how much resistance it offers. If you are a senior or you have just begun exercising, resistance bands and tubes are a great fitness accessory to have.

Dumbbells/Kettlebells: Once you are comfortable with resistance bands and tubes and your muscles are conditioned, you can move onto free weights. You can buy dumbbells in a variety of weights — or save yourself time and space with adjustable dumbbells. Kettlebells are bowling ball-sized cast iron weights with a single looped handle on top.

AGY Hammock: It is a soft fabric hammock that supports you in yoga and allows you to swing. It's biggest advantage is that it is extremely useful in decompressing the spine.

Balance Pads: Training on this can improve balance, ankle stability, and strength. Use them to perform squats, lunges, push-ups and one- or two-legged balance moves with comfort. It is used by physiotherapists and trainers for rehabilitation and for sports conditioning.

Wobble Board: It can help retrain the proprioceptors and improve coordination, hence preventing further injury. You have to stand on the board and try to keep it horizontal - without the edges touching the floor.

Stability/Balance/Swiss Ball: No matter what you call it, the bottom line is, it's a large poly-vinyl ball (typically between

18 and 28 inches in diameter). You can use it for just about anything: as a bench for weight training, for ab exercises, stretching. Look for one which is burst resistant and which is the right size for your height. Charts are usually available when buying. This equipment can be used by individuals at all levels of fitness, and helps to work every major muscle group in the body. It also adds the dimension of core strength to your training.

Medicine Ball: Medicine ball training is one of the oldest forms of strength and conditioning training. Medicine balls used to only come in one style: large and leather. Now, they can be found in every imaginable size, style, shape, and colour. They also come in soft variety which is easier to grip.

UGI Ball: The Ugi ball is a modern twist on the old school medicine ball. It's weighted and squishy. The squish factor is what makes it unique. You can use it in your living room, gym, or an outdoor park. The Ugi ball works as a functional fitness training tool because it challenges the exerciser to use entire muscle groups at one time.

BOSU Ball: The BOSU is like an exercise ball that's been cut in half with a platform at the bottom. You can use it dome-side-up for cardio, lower body strength, or core moves. Or you can turn it over and use the platform side for upper body exercises, like push-ups, or more core moves, like planks. The possibilities are endless. I've used it while doing some traditional yoga poses, like warrior and triangle. It made the workouts challenging and interesting. The pink colour BOSU ball is my favourite.

Step Bench: It looks like a long step stool and is used for step aerobics. You'll really get your heart pumping with one of these.

TRX Suspension Trainer Straps: Suspension Training body weight exercise builds all body strength, flexibility, and your core at the same time. You need to go to a certified instructor to know how to use these straps correctly.

Trampoline and Rebounder: Rebounders stand between 8 and 12 inches above the floor and take up approximately 1 square yard of space. Full-sized trampolines come in various sizes, ranging from 8 to 14 feet, and average about 3 feet off the ground. Some rebounders can also be folded up for carrying.

Plank Ab-station: It is perfect if thin gym mats and hard floors are making it difficult for you to hold your form. It is a rectangular foam piece with alignment contouring, and has been designed to be highly durable. It has a textured bottom which has a non-slip grip for added control.

Interval Timer: It takes the guesswork out of interval training, set/rep timing, and CrossFit.

Heart Rate Monitor: It not only helps you keep track of your heart-rate but also of your general health. A heart-rate monitor allows you to detect health problems that you would not notice otherwise. For instance, you might find your heart-rate going up rapidly even though you are just doing light exercises. This is a clear sign that something could be wrong with your health.

Pedometer: It is a device, usually portable and electronic or electromechanical, that counts each step a person takes by detecting the motion of the person's hips. It's a good tool to have if you are an avid walker.

Foam Rollers: It not only stretches muscles and tendons but also breaks down soft tissue adhesions and scar tissues. By using your own body weight and a cylindrical foam roller, you can perform a self-massage. They come in different sizes, half-rounded as well as full-rounded versions.

Agility Ladders and Cones: It is about 8 metre long. This fitness accessory helps improve agility, balance, and coordination. It can be used for walking, running, and hopping drills. You can also add disc cones as hurdles—they are used as targets for drills to mark specific areas of the court or with agility drills. These cones are light and flexible.

Swimming Accessories: Fitness noodle and kick boards are the most easily recognized and most used piece of aquatic equipment. Aqua jogging is a no-impact workout that works well for cross-training or getting through an injury. Aqua jogging essentially uses the same muscles as used when running on land, but because your feet do not 'land' on anything solid—you need an aqua jogging belt. Aqua shoes can help you jog better. For weightlifting in water, you need water weights, webbed water fitness gloves, flippers, and fins.

Skipping Rope: Portable and easiest way to get your cardiovascular activity done.

YOGA ACCESSORIES

Anti-skid Eco-friendly Yoga Mat: For all yoga lovers, you need to get one of these. Stinky, toxic, PVC-laden mats from the local sporting goods store are a big no-no!

Yoga Wall: Some yoga poses require a great deal of balance and flexibility. The Yoga wall was originally designed by BKS Iyengar in the form of ropes attached to wall hooks to assist students in various yoga asana. The wall has a system of adjustable straps and more comfortable pelvic swings to accommodate every height and body type. Iyengar-based system of straps and wall-mounted props creates a greater support base for inversions, backbends, therapeutics, and standing poses. It is an ideal tool for cross-training for athletes.

Organic Mat Wipes or Cleansers: They help keep your yoga mat clean because they come infused with essential oils. They also dry quickly, leaving only a perfumed scent.

Yoga Blocks: It is a shoebox sized yoga prop which helps you to keep balance in challenging yoga poses.

Yoga Strap: This is another yoga prop that helps you to stretch to your limit and achieve poses which are out of your limit.

Yoga Bolsters: It is a foam pillow placed under the knees or the back to provide extra support.

PILATES ACCESSORIES

Pilates Reformer: It is a traditional piece of Pilates equipment comprising of a bed with springs, a sliding carriage, ropes, and pulleys. It is one of the most versatile and effective piece of exercise equipment ever made because the intensity can be varied considerably from one person to the next. The springs that provide much of the resistance from the reformer are generally quite strong.

Rings or Circles: These are soft, rubber-covered rings based on Joseph Pilates' Magic Circles. They provide faster, more targeted toning, improving muscle strength throughout the body especially in problem areas like the inner and outer thighs, upper arms, and chest.

Arc/step Barrel: It is a lightweight and versatile step barrel that packs three exercise tools in one—exercise arc, spine corrector, and a wedge for balance body reformer.

> **Battle ropes:** It is a unique strength and conditioning training method designed by John Brookfield. He is the writer of several bestselling books and a famous world record holder. Battling ropes or battle ropes can be used for full body strength and conditioning and it is only used by advanced fitness enthusiasts. Battling ropes are hefty ropes specially designed to be heavy so that they take effort to control and move. They come in many different styles and lengths, but there are two primary styles available: 25mm and

44mm. Most ropes usually come in lengths of 5m, 10m, and 25m. There are so many battling ropes exercises, but the wave, battle rope slams, and battle rope pulls are the most famous.

- ✓ **Wave:** Continuous wave with battling rope—you can also alternate the waves between your left and right hand.
- ✓ **Battle Rope slams:** Similar to the wave but in this you have to slam the rope every time.
- ✓ **Battle Rope Pulls:** In this exercise you need to pull the rope towards you as quickly as possible. You can pull the rope to both sides at once, or pull both ropes to one side and alternate sides (think of a skier).

Though Battling ropes are relatively new, they are becoming increasingly popular among coaches and their athletes. You can add a big tyre to the end of the rope and pull it.

WHAT TO WEAR AT THE GYM

Good Training Clothes: Don't wear anything you are not comfortable in. It's no fun to pull up or tug down your clothes while you are working out. Your butt may look amazing in those tights, but those low squats are going to be problematic and no joy to the others. Make sure the material is breathable—cotton can absorb sweat but it isn't built to wick the sweat away, leaving you with a sticky sensation. It can even give you the chills and cause irritation. Opt for technologically advanced fabrics that hold moisture away from the body. Cotton in combination with another material such as spandex is a good bet. Nylon and polyester are also viable options—they help circulate the air more effectively than cotton. Avoid baggy clothes as they get caught on exercise machines like stationary bikes. Wear organic, chemical-free fabrics.

Shoes: If you're an advanced lifter, you may prefer lifting shoes to traditional cross-trainers or running shoes. Whatever choice you make, make sure it provides the support you need for the type of training you do.

Socks: Choose sports socks that will help keep your feet dry and help beat blisters. Ideal workout socks regulate moisture and prevent foot odour, keeping you feeling fresh and pain-free. Compression socks are specialized hosiery items designed to provide extra support and increase in blood circulation. Some compression socks manufacturers may also use the term *support socks* to describe their product. They are usually used by runners.

Sports Bra for Women: Finding the right sports bra is like finding the right pair of jeans—you have to sift and sort till you find the perfect bra for your size and activity. There are all kinds now—for the curvy women, for those who aren't—so make sure you take your time to get a good one.

Gym Bag Essentials:

Water Bottles: Make sure they are made from BPA and DEHP-free plastic and are 100 percent leak-proof. If possible, I recommend *SIGG* bottles as they are 100 percent recyclable and contribute significantly to reducing the global carbon footprint. *HydraCoach* has introduced the world's first interactive water bottle. It calculates your personal hydration needs, tracks your real-time fluid consumption—so it's a good motivational tool to achieve and maintain optimal hydration.

Towel: Sweating is normal especially in the gym. Make sure you get a towel to wipe down the equipment after you finish using it. Keep one for personal use.

Gloves: Buy high quality workout gloves to improve your grip.

Knee Wraps: Protect your knees during heavy squats and leg presses.

Power Belt: Intense squats and dead lifts require heavy-duty core and back support.

Wrist Wraps: They offer maximum wrist support for hardcore lifting.

Grip Lifting Strap: will help you pull heavy weight without grip failure.

Music: Get your iPod, use your phone, or an Mp3 player and get some good quality headphones. You will find that it is incredibly motivating to work out to the music you love.

Anti-bacterial Spray/Liquid: Always carry one in your bag to use in the gym.

THINK OUTSIDE YOUR GYM

Working out outdoors is good for you when you are inhaling fresh air, navigating the uneven ground when you are walking or running and absorbing sunshine. All these factors revitalize your body. Outdoor exercises can be of many kinds—it can be as simple as going out for a walk or a run, hiking, riding your bike, swimming, or it can involve taking your usual strength training outdoors.

Most people find that outdoor training in the fresh air is much more invigorating than training in a stuffy gym. Many often feel like working out harder and longer than when training inside. Also, outdoor training for sports, marathons, or other activities can help athletes adjust to working out even in bright, hot climates or cool, rainy conditions.

Functional timeless moves like push-ups, squats, and lunges can just as easily be done outdoors as they can be done indoors. Chair dips, step-ups, and similar activities can all be performed on an empty park bench. Many people also enjoy doing pull-ups on strong tree branches. This is a good way to build your own circuit training routine in the park—you can run or power walk in the park and combine it with intervals of compound moves to build strength. You can also build your own obstacle course by using agility cones and building a drill.

Play around with your cardiovascular activity too. Once you have conditioned your muscles and your body is used to jogging, take it up a notch higher. Hills add another level of difficulty, forcing the body to work harder to reach the top. Using steep hills, trees, or even large rocks can add an incline or decline element into the exercise. Inclines and declines work on different parts of the muscles or even different muscle groups entirely. The smaller stabilizing muscles come into play and the body develops balance and neuromuscular coordination. It's not just your VO2 Max or lung capacity that is increasing. Setting goals to sprint up hills and then jog or walk down can be a motivating way to do interval training.

Fitness boot camps are another form of outdoor training. It usually is a group training programme conducted by trainers or former military personnels. These programmes are designed to build strength and fitness through a variety of intense group intervals. Boot camp training often starts with dynamic stretching and running. It is then followed by a wide variety of interval training, including lifting weights, pulling TRX suspension straps, functional moves like push-ups, and advanced moves like Plyometrics. Sessions usually finish with yoga stretches.

The TRX suspension strap, which works on the factor of total body resistance, is perfect for outdoor training. For athletes who perform sports outside such as cricket, tennis, badminton, football, and so on, the TRX can be strapped to anything from a bar to a goal post or even a very strong tree branch. The most important thing to consider when anchoring the TRX to an any anchor point is to ensure it can bear your full body weight. Always weight-test before beginning your workout. Take the guidance of an expert before trying this.

Training with TRX, fitness boot camps, or even running on the beach is a great way of mixing up your indoor-outdoor workouts. You will find that mixing it up will make your fitness journey much more exciting. Whatever you do, make it a point to take your workouts wherever you want to go. Your body will reward you with the benefits of health, fitness, and a glow of happiness will be visible to all.

I have only talked about common problems like knee issues, lower back pain, abdominals and spine, because I feel these are the most common problems we face on an everyday basis—whether it is for a common man, a gym-goer, or a professional athlete. So incorporate these moves in your daily routine and see what a difference they make to your body.

Conclusion

Weight training is a topic I can write a thesis on. But it's just impossible to talk about each and everything in the book for scarcity of space. Plus, my publishers will run after me with a broom if I don't end here. So even though I might want to talk about a zillion other things, I will have to restrict myself.

Looking back at my life's experiences, I realize how far I've come. From a gawky teenager to a trainer to the stars, my journey has been nothing but exciting. I have had ups and downs, but what has never dwindled is my hunger for knowledge, for learning new methods of fitness, and for keeping myself abreast with the latest developments in the field of health. And this zest will only keep growing.

My father-in-law always said, 'As long as you are alive, you will keep gaining knowledge. Try spreading that knowledge to as many people as you can so they too can benefit from it. If you don't, that means you have an ego.' I have engraved his words in stone and that's why my friends lovingly call me a fitness angel—because I give free advice at the drop of a hat. The bitter truth is that in India, most people pay heed to advice only if it's bought in cash. Educate yourself and start by implementing small changes, one at a time.

Conclusion

Time and again, I hear many people say, 'But Deanne, where is the time?' Or 'I don't know where to get started.' People who say they don't have time to exercise simply don't want to. Your health is one of the most important things in life and you have to take out time for it, come what may. And fitness is no rocket science as I have shown you through this book. Find the right balance between working hard and being healthy. With each healthy choice you make, your body will reap the benefits and you will be thrilled with the payoff.

I'm a firm believer that happiness comes from leading a healthy lifestyle. It's simple—if I'm fit, I'm happy. It's the best feeling in the world to wake up to a body that you love and that you've carved with your own sweat and blood. Today, I stand tall and proud of what I have achieved.

Just think of how amazing you'll feel once you're at your fittest. Want to become a girl magnet? You'll be able to make heads turn with your dreamlike physique. That annual health check-up you've been dreading all week? Your results will come out perfectly normal. The skimpy bikini you've dreamed of wearing on your honeymoon? It will fit you like a dream. Visualize end scenarios like these and make them your motivation to get started. Don't be a quitter. Push past the boundaries you have set for yourself. How will you know your true potential if you quit even before getting started?

Ten years ago, I gave up on red meat because I felt it was harming my body. As I age, I understand that I need to be more careful about my food choices for they could have overreaching impact on my health. Whether you want to age gracefully or lie on a couch with a diseased body—the choice is yours to make.

It's thrilling to see the success stories around me and the small role I have had to play in them—people who have carved out award-winning bodies without falling prey to unnatural supplements; people who have been able to overcome their inhibitions with my coaching and made fitness a lifestyle choice; and people who have developed a sense of self-esteem by achieving their desired body weight.

I find unmitigated joy when I have clients come up to me and profess what a difference I have made to their lives. I realize that my passion for exercising and living a healthy lifestyle has metamorphosed into something greater than what I started with. Trust me, there is no greater feeling in the world than knowing you have been able to make a positive impact in someone else's life.

Thanks to my children, I have a better understanding of why I should be proud of what I have achieved. I keep fit not so that I can compete in a contest on who looks best. I want to be able to partake in my children's activities and not simply watch from the fences like moms usually do. My exercise and dietary choices help me keep up with my kids' energy. I can play a soccer game with Ahaan till game up or go swimming with Alanna and do as many laps as her.

DON'T JUST WORK OUT, LEARN TO PLAY!

The fittest people I know keep active daily doing what they enjoy. Let your imagination run riot. If you like water, go river-rafting or canoeing. Take a snorkelling class. Plan a holiday around scuba diving. If you like nature, try a simple trek over the weekend. Run on the beach. Take a rock-climbing class. Roller-skate. Try hip-hop or take up belly dancing. Learn to let go of your inhibitions and don't stop at your gym. Think fitness. Think fun. Think adventure. Think outside your gym.

As children, we enjoyed running in the park, playing gully cricket, or just monkeying around. But that element of play gets lost somewhere as we get older. Don't make fitness a chore; as adults, we have forgotten what it is to have fun. So try and incorporate play into your daily lives. If you do the

Conclusion

same kind of training day in and day out, of course it will lead to fatigue and boredom. Make it fun by adding variety and adventure sports like canoeing, hiking, trekking, or rock-climbing.

Buy good shoes which will motivate you to get off the couch. Go shopping to gear up for the gym—get the proper gym attire to work out and don't wear that oversized old T-shirt. Read up on exercising, gather knowledge on the right way of training. I guarantee you that you will fall in love with it, just like me.

This is an age of Brazilian butt lifts, body conturing, and tummy tucks, surgeries like stomach stapling, colon cleansing, and liposuctions have all become the norm of the day. Most people give in to quick fixes, assured results, and dangerous substances and surgeries. I can never think of sacrificing my health for anything. I'd rather stick to the basics. Don't stop trying just because you hit a wall. Progress is progress—no matter how small.

As we come to the end of the book, I really hope you have come out feeling a bit more knowledgeable than when you started. I hope to see you make positive changes in your sleep, diet, and forms of exercise. Make fitness and good health a part of your lifestyle. Don't get demotivated if you can't see instant results. You *are* changing from within. And don't only lust after a slim body. Your goal should be to get fit for life. After all, strong is the new skinny.

To say fitness changed my life will be an understatement. This book is my gift to you. Make it your friend, your saviour, your guide. Let it empower you like it has empowered me.

Now that you are motivated enough, sign a fitness pledge. Make a promise to yourself that you will not give up. If you fall off the wagon, just start again. Don't stop. Remember every step counts.

FITNESS FOR LIFE OATH

In the spirit of making fitness a lifelong plan, I hereby agree to consistently work out and train intelligently. I will honour my body and not give in to any unnatural methods, surgeries, or marketing gimmicks. I agree to make a commitment to myself to eat well and train in a disciplined manner to improve my health.

I will make sure that my training has all the 4PFs—strength, endurance, flexibility, and balance. And I will especially make sure that play is a part of my exercise plan. I will make it fun and not a chore.

I agree to Shut up and Train.
Signature
Date

Afterword

Deanne, my sister Baby's friend and my friend Chikki's wife, has taken fitness to great heights.

Fitness to me means to be able to walk, run, and do your work well. In the profession that I am, if I can't look at myself in the mirror, there's no way my fan is going to enjoy the movie. We have to practice a very moderate kind of fitness. You can't look like a bodybuilder or an athlete—you have to look like a normal man. Depending upon the kind of character you are playing in a movie, you have to mould your body accordingly.

Since a movie is a visual medium, one has to be in constant training. Anything that one does every day, one gets bored of. I do different things to keep myself fit—sometimes freehand, sometimes Pilates, sometimes weight training, and sometimes cardio.

Whatever workout you do, the ultimate objective is that you need to look your charming best. Eat well and don't ever overtrain. You shouldn't look too bulky or train so much that you start looking gaunt. For instance, if I am playing a romantic hero, I do not want to look large or bulky or hard. You need to look vulnerable. You should look like you could get beaten up. Similarly if you are playing an action hero, you need to look hard and tough. When you take off your shirt, siti bajni chahiye.

There are different ways to go about building the body that you want. One way is light training, so that you don't hurt yourself. This involves a lot of repetitions and fewer sets combined with a proper diet. This cuts you up. Then there is the heavy stuff where you lift heavy and overtrain. This involves few reps and can get you ripped.

The next step in getting you the body you want is going to a gym, finding the best looking body, and asking the person to train you. Make sure that you are eating correctly because it's 80 percent about the diet.

Do not do things that you can't do and do not try to compete with somebody else. Your heavy weights might be light weights for somebody else, and their light weights may be heavy weights for you. So you have to work out for yourself. Be extremely careful with the weights—especially when you are doing lower back or legs or shoulders.

Over the years, I have suffered from huge amount of injuries. Injuries happen when you haven't warmed up or stretched. It also depends on the way you sleep or sit. I am against new kinds of training like CrossFit or training with kettlebells. It's not for everybody. It will give you a back problem. I think it is really stupid because we have now progressed to such scientific forms of training where each muscle is accounted for. Instead, we are going back to extreme forms of training— for which we are not made.

You have to train your core. You can't just work on your arms. Having thin legs and just big arms is the worst kind of body. Having nice legs and a ripped upper body is fine.

I have done some really stupid things and not let my body recover, and instead just jumped back to working out. Because of this, I messed up my shoulder, my right knee, and my back. So my advice is that whenever you suffer an injury, at whatever age, give your body rest.

Afterword

We used to do silly things before—pop a combiflam, take some painkiller or put muscle relaxants and continue to work out without knowing it is going to mess you up. You may not realize it the moment you are doing it, but one or two years down the line, you will.

Muscles grow when you are resting, not when you are working out. I believe that massages increases your muscle definition and size of the body by 10 percent. It also helps you recover faster.

Along with massages, a good stretch routine is important. Everybody cheats when they are weight training. They all want to pick up heavier weights than they can without doing it correctly. This leads to shorter muscles. You need to do a lot of stretching—especially your back and hamstrings.

A fit body is a thousand times better than an unfit body. If you want to work for long, you need a fit body. If you want to look good, you need a fit body. If you want to woo a girl, you need a fit body. If you want to be a good father and run around and play with your kids, you need to have a fit body. If you need to be a good husband, then you definitely need to have a fit body! If you want heads to turn or be liked in the first impression, or get compliments, then you need a fit body.

Most importantly, stay away from steroids! Supplementation is good—amino acids, protein shakes—all that is fine. But stay away from anything to do with steroids. Lots of people do it because they feel they have the know-how. But the younger generation should stay miles away from it because they don't know how to use it. Even the guys who know how to use it should stay away from it.

Steroids were basically given to old people who were unwell, so that they could recover from illnesses quickly. It was also given to midgets so that they could grow taller. It was meant to be used for medicinal purposes. Now bodybuilders have started misusing steroids for bodybuilding.

I am also against any kind of extremely strenuous working methods like CrossFit. You need to know your fitness levels before doing it. I have had friends or people who I know, who are doing it and they complain about their back and knees.

Remember your trainer will not want your body to become superb or ripped in two months. That's his job—he will want you to be around for longer so that he can get his salary for 10 months or 2–3 years.

Train with your trainer but don't get dependent on him. Or get a training partner who knows his stuff. Or better still, watch and observe somebody who is good and knowledgeable about weight training. Let him do his set and you do your set in another part of the gym by observing him. So start copying him, how many sets he is doing or what is his form while doing that set.

You need to boost your protein intake only if you are doing a very advanced level of bodybuilding. We don't need it. We will not be able to digest it also. Professional bodybuilders do 4–5 hours of training and that is why they require such a high level of protein through supplements and shakes.

I believe in form. Form always goes wrong when you try to lift weights that you cannot carry. When you are trying to impress somebody in a gym with the weight that you can carry, that's when your form goes wrong. When you are impulsive or impatient, or you are filled with enthusiasm and you want to do it before somebody is showing it to you—that is when your form goes wrong. Some people have that ability to get it right in the first go. They are athletic and can get it right because their posture is right. For other people, it takes more time to achieve the right form. Only a correct form can save you from the maximum amount of injuries.

I don't follow a specific diet plan. I eat whatever I can eat—with either one or half a roti, or one tablespoon of rice. I eat subzis and all kinds of meat—chicken, fish, everything, even

Afterword

mutton, though I have cut down on the amount of mutton I eat. I try to eat a lot of salads.

I have always been a light sleeper. In my profession, I don't manage to get enough sleep. I am awake 18–20 hours a day; I sleep only for 4–5 hours. My body is used to that. There are two-three months when I do get to sleep for 8 hours but then I get back to sleeping for just 4–5 hours.

When I was younger, we used to overtrain because there was no know-how. Since we had high metabolic rates in our younger days, that factor worked for us. We didn't have proper knowledge about diet—about protein and carbohydrates. Today, everything has become so scientific.

People should educate themselves about the very basics of things and then stick to it. Once you start getting too technical or too deep into it, things start going haywire. Remember, everybody's body reacts differently. My advice is to keep it simple.

SALMAN KHAN
May 2013

A Note on the Author

Photo credit: Tina Dehal

Deanne Panday is one of the country's foremost fitness experts. She is also the author of the bestseller *I'm Not Stressed: secrets for a calm mind and a healthy body*. She has been shaping up some of the hottest, most successful, and fittest people for the past fifteen years. Some of her clients over the years include Bipasha Basu, John Abraham, Dino Morea, Lara Dutta, Jacqueline Fernandez, Sonakshi Sinha, and Bobby Deol. Deanne has been featured in *Femina*, *Midday*, *DNA*, *Vogue*, and so on. She has set up some of India's finest gyms and even set up Play, her own boutique gym, which consisted of a high-end gym, spa, and yoga studio. Deanne launched Bia Brazil in India, a top lifestyle workout gear for women. She lives in Mumbai with her husband and two children.

'Being fit is a logical way to recover faster'

PHOTO CREDIT: DABBOO RATNANI

'My fitness mantra is that your fitness regimen is as individual to you as your fingerprint'

'Do not do thing that you can't do and do not try to compete with somebody else'

'Work out for fun, not for pain'

PHOTO CREDIT: SUBI SAMIFI

'It's important to work towards something in your head.
It builds a hunger in you'

PHOTO CREDIT: JITU SAVLANI

'For me, fitness means staying healthy, looking good, and not falling ill too easily'

'You need to work with the biomechanics of your body'

Mihir Jogh, a 23-year-old boy who built his body the natural way

'It's about finding a balance, about making it a lifestyle change'

'I have zero supplements'

'Just because someone has a big body doesn't mean he is strong'

'I am motivated by the high energy levels and how my body has changed'

PHOTO CREDIT: KAVISH SINHA

'Those who look at the aesthetic aspect of it are not really into fitness'

'There's no better feeling in the world than working out'

PHOTO CREDIT: TINA DEHAL

'Training has given me a sense of routine and discipline'

'For me, fitness is a way of living—it keeps me happy and active'

PHOTO CREDIT: BB LOVE YOURSELF

'You have to respect the body you are born with'

PHOTO CREDIT: BB LOVE YOURSELF

'I like the fact that I am big-boned and curvy'

'You have to work your butt off to build a body that you dream of having'